Measuring Customer Satisfaction

Also available from ASQ Quality Press

Improving Your Measurement of Customer Satisfaction: A Guide to Creating, Conducting, Analyzing, and Reporting Customer Satisfaction Measurement Programs
Terry G. Vavra

Mapping Work Processes
Dianne Galloway

Quality Quotes
Hélio Gomes

Measuring and Managing Customer Satisfaction: Going for the Gold
Sheila Kessler

Total Quality Service: A Simplified Approach to Using the Baldrige Award Criteria
Sheila Kessler

Customer Retention: An Integrated Process for Keeping Your Best Customers
Michael W. Lowenstein

The Change Agents' Handbook: A Survival Guide for Quality Improvement Champions
David W. Hutton

Creating a Customer-Centered Culture: Leadership in Quality, Innovation, and Speed
Robin L. Lawton

Insights to Performance Excellence 1997: An Inside Look at the 1997 Baldrige Award Criteria
Mark L. Blazey

Understanding and Applying Value-Added Assessment: Eliminating Business Process Waste
William E. Trischler

To request a complimentary catalog of publications, call 800-248-1946.

Measuring Customer Satisfaction

*Survey Design, Use, and
Statistical Analysis Methods*

Second Edition

Bob E. Hayes

ASQ Quality Press
Milwaukee, Wisconsin

Measuring Customer Satisfaction: Survey Design, Use, and Statistical Analysis Methods
Second Edition
Bob E. Hayes

Library of Congress Cataloging-in-Publication Data
Hayes, Bob E., 1963–
    Measuring customer satisfaction: survey design, use, and
statistical analysis methods / Bob E. Hayes.—2nd ed.
        p. cm.
    Includes bibliographical references and index.
    ISBN 0-87389-362-X (alk. paper)
    1. Consumer satisfaction—Statistical methods.   2. Questionnaires.
    I. Title.
HF5415.335.H39   1997
658.8'12—dc21   97-3240
                                                                        CIP

10 9 8 7 6 5 4 3 2

ISBN 0-87389-362-X

Acquisitions Editor: Roger Holloway
Project Editor: Jeanne W. Bohn

ASQC Mission: To facilitate continuous improvement and increase customer satisfaction by identifying, communicating, and promoting the use of quality principles, concepts, and technologies; and thereby be recognized throughout the world as the leading authority on, and champion for, quality.

Attention: Schools and Corporations
ASQC Quality Press books, videotapes, audiotapes, and software are available at quantity discounts with bulk purchases for business, educational, or instructional use. For information, please contact ASQC Quality Press at 800-248-1946, or write to ASQC Quality Press, P.O. Box 3005, Milwaukee, WI 53201-3005.

For a free copy of the ASQC Quality Press Publications Catalog, including ASQC membership information, call 800-248-1946.

Printed in the United States of America

 Printed on acid-free paper

American Society for Quality

ASQ

611 East Wisconsin Avenue
P.O. Box 3005
Milwaukee, Wisconsin 53201-3005

For Marissa.
This book is dedicated to you. I can never say
enough good things about you to the people I meet.
I try, but words don't truly convey what you mean to me.
You are the kindest, sweetest, and smartest kid I know.
The world is a better place because you're in it.
I love you.

Contents

Preface

The first edition of this book was published in January 1992. During that time, there were no books that covered the topic of customer satisfaction questionnaire development and use. Since then, I have noticed a few books on the topic of customer satisfaction measurement and management. The reason I wrote this book was to update the first edition. This edition, like the first edition, includes topics such as customer requirement determination, uses of customer satisfaction questionnaires, reliability and validity of questionnaires, and item generation. This second edition, however, contains new information. First, an entire chapter has been devoted to presenting real-life examples of customer satisfaction questionnaires to let readers see how other companies use the methods outlined in the book to develop and use customer satisfaction questionnaires. Additionally, the second edition provides information on various sampling techniques and methods to increase response rates for mail surveys. Finally, the discussion on reliability of measures has been lengthened to provide a more comprehensive look at the concept of reliability.

As was stated in the first edition, I also wrote this book because I wanted to present important scientific principles in simple, understandable terms. All too often, important scientific principles in textbooks are not presented in a way that allows for easy comprehension. I present these scientific principles in relation to the development of customer satisfaction questionnaires, but these issues are equally applicable in an attempt to develop any attitude measure (for example, employee attitude surveys).

Although I do discuss several topics in scale development, my intent is not to cover the entire content of this area, but to present information directly related to the development of customer satisfaction questionnaires.

The book contains many illustrations and diagrams to help support the written explanations of the scientific principles. These illustrations and diagrams are intended to facilitate the understanding of statistical analyses as well as scale development. I hope these examples will make the material easier to read.

The book contains seven chapters. One chapter discusses the acceptance of the importance of customer satisfaction in the American economy, and the other six chapters cover specific aspects of customer satisfaction questionnaire development and use. The chapters are designed to be complementary and to develop a coherent picture of customer satisfaction questionnaire development and use. The book contains several appendices that present important statistical concepts to aid readers who lack a statistical background. An understanding of the information in the appendices is helpful but not essential to developing customer satisfaction questionnaires.

Chapter 1 introduces the concept of quality and emphasizes the importance of assessing customer satisfaction. Awareness of the importance of customer satisfaction stems from two sources: (1) A national quality award given to outstanding American companies that demonstrate outstanding product and service quality, and (2) The desire to achieve financial security of companies that are able to satisfy their customers and subsequently able to keep them. In addition, this chapter presents a model of customer satisfaction questionnaire development and use designed as an overview for the remaining chapters. This model will help readers see the big picture of customer satisfaction questionnaire development and use before reading about the specific steps in subsequent chapters.

Chapter 2 covers two methods of determining important service or product characteristics as perceived by customers. These methods are called the *quality dimension development process* and the *critical incident technique*. The quality dimensions include those general aspects of the service or product that customers say define the quality of the service or product. The two methods also identify specific examples of these important characteristics that will help determine the types of questions that can be included in a customer satisfaction questionnaire.

Chapter 3 covers measurement issues related to customer satisfaction questionnaires, discusses reliability and validity, and contains formulae to estimate reliability. It is important to evaluate the quality of any measurement system. When we measure parts that come from an assembly line, we want to be sure that the measurement process accurately reflects the true size of the parts we are measuring. Similarly, we want to ensure that the measurement of our customers' attitudes accurately reflects their attitudes. Imprecise measurement can lead to poor business decisions. This chapter shows you how to evaluate the measurement properties of your questionnaires.

Chapter 4 presents guidelines for developing questionnaires, including the types of questions to be included, characteristics of good questions, response formats, and information to be included in the introduction.

Chapter 5 covers different sampling methods. As is often the case, due to financial constraints, it is not possible to administer a survey to all customers. When this occurs, we administer a survey to a small subset of customers and analyze those data to determine the satisfaction level of all of our customers. The process of sampling ensures that the results based on the sample of customers are generalizable to all customers. Additionally, this chapter covers topics to show you how confident you can be in customer satisfaction results and how to determine an appropriate sample size for your customer satisfaction survey. This chapter also covers research that shows how to increase response rates to surveys.

Chapter 6 includes five examples of customer satisfaction questionnaires. The first three involve the manufacturing industry, the service industry, and the software industry. The latter two cover support functions within an organization (an internal statistical support group and a facilities group). This chapter discusses methods of presenting the data and suggests specific uses, including identifying which aspects of the service or product are especially important in customer satisfaction. In addition, this chapter applies customer satisfaction questionnaires to the traditional quality improvement techniques of control charting and describes their use in conducting organizational comparisons.

Chapter 7 includes various real-life examples of customer satisfaction questionnaires. In this chapter, readers are shown how three companies used customer satisfaction questionnaires. These examples are helpful because they show how the approaches in this book are applied to real-life situations. This chapter shows how the various companies developed both long and short customer satisfaction questionnaires, the application of sampling error, confidence intervals, and control charts. Readers will see that the development and use of questionnaires is one of compromise; it may not always be possible to follow all of the guidelines stated in this book. Nonetheless, the companies represented in the examples employed many of the guidelines from this book and were, at least, aware of these guidelines and could make informed decisions regarding what they wanted to do for their particular survey process. Not all customer satisfaction survey processes will be identical, not even within the same organization. It is ultimately up to each reader to use the information contained in this text and decide how he or she will apply it to his or her specific customer survey process. It is hoped that the examples in this chapter will help readers better understand the survey process as it is applied in the real world.

Several appendices are included as well. Each appendix covers a specific topic related to statistical analysis. These appendices aim to help readers understand key statistical concepts that complement the material presented in the main body of the book. These appendices present a very general overview of statistics. Topics include measurement scales, frequencies, descriptive statistics, sampling error, the concept of hypothesis testing, and formal hypothesis testing procedures (*t*-tests, analysis of variance, and regression analysis).

I would now like to take this opportunity to write about things that are important to me. Writing the preface is my favorite part of the writing process of this book. Oh sure, writing about reliability and validity of questionnaires *CAN* be fun, but only after a glass of merlot. Okay . . . a few glasses . . . . In the preface, I can write pretty much what I want to write. This part of the book gives me the opportunity to offer some words of thanks to those who have made a difference in my life.

A lot has happened to me since the publication of the first edition, which was published five years ago. My daughter has grown into a fun little girl. She is still sweet as always. I hope I can say the same thing at the next edition. I finished my graduate education in 1992. Going back to graduate school was one of the best decisions I have made (and there aren't a lot of good ones) in my life. If any of you are contemplating a return to school, either to complete unfinished schooling or to just further your knowledge, do it. It's difficult but worth it. In the past five years, I have made really good friends and met some interesting people. I have shared some incredible adventures with friends and family.

I would like to thank some people for the support they offered me both professionally and personally. Although the support takes various forms (such as dinner purchases, free hugs, critiques about my personal life, advice—which is often unsolicited), it all means the same thing to me: love. I owe my friends so much. I couldn't imagine a life without them. Rob, thanks for being such a cool friend. It's hard to believe that I have known you for nearly 10 years. I look forward to more years as your friend. By the way, how is my eyeliner looking? Hey, Rob! Rob! Robby, are you listening?!? I've known Heidi for a little more than two years now. There is something that not many people know about Heidi. Heidi became a vegetarian because she wanted to be the first person to be able to eat at barbecue cookouts. Heidi, I'm on to you. My friendship with Wade grew after we both left graduate school. Even though he lives nearly 1000 miles from me, we still manage time to get together at least twice per year and laugh. A few years ago, Wade offered me some great advice: "Don't go in there. There's fire in the hole!" You can't get more practical than that! Thanks, Wade. I owe a lot to Carol G. If it wasn't for her, I wouldn't be able to say that I incoherently mumbled some nonsensical words to Jackson Browne. "Rhahahdhaha." Bettina, you're too sweet not to be mentioned here. Thanks for being a friend. To Carol J., I want to mention that no actors were harmed in the writing of this book. Val, bring over the ice cream and two spoons!

There is so much more I want to write here but I am afraid my publisher would remove it in the review process. For those who are interested in what I have to say, you'll have to wait until my next book is published. That book will be something more for the general public to appreciate. It will be about various things such as romantic relationships, friendships, dating, the internet, conversations, statistics, Jackson Browne, fatherhood, and a whole lot more. I just have to get a publisher interested in it. Some possible titles are (1) *Jackson Browne and Me*, (2) *Bob!*, (3) *Stuff*, or (4) *Things People Should Know*. If you're interested in some stuff that might be in the book, you can visit my homepage (http://members.aol.com/bobehayes).

Here are some other people I have met in the last five years who have had an important influence on my life. Their order of appearance is: Susan, Jeff, Jennifer, Chloe, Tara, Julie, Craig, Melissa, and Tamara. To those I have forgotten to mention here, the guilt you no doubt will make me feel when you notice your absence will pale in comparison to my self-inflicted guilt when I realize I have forgotten you.

My family is always there for me. Thanks to all of you. I love each and every one of you. Lauren has the best sales pitch I have ever heard. Jonathan is the only kid I know who needs four notes to play the Three-Note March. Thanks to Stephen for help on my homepage. Is there anything you don't know? Tom, I make a promise now to get to know you again. Lamona, thanks for helping me go in the right direction. Mom, thanks for having me and being there for me when I needed you. In loving memory of my sister, Betty, thanks for making me aspire to do the right thing.

CHAPTER 1

Introduction

There has been an increase in the emphasis on a company's ability to produce high-quality products and/or provide high-quality services. In fact, many companies, in their attempt to compete in the marketplace, form either an organization to address various quality-related issues for the entire company or quality improvement teams to address specific quality-related problems. Not only do companies rely on their own employees for quality improvement, they also rely on consultants who specialize in quality improvement techniques and methodologies. The primary goal of these specialists is to increase the quality of the products and services of the companies they serve.

To increase the quality of products and services, we first need to define quality. I will use the definition presented by Montgomery (1996): Quality is the extent to which products meet the requirements of people who use them. He further distinguishes between two types of quality: quality of design and quality of conformance.

Quality of design reflects the extent to which a product or service possesses an intended feature. For example, an automobile with power steering, a sun roof, and many other luxury options would be considered to have better quality of design than a car without these options. Quality of conformance reflects the extent to which the product or service conforms to the intent of the design.

These aspects of quality can be measured. Such measures give businesses an accurate indication of the "well-being" of their business processes and determine the quality of products and services resulting from these processes. Measures allow a business to: (1) Know how well the business process is working, (2) Know where to make changes to create improvements, if changes are needed, and (3) Determine if the changes led to improvements. Various measurement techniques can index the quality of business processes, products, and services. Measures of quality often focus on objective or *hard* indices. For example, in manufacturing industries, the process of producing parts is conducive to measurements of size (such as parts) and amount (for example, scrap or rework). In nonmanufacturing industries, measurements could include the time to complete a service or the number of written errors on a particular form.

Recently, however, there has been a desire to utilize more subjective or *soft* measures as indicators of quality. These measures are soft because they focus on perceptions and attitudes rather than more concrete, objective criteria. It is often necessary to use these measures because objective indices are not applicable in assessing the quality of services. Also, companies are simply interested in gaining a more comprehensive understanding of their customers' perceptions. These soft measures include customer satisfaction questionnaires to determine customers' perceptions and attitudes concerning the quality of the service or product they received, as well as employee attitude questionnaires that assess employees' perceptions about the quality of their work life.

Knowledge of customers' perceptions and attitudes about an organization's business will greatly enhance its opportunity to make better business decisions. These organizations will know their customers' requirements or expectations and will be able to determine if they are meeting those requirements. To use customers' perceptions and attitudes to assess the quality of products and services, customer satisfaction instruments must accurately measure these perceptions and attitudes. If the instruments are poorly developed and inaccurately represent customers' opinions, decisions based on this information can be detrimental to the success of the organization. On the other hand, organizations with accurate information about customers' perceptions about the quality of the services and products can make better decisions to better serve their customers.

The combination of a competitive marketplace and the Malcolm Baldrige National Quality Award (MBNQA) has heightened the awareness of American companies of the need to focus their quality improvement efforts on customer-related issues. To incorporate customers' perceptions and attitudes into their quality improvement efforts, companies must be able to gauge customers' attitudes accurately. One way to measure customers' attitudes is through questionnaires. These companies should design customer satisfaction questionnaires that accurately assess customers' perceptions about the quality of services or products.

Measuring customers' attitudes has been an important element in the quality movement of American organizations. For instance, the Baldrige Award, given annually to American companies that demonstrate high standards of business practice, includes seven criteria or categories on which companies are judged. From its inception, the Baldrige Award has included customer satisfaction measurement issues as part of its award criteria. In the recent iteration of changes of the criteria, the MBNQA award and point allocations for the respective criteria are structured in the format in Figure 1.1.

As can be seen by the point allocation for each criterion, customer satisfaction issues still remain an important criterion in the MBNQA. Of the 1000 points in the award, customer satisfaction issues account for 21 percent (Customer and Market Knowledge—40; Customer Satisfaction and Relationship Enhancement—40; Customer Satisfaction Results—130).

Each of these three customer satisfaction categories emphasizes the importance of understanding your customers. In Category 3.1, companies are judged, in part, on their method of determining customer requirements, expectations, and preferences. Companies are to show (1) How customer groups are determined and how approaches to listening and learning vary across these groups; (2) How product and service features are determined; and (3) How the company's approach to listening to customers and markets is evaluated and improved. In Category 3.2, companies are judged on their method of determining and enhancing the satisfaction level of its customers. Specifically, companies are asked to demonstrate (1) How the company determines customer contact requirements and how they are communicated to all employees, and how the company evaluates and improves customer contact performance, (2) Their complaint management process, (3) How the company follows up with customers to receive prompt feedback, (4) How the company determines

	Point values
1. Leadership	**110**
1.1 Leadership Systems 80	
1.2 Company Responsibility and Citizenship 30	
2. Strategic Planning	**80**
2.1 Strategy Development Process 40	
2.2 Company Strategy 40	
3. Customer and Market Focus	**80**
3.1 Customer and Market Knowledge 40	
3.2 Customer Satisfaction and Relationship Enhancement 40	
4. Information and Analysis	**80**
4.1 Selection and Use of Information Data 25	
4.2 Selection and Use of Comparative Information and Data ... 15	
4.3 Analysis and Review of Company Performance 40	
5. Human Resource Development and Management	**100**
5.1 Work Systems... 40	
5.2 Employee Education, Training, and Development 30	
5.3 Employee Well-Being and Satisfaction........................ 30	
6. Process Management	**100**
6.1 Management of Product and Service Processes................ 60	
6.2 Management of Support Processes 20	
6.3 Management of Supplier and Partnering Processes 20	
7. Business Results	**450**
7.1 Customer Satisfaction Results...................................130	
7.2 Financial and Market Results...................................130	
7.3 Human Resource Results 35	
7.4 Supplier and Partner Results 25	
7.5 Company-Specific Results 130	
Total Points	**1000**

Figure 1.1. 1997 Malcolm Baldrige National Quality Award criteria.

customer satisfaction levels and how they are used, and (5) How the company obtains customer satisfaction data regarding its competitors. In Category 7.1, companies are judged on their customer satisfaction results are asked to specifically summarize their customer satisfaction results.

The purpose of this book is to outline some guidelines that will aid in the development of customer satisfaction questionnaires. In addition, this book contains specific examples applying these guidelines. These guidelines are based on information combining both practical standards and scientific standards (AERA, APA, and NCME 1985). This book is written for professional practitioners in quality-related or marketing fields, which can use customer attitude measurements. In addition, companies with quality improvement programs will find this book useful in developing measures to assess their clientele's level of satisfaction.

It should be mentioned that the use of customer satisfaction questionnaires seems most appropriate for organizations in the service sector or other nonmanufacturing fields. Unlike the manufacturing industry, in which quality can be assessed by an objective index like the size of produced parts, the service sector offers little in the way of objective quality measures. Even *hard* measures (for example, time) used in the nonmanufacturing environment might not reflect the true quality of the service. For example, if the transaction completion time for a service is measured by a stopwatch and indicates a fast completion time, this does not ensure that customers perceive the completion time as fast. The customer may have expected an even faster time. Because quality is determined, in part, by the extent to which goods meet the customers' requirements, the measurement of quality in nonmanufacturing settings is probably best indexed by customers' perceptions of the service they received.

Due to the differences in the output between manufacturing and nonmanufacturing companies, customer satisfaction questionnaires will more likely find greatest use in nonmanufacturing settings. However, questionnaires can still be applied in manufacturing environments. For example, although the quality of manufactured products is assessed by objective indices (in fact, automobiles are rated in *Consumer Reports* by objective indices such as number of repairs), automobile manufacturers are using the term *customer satisfaction* to advertise their automobiles. Some automobile manufacturers claim they are designing their cars to make the driver feel better. Although customers' perception of quality is probably correlated with objective indices of quality, automobile companies that make statements concerning customers' perceptions about their car can and should use customer satisfaction measures to assess the customers' perception about the quality of their cars.

Therefore, customer satisfaction questionnaires can be used in both nonmanufacturing and manufacturing fields. The use of customer satisfaction questionnaires offers companies another approach in the assessment of the quality of their goods. It focuses an organization's attention on the customers and how they perceive the organization's products and services.

The entire American economy seems to be revolving around the phrase *customer satisfaction.* There is a strong desire to establish and use measures of customers' attitudes as indices of the company's quality. Often, this desire stems from the lack of quality measures available to some companies (especially service companies) or results from an interest in satisfying customers. This desire to measure customers' attitudes should be paralleled by the knowledge of customer satisfaction questionnaire development. To enable companies to assess their customers' attitudes, technical guidelines on the development of customer satisfaction questionnaires must keep pace with this ever-increasing emphasis on customer satisfaction issues. The following chapters contain guidance on an appropriate method for developing and using questionnaires.

Model of Customer Satisfaction Questionnaire Development and Use

As an introduction to the remainder of the book, I would like to present a model describing the development and use of customer satisfaction questionnaires. This model appears in Figure 1.2 and illustrates the process in general. Each phase of the process contains specific steps, each focusing on an important element in the understanding of customers' opinions. As you read the book, it might be beneficial to keep this model in mind. It will help you incorporate the details of each chapter into a "big picture." This model also allows you to see how different parts of each chapter are interrelated.

Figure 1.2. A general model for the development and use of customer satisfaction questionnaires.

Step 1 in the process is identifying customers' requirements or quality dimensions, the important characteristics of a product or service. Customer requirements define the quality of your products or services. In this step, not only do you identify the quality dimensions, you also identify specific examples of these dimensions.

Knowledge of customer requirements is essential for two reasons. First, it provides a better understanding of the way your customers define the quality of your services and products. If you understand customer requirements, you are in a better position to know how to satisfy your customers. Second, knowledge of customer requirements will facilitate the development of the customer satisfaction questionnaire. Its questions should assess the extent to which customers are satisfied on each of the quality dimensions. Chapter 2 includes information on identifying customers' requirements.

Step 2 in the process is developing the questionnaire. This step includes many specific components. The ultimate goal of this step is to develop a questionnaire that allows the assessment of specific information about your customers' perceptions. The specific information should correspond to the underlying customer requirements you identified in Step 1. Chapter 3 includes information concerning the evaluation of questionnaires. Chapter 4 covers the development of the questionnaire, including the selection of questions for the questionnaire (characteristics of good items), the choice of response formats, and the method of selecting the best items to be included in the questionnaire. Chapter 5 covers various sampling methods and shows you how to determine an appropriate sample size to obtain reliable results.

Once the questionnaire has been developed, the next step is to use it. Step 3 represents the many specific uses of customer satisfaction questionnaires. Each use allows you to obtain specific information about your customers' perceptions. The uses vary from identifying the current status of customer satisfaction to assessing customer satisfaction over time. Chapter 6 includes some specific use of customer satisfaction questionnaires. Chapter 7 includes examples of customer satisfaction questionnaires.

Tables at the end of Chapters 2, 4, and 6 summarize the text of each chapter. These tables provide practical guides and a general outline in the development and use of customer satisfaction questionnaires; consult the text to obtain the exact procedures involved at each general step.

All survey processes within an organization (for example, employee, customer) should be documented in a written format. This written document is designed to help the organization understand how and why the survey process was developed and to help you present your survey process to interested parties. For example, the Baldrige Award could use this written documentation to help decide the extent to which you truly understand your customers' satisfaction level. This book not only offers guidelines regarding the customer survey process, but it can also help you organize and present your survey process in a documented format. By following the guidelines in the book, you should be able to demonstrate, in a clear and straightforward manner, a written document that outlines the customer survey process, from the determination of the customer requirements, the development of the sampling plan, and creation of the survey, to the use of the information gained from the customer survey, to name a few. This type of information is designed to show readers the exact process and methodology that were used to develop the survey process. Only through clear written documentation can you support the quality of the entire survey process and lend credibility to the people who developed the survey.

CHAPTER 2

Determining Customer Requirements

We usually describe a product or service in terms of several dimensions or characteristics. For example, after receiving a service, we might describe the service provider as fast, always available when needed, and unpleasant. These descriptions represent three different aspects of the service: *responsiveness, availability,* and *professionalism,* respectively. These are a subset of all possible dimensions by which the service can be described. The composite of all possible dimensions describes the entire product or service.

We can regard customer requirements as those characteristics of the product or service that represent important dimensions. They are the dimensions on which customers base their opinion about the product or service. I will use the term *quality dimensions* to describe these important dimensions. Also, I will interchange the terms *customer requirements* and *quality dimensions* throughout the book.

The purpose of determining customer requirements is to establish a comprehensive list of all the important quality dimensions that describe the service or product. It is important to understand the quality dimensions so that you will know how customers define the quality of your service or product. Only by understanding the quality dimensions will you be able to develop measures to assess these quality dimensions.

Although there may be some standard quality dimensions that generalize across many products or services, some dimensions will apply only to specific types of products or services. Quality dimensions applicable to many service organizations include availability, responsiveness, convenience, and timeliness (Kennedy and Young 1989). These quality dimensions seem applicable to many service industries, such as the banking, hotel, and hospital industries. This list of quality dimensions, however, is not comprehensive for each of these industries. The hospital industry might include additional quality dimensions such as quality of food and quality of care. Similarly, other industries may possess quality dimensions that uniquely define their services and products. It is important that each company identify all quality dimensions to ensure understanding of the definition of quality for its products or services. Analyzing the services or products will provide a comprehensive picture of these dimensions.

This chapter will present two methods designed to identify important quality dimensions of products or services. The first method is the *quality dimension development approach*. This approach calls for the provider to establish the quality dimensions of its service or product. The second method is the *critical incident approach* (Flanagan 1954) and involves customers in determining the quality dimensions.

Quality Dimension Development

This method involves the people who provide the service or product. They should be in a good position to understand the purpose and function of the service or product. These people could range from individuals within a quality circle addressing a particular problem to individuals working independently to better understand their customers' requirements. In either case, these people are closely involved with the business process. Essentially, this process involves two steps: identifying the dimensions and defining these dimensions with specific examples.

Identification of Quality Dimensions

The first step involves identifying the dimensions that define the quality of the service or product. This list of dimensions can be generated in various ways, using different sources of information. One way is to investigate literature (such as scientific, professional, and trade journals) that discusses specific industries. These publications might provide dimensions of the service or product.

As an example of information found in scientific journals, researchers (Parasuraman, Zeithaml, and Berry 1985) have concluded that service quality can be described on the basis of 10 dimensions. Attempts to measure these 10 dimensions, however, reveal that customers can only distinguish between five dimensions (Parasuraman, Zeithaml, and Berry 1988), suggesting that the original 10 dimensions overlap each other considerably. The five dimensions of service quality are *tangibles, reliability, responsiveness, assurance,* and *empathy.* Definitions of these dimensions are available in a publication on service quality by Zeithaml, Parasuraman, and Berry (1990).

Some trade journals often include articles that pertain to a particular industry. For example, various quality dimensions of staff support areas were presented by Kennedy and Young (1989). Five dimensions of staff support and their definitions appear in Figure 2.1. These quality dimensions were identified as important characteristics of staff support areas.

Both of these examples demonstrate the usefulness of examining journals to obtain information for establishing a list of quality dimensions. By reading journals, you can gain insight from many knowledgeable people who have extensive experience in a particular field. Journals, either scientific or trade, provide an excellent resource for identifying quality dimensions.

---

1. *Availability of support:* the degree to which the customer can contact the provider

2. *Responsiveness of support:* the degree to which the provider reacts promptly to the customer

3. *Timeliness of support:* the degree to which the job is accomplished within the customer's stated time frame and/or within the negotiated time frame

4. *Completeness of support:* the degree to which the total job is finished

5. *Pleasantness of support:* the degree to which the provider uses suitable professional behavior and manners while working with the customer

---

Figure 2.1. Some quality dimensions for staff support areas and their definitions.

Another way to establish a list of quality dimensions is to study the service or product. This study should include people involved in the business process. These people are in a good position to understand the purpose or function of their job in relation to meeting customers' expectations. This examination of the service or product should lead to a list of many dimensions.

Some dimensions might include those found in Figure 2.1, or, again, the dimensions might be specific to a particular industry or organization. The initial list of dimensions will be in general terms such as *timely* or *professional*. These terms are to be used as guides toward understanding the dimensions of the service or product. Each term represents a particular quality dimension or customer requirement.

It is important to define these terms so that someone reading the definitions will understand precisely what is meant by each dimension. To clarify the definitions of the quality dimensions further, write specific examples for each quality dimension. This process follows.

Establishing Specific Examples of Quality Dimensions

The process of clarifying the quality dimensions is one of generating specific examples of the quality dimensions. Each example defines a particular quality dimension, and each dimension could include multiple examples. These examples are specific declarative statements, each describing a specific instance of the quality dimension it represents. The statements could be a specific task or behavior performed by a person within the process or could describe a specific example illustrating the dimension. The former type of statement should include an action verb describing a specific behavior of the service provider or product. The latter statement should include a specific adjective reflecting the content of the dimensions. Example statements that contain both specific behavior and specific adjectives are included in Figure 2.2. These statements were generated by the author using definitions presented by Kennedy and Young (1989).

These statements should reflect instances of performance by the staff or product that customers can assess. It is important that your list include all possible examples for a particular dimension. This list of examples reflects the content of the dimensions, so if the list is deficient, a complete understanding of each dimension will also be deficient. You should try to

Availability of support
1. I could get help from the staff when I needed.
2. The staff was always available to help.
3. I could contact the staff at any time I needed.
4. The staff was there when needed.
5. I could arrange convenient meeting times with the staff.

Responsiveness of support
1. They were quick to respond when I asked for help.
2. They immediately helped me when I needed help.
3. I waited a short period of time to get help after I asked for it.

Timeliness of support
1. They completed the job when expected.
2. They met my deadline(s).
3. They finished their responsibilities within the stated time frame.
4. The project was completed on time.

Completeness of support
1. They ensured that every aspect of the job was completed.
2. They completed everything they said they would do.
3. They were there to provide help from the beginning to the end of the project.

Professionalism of support
1. The staff members conducted themselves in a professional manner.
2. The staff listened to me.
3. The staff was courteous.
4. The staff cared about what I had to say.

Overall satisfaction with support
1. The quality of the way the staff treated me was high.
2. The way the staff treated me met my needs.
3. The way the staff treated me met my expectations.
4. I am happy with the way the staff treated me.
5. I am satisfied with the way the staff treated me.

Overall satisfaction with product
1. The quality of the final job they provided was high.
2. The job met my expectations.
3. I am satisfied with the job the staff provided.

Figure 2.2. Declarative statements describing the quality dimensions of staff support areas.

include at least four or five statements for each dimension. After generating the list of statements, you may take the additional step of combining some quality dimensions that seem redundant. Some of the statements may overlap considerably and may not warrant separate dimensions.

The two steps in this process (generating dimensions and developing specific examples), although presented as independent of each other, are sometimes done simultaneously. Also, sometimes you may first generate specific examples that, in turn, lead to the generation of customer requirements. In either case, it is important that quality dimensions be defined by specific examples. Ultimately, the quality dimension development process will result in a list of customer requirements or quality dimensions, each defined by specific statements. The following example illustrates the process and outcome of the quality dimension development process. The example involves the software industry.

Software Industry

Murine (1988) discusses the measurement of software quality and lists 13 software quality factors. These factors are user-oriented and can be evaluated by the customer. I have extracted the dimensions and their definitions directly from the article and have written statements to provide specific examples of each dimension. The dimension, a brief definition, and the specific statements are presented in Figure 2.3. These specific statements are only a small portion of the possible statements that could have been generated. Other questionnaire developers, examining the same quality dimensions, could generate more statements similar in content to the ones presented here.

Summary

Quality dimension development is a process of identifying customer requirements through various sources. One source is published literature covering specific industries that might contain information concerning some quality dimensions or customer requirements. Another potential source involves asking people within the company to examine the business process and determine the key quality dimensions of the service or product they provide. In addition to determining these dimensions, you should generate specific examples illustrating exactly what is meant by the

I. Correctness: the degree to which the software meets customers' specifications
    1. I am able to complete my job with this software.
    2. The software meets my specifications in getting my job done.

II. Reliability: the extent to which programs perform intended functions with precision
    3. I am able to perform functions with precision.
    4. The software allows me to perform functions accurately.

III. Usability: effort required to understand output from programs
    5. I was able to learn about the output from programs in a short amount of time.
    6. The output of the programs is easy to understand.

IV. Maintainability: effort required to find and correct an error in operational programs
    7. Locating an error in the operational program is easy.
    8. Fixing an error in the operational program is easy.

V. Testability: effort required to test programs to ensure they perform intended function
    9. The testing of the program required a short amount of time.
    10. Testing the program to ensure it performed functions was easy.

VI. Portability: effort required to transfer programs between hardware configurations and/or software environments
    11. Transferring the program between different hardware configurations is easy.
    12. I am able to transfer programs between different software environments with little problem.

VII. Interoperability: effort required to couple one system to another
    13. Coupling one system to another is easy.
    14. The software allows for simple coupling between systems.

VIII. Intra-operability: effort required to communicate between software components
    15. Communicating between software components is simple.
    16. I am able to communicate between software components easily.

IX. Flexibility: effort required to modify operational programs
    17. I am able to modify the operational program with little effort.
    18. Changing the operational program is easy.

Overall satisfaction:
    19. I am very happy with the software.
    20. The software meets my expectations.

Figure 2.3. Quality dimensions, their definitions, and statements for the software industry.

dimensions. This process will lead to the development of a list of customer requirements, each defined by several specific statements.

Critical Incident Approach

The critical incident technique (Flanagan 1954) is another approach for determining customer requirements. It has been used in establishing performance dimensions in performance appraisal systems (Latham, Fay, and Saari 1979; Latham and Wexley 1977). This method is not only applicable in developing customer satisfaction questionnaires, but is equally valuable in any business process analysis in which companies attempt to define and understand their customers' requirements. The present method can greatly facilitate this process of definition and understanding.

The critical incident approach focuses on obtaining information from customers about the services and products they receive. *Customers* is a generic term referring to anybody who receives a service or product from some other person or group of people. It is clear that various customer satisfaction questionnaires can be developed for different types of customers and that customers can be people who are external to an organization or people from a different department within the same organization. In either case, the critical incident approach can identify customer requirements.

The strength of the critical incident approach lies in its utilization of customers in defining customer requirements. Customers are in a good position to help you understand these requirements because they are the recipients of your services or products. Relying solely on organization or department standards in determining customer requirements might lead to a poor list that does not include factors important to customers. Also, such a list may reflect customer requirements that should not be included. The critical incident approach identifies specific performance examples that illustrate organizational performance related to the services or products which they provide.

Critical Incidents

A critical incident is an example of organizational performance from the customers' perspective. That is, critical incidents are those aspects of organizational performance in which customers come in direct contact.

As a result, these incidents usually define staff performance (in service organizations) and product quality (in manufacturing organizations).

A critical incident is a specific example of the service or product that describes either positive or negative performance. A positive example is a characteristic of the service or product that the customer would like to see every time he or she receives that service or product. A negative example is a characteristic of the service or product that would make the customer question the quality of the company.

A good critical incident for defining customer requirements has two characteristics: (1) It is specific and (2) It describes the service provider in *behavioral terms* or describes the service or product with *specific adjectives.* These characteristics should be explained to those responsible for generating the critical incidents.

A critical incident is *specific* if it describes a single behavior or characteristic of the service or a single characteristic of the product. The incident should be written so that it is interpreted the same way by different people. The critical incident is not specific if it describes several aspects of performance. For example, a bad specific critical incident might say

> *I went to the bank to cash a check and waited in line for a long time. While I was waiting, I noticed that the teller was quickly servicing her customers.*

This critical incident is not specific because it describes two different incidents. The reader would not know whether to focus on the fact that the customer waited a long time or that the teller was quick in the service she provided. Examples of good critical incidents would be to divide the previous example into two separate incidents.

1. I waited in line for a long time.

2. The teller was quickly servicing her customers.

A critical incident should also focus on *behaviors* of the service provider or specific *adjectives* that describe the service or product. An incident such as "the teller was not able to help me" does not specify what the teller did and why the teller was unable to help. Good incidents are

1. The teller carefully listened to my request.

2. I received immediate service for my transaction.

The first critical incident describes a behavior of the teller while the second incident uses a specific adjective to describe the service.

Generating Critical Incidents

This procedure involves two steps. In the first, customers are interviewed to obtain specific information about the service or product. In the second, this information is categorized into groups, each group reflecting a quality dimension. A detailed discussion of both steps follows.

Interview

There are two approaches for obtaining critical incidents: group interviewing and individual interviewing. The major difference is that either groups or individuals are the focus of the generating process. A minor difference is that individual interviews can be conducted either in person or over the telephone. In either group or individual interviewing, the method of generating critical incidents is the same, and the following procedure is equally applicable.

For the first step, it is essential that you obtain the input of people who have received the service or product. These people must be actual customers who have had several interactions with the service provider or the product, since they will be providing specific examples of service or product quality.

The recommended number of customers to be interviewed ranges from 10 to 20 people. This high number of interviewees is recommended so that the possibility of deficient information from one interviewee will be offset by sufficient information from another interviewee. Thus, information obtained from the interviews will more likely completely cover the spectrum of customer requirements. Also, if group interviews are conducted, critical incidents stated by one person may stimulate incidents from other group members.

The interviewer should ask each interviewee to describe five to 10 positive instances and five to 10 negative instances of that service or product he or she received in the past. These positive and negative instances constitute the critical incidents that define good and poor service or product quality.

Recall that the interviewee should avoid using general terms to describe critical incidents. If the interviewee uses general phrases such as "the service was nice" or "the product was good," the interviewer should determine what the merchant actually did, in behavioral terms, that made him or her "nice" or which aspects of the product made it "good."

For example, two critical incidents a customer could provide are "The merchant was quick to respond when I arrived" and "The merchant was good." The latter critical incident does not specify why the merchant was good. The former critical incident specifically describes why the merchant was nice: the merchant was quick in responding to the customer. By pressing the interviewees to supply specific examples of performance or specific adjectives of the service or product, the interviewer obtains critical incidents that more efficiently define customer requirements. In addition, specific critical incidents will facilitate the development of the customer satisfaction questionnaire.

Categorization of Critical Incidents

After interviewing 10 people, you may obtain a list of approximately 200 critical incidents. This list will contain incidents that are similar to each other. These should be grouped together. The key to categorizing these critical incidents is to focus on a specific adjective or verb they share. After forming the clusters, write a phrase for each cluster which reflects the content of its incidents. This phrase is called a *satisfaction item.* One guideline in writing the satisfaction items is that they should contain a specific descriptive term of the service or product or a verb that describes an annual event involving the service or product. For example, the following three critical incidents, each from different people, would fall under one satisfaction item.

1. I waited too long before I was helped.

2. I was in a big hurry but had to wait in line for a very long time.

3. I waited in line for a very short time.

A satisfaction item that would encompass these three similar incidents could be

I waited a short period of time before I was helped.

As indicated by this example, both positive and negative critical incidents can be included under one satisfaction item. The three critical incidents just listed, even though they reflect positive and negative aspects of service, are all reflected by the verb *wait*. Therefore, the satisfaction item was written to include the word *wait*.

Writing satisfaction items may take some practice. The most important thing to remember is that satisfaction items, like critical incidents, should be specific in describing the service or product. Quite often, the satisfaction item might even be one of the critical incidents.

Once all the critical incidents are categorized into their respective satisfaction items, repeat the categorization process using the satisfaction items. Now, group similar satisfaction items to form a specific customer requirement or quality dimension. Label these customer requirements with phrases or a single word describing the content of the satisfaction items. These summary labels reflect the specific quality dimensions. Unlike the satisfaction items, these labels do not have to be specific. The only requirement is that the label should reflect the content of the satisfaction items. Using the previous example, we may generate a second satisfaction item that results in these two satisfaction items.

1. I waited a short period of time before I was helped.

2. Service started promptly when I arrived.

Both of these satisfaction items would be included under one customer requirement category labeled *Responsiveness of service.*

Thus, after finishing all the groupings, you will obtain a hierarchical relationship representing three levels of specificity. The three levels fall on a specific-general continuum. The critical incidents fall on the specific end of the continuum, the satisfaction items fall somewhere in between the ends, and the customer requirements fall on the general end of the continuum.

Although the outlined process leads from critical incidents directly to satisfaction items that lead, in turn, to customer requirements, this is not the only order in which the critical incidents approach can flow. It may be easier to first categorize the critical incidents directly into the customer requirement categories. Next, within each customer requirement category, categorize critical incidents into various satisfaction items. Thus, both methods result in a hierarchical relationship between critical incidents, satisfaction items, and customer requirements. This hierarchical relationship is illustrated in Figure 2.4. Customer requirements are defined by satisfaction items that are, in turn, defined by critical incidents.

Three forms are presented in Appendices A and B to help you conduct interviews to determine the critical incidents. These forms are designed to facilitate each step in the critical incidents approach. The first form (Appendix A) will help you divide positive and negative aspects of the service and will make it easier to list all the critical incidents in a simple format. After you have conducted all the interviews, you can cut out the critical incidents and allocate them into separate satisfaction items. The second form (Appendix B) will allow you to place critical incidents into clusters and write satisfaction items as headings for each cluster. After writing all the satisfaction items, you can place similar satisfaction items in one customer requirement category. The third form (Appendix B) allows you to list satisfaction items that fall under a particular customer requirement.

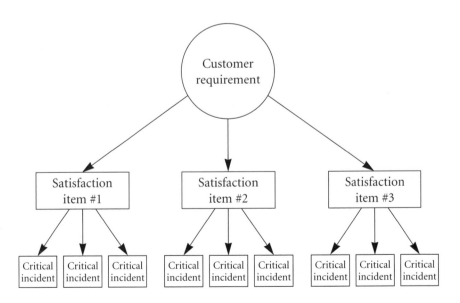

Figure 2.4. Hierarchical relationship among critical incidents, satisfaction items, and customer requirements.

Quality of the Categorization Process

The allocation process (from incident to satisfaction item, and from satisfaction item to customer requirement category) is very critical in understanding quality dimensions. Since the resulting customer requirements are derived from the allocation process of critical incidents, it is important to determine the quality of this allocation process.

The quality of both steps of the grouping processes can be established by having two people involved in the allocation process. These people will be referred to as *judges* since their role involves judging the similarity of critical incidents and satisfaction items. The first judge will follow the previously described process, grouping the incidents into satisfaction items and then grouping the satisfaction items into customer requirement categories. The second judge is given the customer requirement categories established by the first judge and asked to allocate the critical incidents directly into them, bypassing the satisfaction items.

Interjudge Agreement

The quality of the allocation process is indicated by the extent of agreement between the two judges. This "interjudge agreement" is the percentage of incidents both judges place in the same customer requirement category. Interjudge agreement is calculated by dividing the number of same incidents both judges place in the same customer requirement category by the total number of redundant and distinct incidents both judges place in the category. The index can range from 0 to 1.0. As this index approaches 1.0, it indicates that the judges are in high agreement. When the index approaches 0, it indicates that the judges are in low agreement. An index of approximately .8 should be used as a cutoff to determine if the customer requirement was acceptable. This criteria has been suggested elsewhere (Latham, et al. 1979).

Let's look at an example to illustrate this index. Suppose the first judge grouped 100 critical incidents into 20 satisfaction items. Next, assume that this judge allocated two satisfaction items (a total of seven incidents) into one particular customer requirement category. Specifically, judge 1 included incidents 1, 4, 6, 7, 9, 13, and 40 into the customer requirement category of *availability*. Next, the second judge would allocate all 100 critical incidents directly into the customer requirement categories that were established by the first judge, skipping the allocation of incidents into satisfaction items. Suppose that judge 2 included incidents 1, 2, 4, 6, 7, 9, 13, and 40 into the availability customer requirement category. The interjudge agreement for this particular category would be .88 (7/8). The interjudge agreement index would also be calculated for the remaining customer requirement categories.

If the criteria of .8 is not obtained, one or both judges may have made an error in the categorization process. A judge may have accidentally included/omitted a critical incident because he or she did not read the incident or category correctly. Thus, a brief check of the critical incidents could correct this problem. Also, a low interjudge index could occur when a small number of incidents make up one customer requirement. Therefore, if one judge omitted one incident from a total possible set of four incidents, the resulting interjudge agreement would be .75 (3/4). Although this value is below the recommended cutoff of .8, it seems to be an acceptable value given the small number of incidents that comprise the customer requirement category.

If a low interjudge agreement index is apparent, both judges should discuss their disagreement and come to a consensus as to the appropriate incidents that compose a particular customer requirement category. If they cannot agree, a third judge could be included to categorize the incidents into the categories. This third judge could highlight the differences between the first two judges, which will lead to some consensus.

Comprehensiveness of the Customer Requirements

Customer requirements obtained from the interviews should comprehensively define the quality of the service or product. If one important customer requirement category is overlooked during the initial interviewing process, the resulting customer satisfaction questionnaire would be deficient in measuring all customer requirements. In other words, you would be unable to assess your customers' perception on an important element of your service or product. Subsequently, you might not be able to improve overall customer satisfaction, because you do not know why your customers are satisfied or dissatisfied.

You may also establish the quality of the content of critical incidents (Latham, et al. 1979). Do this by removing a random group of approximately 10 percent of the critical incidents from the initial list *before* they are categorized into satisfaction items and customer requirement categories. After the entire allocation process is completed with 90 percent of the critical incidents (determining customer requirements category), examine the remaining 10 percent to see if they can be placed in the customer requirements categories.

If the 10 percent clearly can be placed into the customer requirement categories, then the categories are probably a comprehensive list of all possible customer requirement categories for that organization or group. If one or more of the 10 percent cannot be placed into any customer requirement categories, then the list is probably deficient in defining all possible customer requirement categories. This problem can be handled by interviewing more customers to obtain more critical incidents. The recommended number of additional interviews, however, will depend on the extent of the deficiency; the more deficient, the more interviews are needed. As a general rule, you should conduct five additional interviews for every critical incident that could not be allocated in the initial list of customer requirements. Once you have conducted these additional interviews, reallocate all critical incidents into satisfaction items, then into customer requirement categories.

The next part of this chapter illustrates the use of the critical incidents technique to determine customer requirements in the service and manufacturing sectors. The service sector is represented by the banking industry, and the manufacturing sector is represented by the automobile industry. In addition, because customers can be internal to an organization, there is an illustration of the critical incidents approach as applied to a department that provides statistical support to other departments in the organization.

Banking Industry

The first step in this process included interviews of 10 people who have had interactions with the bank's service. Critical incidents are confined to those related to customer interactions with personnel in the banking facility.

Critical incidents obtained from each person resulted in a total of 146 incidents. Some of these incidents appear in Figure 2.5. In addition, the figures includes the 10 satisfaction items (preceded by Roman numerals)

Responsiveness of Service

I. I waited a short period of time before I was helped.
1. I waited too long before I was helped.
2. Lines were too long.
3. I waited in line for a very long time.

II. The service started immediately when I arrived.
4. I went into the bank and the teller responded immediately to me.
5. I received immediate service for my transaction.
6. I could not get the teller's attention even though I was the only one in line.

Speed of Transaction

III. The teller handled transactions in a short period of time.
7. The teller handled transactions fast.
8. The handling of the transaction was quick after I told him or her what I wanted.

IV. The teller took a long time to complete my transaction.
9. The entire transaction took too long.
10. I waited a long time once I got to the window.

Availability of Service

V. The financial consultant was available to schedule me for an appointment at a good time.
11. I was able to set up an appointment with a financial consultant at a good time.
12. The appointment time with the financial planner was when I wanted it.

VI. My appointment with the financial consultant was at a convenient time.
13. The financial planner was available at a convenient time.
14. My appointment was at an inconvenient time.

Professionalism

VII. The teller talked to me in a pleasant way.
15. The teller took the time to talk to me to get all my requests completed.
16. The teller was rude to me (specifically, he or she was short with me).
17. The teller yelled at me when I could not open the depository canister.

VIII. The teller was very personable.
18. The teller gave a personal compliment on my appearance.
19. The teller had a friendly smile.
20. The teller was not personal (did not say hello or goodbye).

IX. The teller carefully listened to me when I was requesting a transaction.
21. The teller carefully listened to my request.
22. The teller took the time to listen to me when I requested a lot of things.

Figure 2.5. Critical incidents, satisfaction items, and customer requirements related to the banking industry.

X. The teller knew how to handle the transactions.

23. The teller knew how to handle a special transaction I requested.

24. The teller had to ask for help from another teller for a special transaction I asked for.

25. The teller looked confused when I asked for a special transaction.

Overall Satisfaction with Service

XI. The quality of the way the teller treated me was high.

XII. The way the teller treated me met my expectations.

XIII. I am satisfied with the way the teller treated me.

Figure 2.5. *Continued.*

that represent their respective critical incidents. Furthermore, satisfaction items are grouped into four customer requirement categories.

There is also a category labeled *Overall Satisfaction with Service*. The satisfaction items for this category are less specific than the items in different customer requirement categories and are not based on any critical incidents. This category represents overall service quality; it is not focused on any particular quality dimension. The value of these items will become clear in Chapters 3 and 6.

It is important to note that customer requirements reflect only aspects of the banking industry that are related to financial personnel. Additional incidents could have been included from other aspects of the banking industry, such as phone transaction banking, automatic teller machines, and banking statements.

Automobile Industry

The next illustration of the critical incidents technique applies to the automobile industry. Critical incidents were confined to the aspects of the automobile's interior and its "drivability." Aspects of car driving quality were gathered in customer interviews. The critical incidents, satisfaction items, and customer requirements appear in Figure 2.6. The categorization process resulted in three customer requirements.

Interior Quality

I.   The seating position was very comfortable.
1. The seats are comfortable.
2. The seats were very uncomfortable.
3. There is ample leg room.

II.   The visibility through the window was good.
4. There were many blind spots from the driver's seat.

III. The inside of the car was noisy.
5. There is loud interior noise.
6. The interior noise interfered with the sound of the stereo.
7. Air whistles through the window.
8. There was little noise while I was driving.

Instrumentation

IV.   The instrumentation panel was simple to understand.
9. The instrumentation panel is difficult to read.
10. The dials for the accessories were too complex to understand.
11. The dials for the controls were easy to understand.

V.   The instrumentation panel was clearly visible from the driving seat.
12. I could clearly see all the instruments and gauges.
13. I had a clear view of the instrumentation.
14. Instruments are within good reaching distance.

"Drivability"

VI.   The car stopped smoothly when I applied the brakes.
15. The car did not brake well. (It would vibrate when I was braking.)
16. The car vibrated when I applied the brakes.
17. The car stopped smoothly when I applied the brakes.

VII. The car vibrated at high speeds.
18. The car vibrated at high speeds.
19. The car rides smoothly, even at high speeds.

VIII. The car handled corners well.
20. The car handles corners well.
21. I could negotiate corners very well.
22. The car would consistently skid around tight corners.

Overall Satisfaction with Automobile

IX.   I enjoyed driving the car.

X.   I liked the overall driving experience of the car.

XI.   The drive was excellent.

Figure 2.6. Critical incidents, satisfaction items, and customer requirements related to the driving quality of automobiles.

Another way to conceptualize the groupings of these satisfaction items is to place them all into one customer requirement category called *perception of driving quality*. This customer requirement could be paralleled by another aspect of car quality such as *reliability of car*. This customer requirement might be measured by more objective indices such as the number of repairs, amount of money spent on repairs, or number of breakdowns. Therefore, using this conceptualization, there could be two customer requirements: (1) The customers' perception of driving quality and (2) The car's reliability.

Statistical Support

The next illustration of the critical incidents technique applies to a statistical department that provides support to other departments within the organization. A total of nine customers who have had previous contact with the staff in this department were interviewed. The categorization process resulted in five customer requirements. A partial list of the critical incidents, satisfaction items, and customer requirements is included in Figure 2.7.

Statistical Support

I. The staff person explained the statistical tests in understandable words.
    1. There was good explanation of the statistical tests.
    2. I received good explanation of the statistical analyses.

II. The statistical analyses were thorough.
    3. There was good analysis of data.
    4. Statistical help was minimal.
    5. The data analysis was incomplete.

III. The staff understood my software requirements.
    6. The software problem was never resolved.
    7. The staff understood the kinds of software I needed.

Figure 2.7. Critical incidents, satisfaction items, and customer requirements related to the quality of a statistical support department.

Enthusiasm

IV. The staff person was always willing to help.
　　8. The person was always willing to help.
　　9. The person would always help when I asked.

V. The staff person went out of his or her way to help.
　　10. The person did not do the tasks.
　　11. The person refused to do the project.
　　12. The person did not do the project I asked him or her to do.

Final Written Report

VI. The written report was sufficiently detailed.
　　13. The writeup of the project was not detailed.
　　14. The written report was not complete.
　　15. The document needed to be more comprehensive.

VII. The written report contained what I needed.
　　16. Everything I asked for was in the final report.
　　17. The report contained everything I asked for.

Responsiveness

VIII. The staff person completed the job quickly.
　　18. Projects are completed quickly.
　　19. The project started very late.
　　20. I received fast turnaround time on my project.

Project Management

IX. The staff person finished the project in the stated time frame.
　　21. The staff person did not meet the specified deadlines.
　　22. The staff person did not have the job completed for a meeting.
　　23. The project was turned in late.

X. The staff person planned the entire project through its completion.
　　24. The planning of the project was complete.
　　25. The project was well-organized.

XI. The staff person understood how much time the project required.
　　26. The person did not understand my requirements.
　　27. The person understood the magnitude of the project.

Overall Satisfaction with Support

XII. I am satisfied with the service I received.

XIII. The quality of the service met my expectations.

Figure 2.7. *Continued.*

Chapter Summary

This chapter demonstrated two techniques for determining customer requirements, those aspects of your service or product that define its quality. The first technique, the quality dimension development process, involves people closely linked to the service or product. These people should be knowledgeable in understanding the needs of the customers and the function and purpose of the service or product. These people are responsible for determining quality dimensions, definitions of the quality dimensions, and specific examples of each dimension.

The second technique, the critical incident technique, involves obtaining information from customers about actual incidents they consider to define good and bad aspects of the product or service. These incidents define the satisfaction items, and the satisfaction items, in turn, define the customer requirements. Some examples demonstrated the effectiveness of the critical incidents approach in establishing customer requirements for both nonmanufacturing and manufacturing organizations and internal customer support groups.

Figure 2.8 presents the basic steps to follow for each method when establishing your customer requirements. This figure includes some important points at each step to facilitate the process of establishing customer requirements.

The next chapter will discuss measurement issues related to questionnaire development and use. These measurement principles should be considered when evaluating any type of questionnaire designed to measure people's opinions, perceptions, and attitudes.

Quality Dimension Development	
Steps	Important Points
1. Create list of quality dimensions.	• Read professional and trade journals to obtain list of quality dimensions.
	• Generate list from personal experience.
2. Write definitions of each dimension.	• Definition can be in general terms.

Figure 2.8. Procedures for establishing customer requirements.

3. Develop specific examples for each quality dimension.	• Examples should use specific adjectives reflecting the service or product.
	• Examples should include specific behaviors of the provider.
	• Examples should use declarative statements.

Critical Incidents Approach

Steps	Important Points
1. Generate critical incidents.	• Interview customers.
	• Critical incidents should be specific examples of good or poor service or product quality.
	• Each critical incident reflects only one example.
2. Categorize critical incidents into clusters.	• Categorization is based on similarity in content of the incidents.
3. Write satisfaction items for each critical incident cluster.	• Each satisfaction item should be a declarative statement.
	• Satisfaction items should be specific.
4. Categorize satisfaction items into clusters, each cluster representing a customer requirement.	• Categorization should be based on similarity of satisfaction items.
	• Customer requirement must reflect the content of satisfaction items.
5. Determine the quality of the categorization process.	• Two judges should do categorization steps.
	• Calculate interjudge agreement.
6. Determine the comprehensiveness of customer requirements.	• Remove 10 percent of the critical incidents before establishing customer requirements.
	• Determine if the 10 percent can be placed into the customer requirements.

Figure 2.8. *Continued.*

CHAPTER 3

Reliability and Validity

Measurement instruments can help us better understand and make predictions about our world. For example, we may be interested in measuring our customers' level of satisfaction to uncover any perceived problems with our services or products. In addition, we might want to change our customers' opinions about our services or products. To know our customers' current level of satisfaction and to realize if changes in their opinion do occur, we need a measure that accurately assesses customer attitudes. When we develop questionnaires, it is important to ensure that the data obtained from them reflect reliable and valid information. This chapter presents measurement issues that demonstrate the importance of careful thought when designing questionnaires to measure perceptions and attitudes.

The Meaning of Customer Perception and Attitude

Customers' perceptions of the quality of a service and their overall satisfaction have some observable indicators. Customers may smile when they talk about the product or service. They may say good things about the product or service. Both these actions are manifestations or indicators of an underlying construct we might call *customer satisfaction*. The terms *customer satisfaction* and *perception of quality* are labels we use to summarize a set of observable actions related to the product and/or service.

This idea of constructs and their relationship to observable variables is depicted in Figure 3.1.

As indicated by Figure 3.1, various observable criteria (such as items) might be manifestations of an underlying dimension (for example, customer requirements). For example, we could make inferences about people's happiness by obtaining several types of observable indicators of the underlying *happiness* construct. Observable indicators could include smiling, laughing, and saying positive things. If a person is laughing, smiling, and saying positive things, we draw the conclusion that this person is happy. We have, in fact, concluded that this person is happy by examining the observable criteria.

Similarly, we draw conclusions about customers' perceptions and attitudes about products or services by examining observable manifestations related to the product or service. These observable manifestations are the responses the customers give on a customer satisfaction questionnaire. If people indicate good things about the product on the customer satisfaction questionnaire and demonstrate other indications of positive

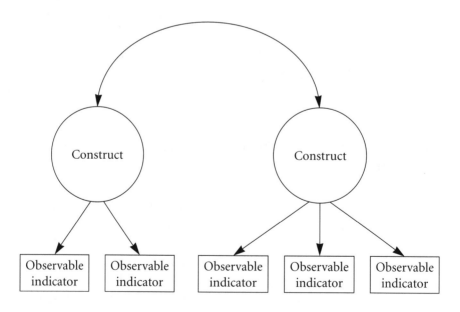

Figure 3.1. The relationship between observable indicators and the underlying constructs and the relationship between the constructs.

behavior, we can draw the conclusion that they are satisfied with the product.

From Figure 3.1, we can make some conclusions about the concept of customer perception and attitude. First, we can never really know the true underlying satisfaction level of our customers. We develop measures to make inferences about the underlying construct, satisfaction. Second, we are interested in the relationship between underlying dimensions or constructs (such as customer satisfaction or perceived responsiveness). We want to understand how these underlying constructs, or customer requirements, are related to each other.

When constructing a questionnaire or scale that assesses customer attitudes and perceptions toward customer requirements, it is necessary to consider measurement issues to ensure that scores derived from such instruments reflect accurate information about these underlying constructs. The emphasis on measurement issues in customer satisfaction is similar to the importance of measurement issues concerning instruments designed to measure tangible objects, such as parts of a machine. Gauge repeatability and reliability (gauge R&R) indices, for example, are designed to reflect the quality of the measurement process in industrial settings. Similarly, statistical indices can reflect the quality of measurement of satisfaction questionnaires. Two important measurement issues to consider when developing questionnaires are reliability and validity.

Reliability

I will introduce the concept of reliability using a simple measurement example. We could use a ruler to measure the length of one particular part. We could measure the part five times, obtaining five scores. Even though the part can be characterized by one true length, we would expect the five scores to be slightly different from each other. The deviation could be due to various random factors in the measurement process, such as variations in use of the ruler with each measurement or change in ruler length with each measurement. To the extent that random factors are introduced into the measurement process, any one score we obtain may not reliably reflect the true score.

When we develop a questionnaire that assesses customers' perception of the quality of the service or product, we want to be sure that measurements are free from random error. That is, we want to be sure the true underlying level of perception of quality or satisfaction is accurately reflected in the questionnaire score. When random error is introduced into measurement, the observed score is less reliable in estimating the true underlying score. Errors of measurement are examined under the context of reliability.

Reliability is defined as the extent to which measurements are free from random-error variance. Random error decreases the reliability of the measurement. If we want to feel confident that scores on our questionnaire reliably reflect the underlying dimension, we want the questionnaire to demonstrate high reliability. There are three general forms of reliability: test-retest reliability, equivalent form reliability, and internal consistency. Discussions of reliability also appear in various textbooks (Anastasi 1988; Brown 1983; Guion 1965; and Gulliksen 1987). I will first review information concerning classical measurement theory, and then I will discuss indices used to estimate the reliability of questionnaires. A more detailed discussion of classical measurement theory, including underlying statistical assumptions, appears in various books (such as Gulliksen 1987).

Classical Measurement Theory

When assessing a customer's level of satisfaction, the best we can do is to ask the person to respond to some questions. From the answers, we obtain a score that indicates that person's level of satisfaction with the product or service. However, this only gives us an observed score of that person's level of satisfaction. According to classical measurement theory, this observed score is composed of a true score (which is the actual level of satisfaction) and a component of measurement error. Error is assumed to be random and is unrelated to the true score. The basic equation of classical measurement theory, known as the classical measurement model, describes the relationship between observed scores, true scores, and error. The model is

$$X = T + E$$

where X is the observed score, T is the true score, and E is error of measurement. To the extent that we have small error of measurement, this observable measure (X) is highly representative of the underlying true score, T.

An illustration concerning the relationship between these three components might make things clear. In Table 3.1, we have a hypothetical example of some data collected from 10 customers. The first column (X) represents the score these people received on the questionnaire (their observed score) and indicates their level of satisfaction: the higher the number, the higher their satisfaction. Now, let's assume that we were somehow able to obtain the customers' true level of satisfaction (the customers' true score)—perhaps we know God, and He informed us of the true level of satisfaction for each customer. The second column (T) represents the customers' true level of satisfaction. Finally, the last column (E) represents the random error and is calculated by subtracting the values in column T from the values in column X.

There are two approaches we can take in explaining reliability. One approach focuses on correlational analysis (see Appendix J), and the

Table 3.1. Hypothetical example illustrating observed scores, true scores, and error.

Customers	X	T	E
1.	5	5	0
2.	3	4	−1
3.	4	3	1
4.	3	2	1
5.	1	1	0
6.	5	5	0
7.	5	4	1
8.	2	3	−1
9.	1	2	−1
10.	1	1	0
	$M_X = 3.0$	$M_T = 3.0$	$M_E = 0.0$
	$\text{Var}(X) = 2.88$	$\text{Var}(T) = 2.22$	$\text{Var}(E) = 0.66$

Average for

$X = M_X = \Sigma X_i/n$
$T = M_T = \Sigma T_i/n$
$E = M_E = \Sigma E_i/n$

Variance for

$X = \text{Var}(X) = \Sigma(X_i - M_X)^2/n$
$T = \text{Var}(T) = \Sigma(T_i - M_T)^2/n$
$E = \text{Var}(E) = \Sigma(E_i - M_E)^2/n$

other focuses on variance for each of the components in the classical theory equation (*X*, *T*, and *E*). I will present the correlational approach first.

Using correlational analysis, we can determine the degree of agreement between the observed scores (*X*) and the true scores (*T*). We can calculate the correlation coefficient between *X* and *T* scores. A correlation coefficient can range from –1 to 1. A negative correlation indicates that, as one variable increases, the other variable decreases. A positive correlation indicates that, as one variable increases, the other variable also increases. A correlation of zero indicates there is no linear relationship between the two variables. A perfect negative or positive correlation indicates a perfect negative and positive relationship, respectively.

Using the data in Table 3.1, the correlation coefficient between the *X* and *T* scores is calculated to be .88. This suggests that the differences in true scores are closely matched by differences in observed scores. That is, people who have truly high scores (true scores) also obtain relatively high scores on the questionnaire (observed score). Also, people who have relatively low true scores also obtain relatively low observed scores on the questionnaire.

Therefore, a form of reliability would be the correlation between observed and true scores. As the correlation between *X* and *T* increases, the differences in people's *X* scores more closely approximates the differences in people's *T* scores. When the correlation between *X* and *T* is 1.00, there is perfect linear agreement between *X* and *T*; that is, differences in *X* scores exactly match the differences in *T* scores. When the correlation between *X* and *T* is 0, there is no linear relationship between *X* and *T*; that is, there is no agreement between *X* and *T* scores.

We could also examine reliability of the measurement instrument by focusing on variance of the specific components (in other words, observed, true, and error components). Variance is an index that reflects the spread of the data around the arithmetic average of the data. (See Appendix E for a discussion of average and variance.) The larger the variance, the larger the spread of the data around the average. The formula for variance is presented in Table 3.1, and the variance for each component has been calculated. The variances for each of the sets of variables are related in a similar fashion as the variables themselves.

$$\mathrm{Var}(X) \;=\; \mathrm{Var}(T) \;+\; \mathrm{Var}(E)$$

where $\mathrm{Var}(X)$ is the variance associated with the set of observed scores, $\mathrm{Var}(T)$ is the variance associated with the set of true scores, and $\mathrm{Var}(E)$ is the variance associated with the set of errors.

As error variance decreases, as is indicated by the equation, the variance of the observed score approaches the variance of the true score; that is, as error decreases, the differences in observed scores between people become a *reliable* reflection of differences in their true scores. If the error variance is large, however, the observed score is not reliably related to the true score.

Reliability estimates can be indexed by a number that represents the percentage of variance of observed scores that is accounted for by the variance in true scores. In mathematical terms, this corresponds to the following equation.

$$\text{Reliability } (r_{xx'}) \;=\; \mathrm{Var}(T) \;/\; [\mathrm{Var}(T) \;+\; \mathrm{Var}(E)]$$

where $\mathrm{Var}(T) + \mathrm{Var}(E) = \mathrm{Var}(X)$.

This reliability index can range from 0 to 1.0. A reliability index of 1.0 indicates there is no measurement error; observed scores can be perfectly predicted by true scores. This is a highly desirable situation. A reliability index of 0 indicates there is no true score variation or that the variation in the observed scores can be completely explained by random error. This is a highly undesirable situation. For the data in Table 3.1, we can calculate the reliability of the observed score (X), which is $r_{xx'} = 2.22/2.88 = .77$. This indicates that our observed scores are somewhat related to the underlying true scores for the customers. In fact, the correlation between the X and T scores can be calculated by taking the square root of the reliability ($r_{XT} = \sqrt{.77} = .88$). Conversely, reliability is the squared correlation between the observed scores and true scores.

Reliability, then, can be discussed in terms of both the relationship between observed and true scores, and the variance of components of the classical measurement model. The two approaches should not be interpreted as representing two different types of reliability. They are merely two different ways of conceptualizing the degree to which observed scores are related to true scores (or the degree to which observed scores are free from random error). Readers are offered both approaches to help facilitate understanding of this important concept.

Standard Error of Measurement

Measurement error is often discussed in terms of the standard error of measurement (SEM). The SEM could be calculated for a given individual by administering the questionnaire or test to that individual many times (say, 100 times). Due to measurement error, the person might not get the same score on each administration of the test. Thus, these observed scores would form a distribution that would approximate a normal distribution described by a mean and a standard deviation (see Appendix F). The mean of this distribution would be our best estimate of the person's true score. The standard deviation of this distribution is technically called the *standard error of measurement* and describes the amount of measurement error we have. Theoretically, we could calculate the SEM for each individual, but this would be tedious, if not impossible. We can more easily calculate SEM from the reliability of the questionnaire. The equation for the SEM is

$$\text{SEM} = s_x \times \sqrt{(1 - r_{xx'})}$$

where s_x is the standard deviation of observed scores for the sample of people to which the questionnaire was administered, and $r_{xx'}$ is the reliability of the questionnaire.

As this formula illustrates, SEM is inversely and monotonically related to reliability. That is, for a given s_x, an increase in reliability always leads to a decrease in SEM. As reliability approaches 1.0 (observed scores, X, are perfectly correlated with true scores, T), SEM goes to zero. Conversely, as reliability approaches zero (X scores are not related to T scores), SEM will equal the s_x.

The meaning of SEM and the relationship between reliability and SEM is illustrated in Figure 3.2. The top portion of the figure presents the expected distribution of random errors for a given individual using a particular questionnaire. The SEM describes the degree of errors for observed scores we would expect for a given true score. As the SEM decreases, the more confident we are that the observed scores are a good reflection of the true scores. For example, if the SEM for a given questionnaire was .50, then we could say with a 95 percent degree of confidence that, for a person

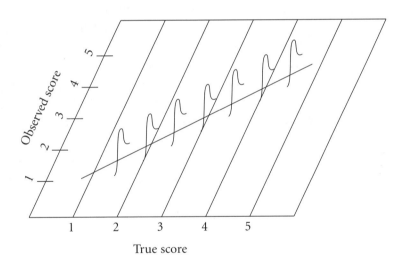

Figure 3.2. The top portion illustrates an expected distribution of observed scores for a given person. The bottom portion illustrates the relationship between observed scores and true scores and incorporates the standard error of measurement.

with a true score of 4, his or her observed score would fall between 3.0 = (4 − (2 × .5)) and 5.0 = (4 + (2 × .5)). If the SEM was .25, we could say with the same degree of confidence that the person's observed score falls between 3.5 and 4.5.

The bottom portion of Figure 3.2 demonstrates the relationship between X and T scores and shows how SEM is incorporated into this relationship. As this illustration indicates, if we have a high degree of measurement error, we are less confident that a particular observed score is associated with any one true score. For example, if SEM is high, which would be reflected in the widening of the distributions, then an observed score of 4 might represent a true score of 4 or it might also represent a number of other true scores. If SEM is low, which would be reflected in the narrowing of the distributions, then an observed score of 3 would most likely represent a true score of 3, and the possibility of the observed score representing other true scores is greatly decreased.

Some simple scatter plots of the relationship between the X and T scores are presented in Figure 3.3. Although T scores can never be assessed, a hypothetical scatterplot of the T scores with the X scores can be presented given a certain value of the reliability. In general, as reliability increases, the precision in predicting X scores from the T scores increases. In other words, as reliability increases, the variability in X for any given T score (represented as SEM) decreases. As seen in Figure 3.3(a), a reliability of 0 indicates that changes in X scores are unrelated to changes in T scores. In other words, a given observed score, X, could reflect many possible true scores, T. As seen in Figure 3.3(b), a reliability of .81 indicates that an observed score (X) is highly related to the underlying true score (T). Consequently, a given observed score is likely to reflect a limited number of true scores. Figure 3.3(c) illustrates a measure with a low degree of reliability.

Sources of Error and Reliability Estimates

The term *reliability* is a generic term used to describe the degree of error associated with a measure. Because we can never know the exact degree of true variance and error variance, we can never directly calculate the level of reliability for a set of scores. We can, however, estimate reliability. We will see that there are different methods of estimating reliability. These different forms of reliability are different depending on what type of measurement error you want to examine. Next, I will cover the different type of estimates of reliability and the errors associated with them. There are three general classes of reliability: stability, equivalence, and internal consistency.

Figure 3.3. The hypothetical relationship between true scores and observed scores with varying degrees of reliability (a: $r_{xx'} = 0$; b: $r_{xx'} = .81$; c: $r_{xx'} = .25$).

Measures of Stability and Test-Retest Reliability

It is possible to administer the same survey at two different times (time 1 and time 2) to the same set of people. The difference between their scores at time 1 and time 2 reflects error associated with a change in the characteristic that is being measured by the survey. Changes from time 1 to time 2 indicates one of three things: (1) There may have been a change in the true score being measured, (2) There may have been measurement error, or (3) Both (1) and (2).

An index of reliability to assess the stability over time is referred to as *test-retest reliability*. This index of reliability is essentially the correlation between the survey scores for time 1 and time 2. As is seen in Table 3.2, we have a set of 10 people, each receiving a survey at two separate times. Their

Table 3.2. Test-retest reliability for survey X.

Person	Time 1 (X)	Time 2 (X')
B. Hinderer	4.5	5.0
J. Close	4.0	3.4
T. Hayes	2.0	3.0
M. Hayes	5.0	5.0
C. Silva	1.5	3.0
H. Turner	5.0	3.0
R. Schneider	4.0	4.0
T. Garcia	2.6	3.5
L. Foster	2.0	1.0
C. Berry	4.5	4.0
Mean of X and X'	3.51	3.49
SD	1.35	1.16
ΣX and $\Sigma X'$	35.10	34.90
ΣX^2 and $\Sigma (X')^2$	139.51	133.81
$\Sigma (X X')$	131.70	

$$r = \frac{10(131.7) - (35.10 \times 34.90)}{\sqrt{([(10 \times 139.51) - 35.10^2][(10 \times 133.81) - 34.90^2])}}$$

$$r = .657$$

respective scores for each time period are listed. Using the formula in Appendix J to calculate the correlation, we see that the test-retest reliability is .66. This reliability estimate indicates that scores are relatively stable across the two time periods. People who have low scores at time 1 also tend to have low scores at time 2. People who have high scores at time 1 also tend to have high scores at time 2.

The stability of customer satisfaction over time might depend on the time interval between the administration of the survey. Given a short time interval between the first and second administration of the survey, there may be carry-over effects to the second survey session. That is, customers may remember their scores in the first session and simply duplicate them in the second administration of the survey. Thus, a high test-retest correlation (say, .90) between the two sets of scores might not be due to the stability of the customer satisfaction being measured but reflect carry-over effects. On the other hand, when there is a long interval between two administrations of the survey, many intervening variables can come into effect and, consequently, influence customer satisfaction scores. For example, customers could be given a survey one month after they purchase a product and then given the same survey one year later. If we see a low correlation (say, .40) between these two scores, there are competing explanations for this result: (1) There is a change in the customer satisfaction level over this time period, (2) The customer survey is not highly reliable, or (3) Both.

Even though interpretations of the test-retest correlation can be problematic for either short or long time intervals between administrations, there is still no standard rule for an appropriate length of time between survey administrations. A general rule would be that, when determining an appropriate time period between survey administrations, one must be cognizant of the types of factors that can influence survey scores and adjust the time interval accordingly.

With customer satisfaction surveys, test-retest reliability is not commonly calculated due to the difficulty in designing a survey process that allows for the administration of the survey to the same set of individuals across two time periods. Each customer must be identified so that his or her scores for time 1 and time 2 can be linked together in order to calculate the correlation between the two sets of scores. For research purposes, this type of reliability estimation might be useful to see if, in fact, customer satisfaction does not change over time. For practical purposes, however, this method of estimating reliability may not be worthwhile. However, test-retest reliability could be conducted at the group level of analysis to determine the stability of customer satisfaction across different office locations. For example, if a bank has hundreds of locations, it would be possible to calculate the average satisfaction scores for each bank branch across two different times. The correlation between the two sets of bank branch scores would indicate the degree of stability we see across time. A high correlation would indicate that customer satisfaction levels for branches are the same over time. A low correlation would indicate that customer satisfaction levels for branches change over time.

Measures of Equivalence and Parallel Forms Reliability

A survey contains a specific set of questions that are designed to assess a particular construct (such as service quality). When developing this survey of service quality, you include various specific questions to measure service quality. Our goal in developing the survey is to be able to generalize from the specific items in our measure to the content domain from which the items were drawn. The set of items used in the survey are just a small sample of possible items we could have used in the service quality survey. To the extent that scores derived from this survey are unique to the items within the survey, we have error associated with the selection of those particular items.

An index of reliability to assess the extent to which scores are free from error associated with a particular set of items is referred to as *parallel forms reliability*. Essentially, this form of reliability indicates whether the scores of the survey can generalize beyond the specific items that are in the survey to the domain of all possible items. For this form of reliability, we compare two equivalent forms of a survey designed to measure the same construct. For example, it is possible to develop two different surveys of service quality, each survey containing slightly different questions to measure the same underlying construct of interest. To calculate parallel forms reliability, two surveys measuring the same construct are administered to the same set of people. The correlation between the two sets of scores is used as the estimate of reliability. If there is not much error associated with the item selection process, the two different surveys should be highly correlated with each other. Table 3.3 contains the scores of two different surveys that measure service quality for 10 people. The correlation between the two surveys is .93, suggesting that there is little error associated with the selection of the specific items within each survey. A low correlation between the two measures could suggest that scores from one or both of the measures are not generalizable beyond the items in the scale.

Internal Consistency

Internal consistency is concerned with the degree to which the items in the survey are measuring the same thing. For example, in a customer survey,

Table 3.3. Parallel forms reliability for survey X.

Person	Survey 1	Survey 2
B. Hinderer	4.5	5.0
J. Browne	4.4	4.0
T. Hayes	2.0	1.5
M. Hayes	5.0	5.0
C. Silva	1.5	2.0
H. Turner	5.0	4.0
R. Schneider	3.8	4.0
T. Garcia	2.4	3.0
L. Foster	2.0	1.5
C. Berry	4.5	4.0
Mean of X_1 and X_2	3.51	3.35
SD	1.38	1.27
ΣX_1 and ΣX_2	35.10	33.50
ΣX_1^2 and ΣX_2^2	140.31	126.75
$\Sigma(X_1 X_2)$	132.25	

$$r = \frac{10(132.25) - (35.10 \times 33.50)}{\sqrt{([(10 \times 140.31) - 35.10^2][(10 \times 126.75) - 33.50^2])}}$$

$$r = .93$$

we could combine some items to get a single score of some quality dimension. The items that are combined should be assessing the same thing. If the items are not measuring the same thing, then the overall score would be meaningless. To the degree that the items in the survey are measuring the same thing, we have little measurement error. Two estimates of internal consistency will be presented next.

Split-Half Reliability Estimate

This method estimates internal consistency by dividing the scale into halves (for example, odd versus even items, or first half of scale versus last half of scale), then correlating the scores on these halves. A high correlation indicates that the two sets yield consistent information; that is, if a person scores high on one set of items, then that person also scores high on the other set. Thus, the items are likely measuring the same thing.

When using the split-half method to estimate reliability, it is necessary to include a correction factor. Reliability estimates are affected by the length of the scale: the more items on the scale, the higher the reliability. Using the split-half method, we actually estimate the reliability for a scale that was half the original length (because the scale was divided in half). To control for test length, we use a correction formula, the Spearman-Brown formula, which results in a corrected reliability estimate. The general formula is

$$r_{cc'} = (nr_{12}) / (1 + (n - 1)r_{12})$$

where $r_{cc'}$ is the corrected reliability estimate of the questionnaire, r_{12} is the correlation between the two halves of the same questionnaire, and n is the number of items in the overall scale divided by the number of items in each of the halves

For example, we may want to calculate the reliability of a questionnaire that has 10 items. Using the split-half method, we divide the questionnaire into halves containing five items each and calculate the correlation between the halves. Suppose we found that the correlation was $r_{12} = .7$. Next, because reliability estimates are affected by the length of the scale, we would correct this value to obtain a better estimate of reliability. The final reliability estimate, corrected for length, would be $r_{cc'} = .82$ ($r_{cc'} = (2 \times .7)/(1 + .7)$).

Cronbach's Alpha Estimate

The Cronbach's alpha estimate also tells us how highly the items in our questionnaire are interrelated. Unlike the split-half reliability method, however, this estimate does not have to be corrected for length. Calculation of Cronbach's estimate is usually done with the help of a statistical package designed to calculate this reliability estimate. Statistical packages are usually used if questionnaires have many items. Cronbach's (1951) estimate of reliability is calculated using the variance of individual items and covariances between the items. This estimate, however, also can be calculated using the correlations between the items. Given that items within a questionnaire use the same scale, both approaches give similar estimates. The latter approach is easier to understand and is presented here. Generally, the formula for Cronbach's reliability estimate is

$$r_{xx'} = (K/(K - 1)) \times (1 - [(\Sigma X_{ii}) / (\Sigma X_{ii} + \Sigma X_{ij} \text{ where } i \neq j)])$$

where X_{iis} and X_{ijs} are the elements in the covariance matrix or correlation matrix, and K is the number of items within a given dimension. The numerator, (ΣX_{ii}), indicates that the elements in the diagonal of the covariance (correlation) matrix be added together. The denominator, $(\Sigma X_{ii} + \Sigma X_{ij})$, indicates that all the elements in the covariance (correlation) matrix be added together.

Table 3.4 represents a correlation matrix using actual data for the items from Figure 4.5 in Chapter 4. Customers responded to each item using a five-point scale ("1" represented strong disagreement, and "5" represented

Table 3.4. The correlation matrix of the items from Figure 4.5.

	Avail 1	Avail 2	Avail 3	Resp 1	Resp 2	Resp 3
Avail 1	1.00	.92	.80	.23	.00	.34
Avail 2	.92	1.00	.51	.49	.16	.49
Avail 3	.80	.51	1.00	−.25	−.25	.00
Resp 1	.23	.49	−.25	1.00	.78	.83
Resp 2	.00	.16	−.25	.78	1.00	.67
Resp 3	.34	.49	.00	.83	.67	1.00

strong agreement). With this questionnaire, we think we are measuring two customer requirements, perception of availability (items 1 through 3) and perception of responsiveness (items 4 through 6). Therefore, we can combine the items in their respective scales (average of the items within each scale) to obtain two observed scores, each representing a customer requirement. We now want to see if these observed scores are reliable indicators of an under-lying dimension. The reliability estimate is $.897 = [1.5 \times (1 - 3/7.468)]$ for perception of availability and $.904 = [1.5 \times (1 - 3/7.556)]$ for perception of responsiveness. As indicated by these reliability estimates, the composite of the three items for each dimension gives us an overall observed score that is a reliable measure of the underlying dimension.

Types of Error and Reliability Estimates

Reliability indicates the degree to which measures are free from random error. As we have seen, however, there are different sources of error and corresponding estimates of reliability. Table 3.5 summarizes these differ-ent sources of error and the methods of estimating reliability. One type of measurement error is associated with time sampling. A survey given on two separate occasions might result in different scores. The method to determine the degree of this error is the test-retest method of estimating reliability. Another form of measurement error is associated with the spe-cific items used in a given measure. Different items are used in two differ-ent surveys that measure the same thing. If both surveys are measuring the same thing, the sample of items from both surveys should be representa-tive of the same larger population of items. The extent to which results from the survey are item-specific, we have error associated with item sam-pling. Parallel forms reliability is the method to determine the degree of this type of error. Finally, if we develop a survey that is designed to mea-sure a single thing, then all the items in that measure should be highly cor-related with each other. Internal consistency estimates indicate the degree to which the items in the survey measure the same thing.

It is clear that the term *reliability* means different things, depending on what source of error you are estimating. It is important that you are aware of the distinction among the sources of error and methods to esti-mate reliability. It is possible that each source of error would occur in a single instance in the use of a survey. For a given situation, a survey could be assessed on the error associated with time-specific factors as well as item-specific factors. Corresponding reliability estimates could be calculated for these respective sources of error. Be aware of the sources of error associated with these reliability estimates and what they mean.

Benefits of Scales with High Reliability

There are two benefits of having a scale with high reliability: (1) It distinguishes between varying levels of satisfaction better than a scale with low reliability, and (2) It makes it more likely that we will find significant relationships between variables that are truly related to each other.

Detection of Differences in Satisfaction Levels

Reliability indicates the degree to which observed scores are related to true scores. Therefore, if we use a scale with a high level of reliability, we can better distinguish between people on the continuum of customer satisfaction. As illustrated in the scatter plot in Figure 3.3(c) representing a scale

Table 3.5. Sources of error and methods of estimating reliability.

Source of error	What are we asking?	Estimate of reliability	How to calculate reliability estimate
Time-specific	Is there stability in customer satisfaction over time?	Test-retest	Correlation between same survey given on two occasions
Item-specific	Can the items in the survey generalize to all possible items?	Parallel forms	Correlation between two different surveys designed to measure the same thing
Internal consistency	Do the items in the survey measure the same thing?	Split-half	1. Corrected correlation between two halves of the same survey
		Cronbach's alpha	2. See text

of low reliability ($r_{xx'} = .25$), we would have considerable error of measurement. Consequently, we could find that customer 1, who has a true score of 3, could have an observed score between 1.0 and 4.5. Also, customer 2, who has a true score of 5.0, could have an observed score as low as 3.0. Although these two customers actually differ with respect to customer satisfaction (*T* scores), we might not be able to distinguish between them because our scale is unreliable. It is possible that customer 2 with a higher true score of customer satisfaction might get an observed score that is lower than the observed score of customer 1. With low reliability, there is a great deal of uncertainty as to what the observed score indicates for any person. This would limit the strength of the conclusions we can make about people's scores.

If we use a scale with high reliability such as $r_{xx'} = .81$ [see Figure 3.3(b)], we would have little error in measurement. Therefore, we would be able to distinguish between people whose satisfaction levels are close. Now, customer 1, who is truly less satisfied than customer 2, will more likely get an observed score that is lower than the score of customer 2. In the situation where reliability equals 1.0, customers who have a true score of 3 will get an observed score of 3, and customers who have a true score of 5 will get an observed score of 5.

In summary, when using scales with low reliability, only true differences that are very large are likely to be detected. A scale with high reliability will likely detect true differences that are either very large or very small. The strength of this detection is directly related to the reliability of the scale. Therefore, to increase the ability to make distinctions between customers, we need to increase the reliability of the scale.

Detection of Significant Relationships Between Variables

We might want to determine if perceptions of availability are linked to overall customer satisfaction. This might be important to know if we wanted to determine where to allocate some resources to increase overall customer satisfaction. We would allocate resources to increase availability of the service if, in fact, it did significantly predict overall customer satisfaction. We could determine how strongly these two variables are related to each other by calculating the correlation coefficient (see Appendix J) between them.

Even though we have an observed correlation between these two variables, we are really interested in the true correlation between them. Our observed scores possess some amount of measurement error that will decrease the correlation between these two variables. Due to error in measurement of the variables, observed correlations between variables are always smaller than the true correlations. The relationship between the true correlation and the observed correlation is

$$r_{X_oY_o} = r_{X_tY_t} \sqrt{r_{XX'}} \sqrt{r_{YY'}}$$

where $r_{X_oY_o}$ is the observed correlation between variables X and Y, $r_{X_tY_t}$ is the true correlation between variables X and Y, and $\sqrt{r_{XX'}}$ and $\sqrt{r_{YY'}}$ are the reliabilities for variables X and Y, respectively.

From this equation, we see that the observed correlation decreases as the reliability of either or both scales decreases. Also, as the reliability of both scales approaches unity, the observed correlation approaches the true correlation. Using the previous example, even though there might be a true relationship between availability and overall customer satisfaction, poor measures (low reliability) of either variable would attenuate the correlation and lead us to the wrong conclusion about the relationship between these two variables.

For example, let's suppose that we assessed the satisfaction level of 50 of our customers using a measure that included scales assessing perception of availability and overall customer satisfaction. The reliability of each of these scales is .50. Suppose that the true correlation between these two variables is $r = .40$. With our sample of 50 customers, however, we might find an observed correlation of $r = .20 = (.40 \times .71 \times .71)$. Calculating the significance of this observed correlation coefficient, we find that it is not statistically significant from zero, $t(48) = 1.41$, $p > .05$ (see Appendix J for an explanation of t-tests for correlation coefficients). Thus, we incorrectly conclude that there is no relationship between these two variables even though a true relationship exists. With this misleading information, we may not allocate the necessary resources to availability and would miss an excellent opportunity to increase the satisfaction level of the customers.

An acceptable level of reliability will depend on how the questionnaire is used (see Nunnally 1978). For basic research, as illustrated in the preceding paragraph, reliabilities should be .80 or higher. It has been stated, however, that increasing reliabilities above .80 will not dramatically affect the correlation between scales (Nunnally 1978).

In summary, reliability of the scales will necessarily influence the magnitude of the correlation found between any two scales. The correlation is attenuated as the reliability of the scales decreases. Incorrect conclusions about the relationship between two variables are likely when the reliability of either or both scales is low.

Factors Affecting Reliability

Various factors affect the reliability of scales. Two of them are the number of items in the scale and the sample of people on which the reliability estimate is calculated.

Number of Items in the Scale

We can increase reliability by increasing the number of items in the scale. This is similar to the concept of decreasing sampling error by increasing sample size (see Appendix F). The more observations we have in our sample, the more confident we are that the sample mean is an accurate reflection of the population mean. Similarly, the more items we have in our questionnaire, the more confident we are that people's observed scores are accurate reflections of their true scores.

If increased reliability is to be realized by adding more items to the scale, the additional items must be representative of the same concept that is being measured. For example, if we have two dimensions in our questionnaire, professionalism and responsiveness, we could increase the reliability of the responsiveness scale by adding more items related to the responsiveness concept. These items, however, would not necessarily increase the reliability of the professionalism scale because they do not reflect that concept.

Sample of People

A sample of people who are similar with respect to their level of satisfaction might yield low reliability estimates of the scales. If a scale has potential scores ranging from 1 to 5, and everybody in the sample has a true score of 5, then, theoretically, there is no true score variance in this sample. Recall that reliability is the true score variance divided by the observed score variance. Therefore, in our example, if the true score variance is 0, then reliability would be calculated to be 0.

If we are to obtain high reliability estimates, we must base reliability estimates on a sample of people who are heterogeneous (they differ amongst themselves) with respect to the concept being measured. If people truly differ with respect to the concept being measured (true scores varying from 1 to 5), there would be true score variance in the sample. Consequently, because there will be considerable true score variance, we would more likely find a high reliability estimate.

The Need for Multiple Items in Measurement

It must be noted that internal consistency indices can only be estimated with measures that have more than one item. In Appendix K, Figure K.1, the first three statements pertain to the dimension of availability. The next three statements pertain to responsiveness. A reader may ask, "Why use all these statements in the same customer satisfaction questionnaire? They seem to be redundant." The point of using multiple items to measure a given dimension is to ensure that our overall score, which is a composite of several observed scores, is a reliable reflection of the underlying true score. Measures that use only one item to assess a person's perception of quality of customer requirement categories or of overall customer satisfaction may be unreliable (not measuring the underlying true score). In fact, the reliability estimates presented previously cannot be calculated for a one-item scale. Therefore, people who use one-item scales to assess the level of satisfaction of various customer requirements run the risk of obtaining information that is not highly reliable; that is, the observed score on their one-item measure is not highly related to the actual levels of satisfaction of their customers.

I think an illustration of the importance of multiple-item scales is warranted. Suppose that you wanted to develop one test to assess both simple arithmetic ability and reading comprehension. One way to assess arithmetic ability is to ask people to solve a mathematical problem, and one way to assess reading comprehension is to have people read a passage and then answer a question related to it. Does it seem reasonable to assess the level of mathematical ability by using a test that contains only one arithmetic question and to assess reading comprehension by using a test that contains only one problem? People who believe that one item reliably assesses the perception of customer requirements may also believe that one question is sufficient in measuring both the level of mathematical ability and the level of reading comprehension.

Mathematical ability and reading comprehension, like customer perceptions, are unobservable constructs measured by instruments (tests) that result in scores of some kind. According to classical measurement theory, these scores are only observable indications of the underlying level of satisfaction or level of mathematical or reading comprehension.

Intuitively we understand that, to get a better indication of arithmetic ability and reading comprehension, we should use more than one question (item) to assess each ability. The more items related to a particular ability, the more confident we feel that the overall scores on that test will be consistently related to people's arithmetic ability and reading comprehension. In other words, we should have a test that has multiple items for each category we are measuring. In fact, with a test that contains multiple items for both arithmetic ability and reading comprehension, the reliability of each subscale can be calculated using the split-half method of estimating reliability. With this test, we would obtain two reliability estimates, one for the arithmetic scale and one for the reading comprehension scale.

The same argument for the importance of multiple items applies to measurement of customers' perceptions and attitudes. We should not feel comfortable with people who design customer satisfaction questionnaires to assess five quality dimensions using one item for each dimension. More than one item should be used when assessing customers' attitudes if we want to determine how reliably each dimension is measured.

Summary

So far, I have discussed issues of reliability of measures. When we are measuring customer perceptions or attitudes, we want scores for that particular scale to be highly reliable. This will give us some confidence that observed scores derived from that measure reflect true levels of customer attitudes. Furthermore, we will be confident that the highly reliable measure will be able to distinguish between people who have a positive attitude and those who have a negative attitude.

Although reliability of a scale is crucial, it is not sufficient in determining the quality of a measure. We should also concern ourselves with the issue of validity.

Validity

Validity refers to the degree to which evidence supports the inferences made from scores derived from measures, or the degree to which the scale measures what it is designed to measure. For example, if we make the inference that scores on a measure reflect levels of customer satisfaction, we need information to assess how well that inference is supported. Although we may have a highly reliable questionnaire, we still may want to question what the observed score actually indicates. Although the scale may reliably distinguish people on some underlying continuum, we still must ensure that the continuum is the correct continuum (for example, customer satisfaction). Unlike mathematical indices of reliability, there is no one statistic that provides an overall index of the validity of inferences about scores. There are several ways to obtain evidence to support the inferences made from test scores. These methods, referred to as *validity-related strategies* (AERA, APA, and NCME 1985), are content-related strategy, criterion-related strategy, and construct-related strategy.

Content-Related Strategy

Content-related strategy is concerned with examining the content of the items of the scale. Content-related evidence is concerned with the degree to which items on the scale are representative of some "defined universe" or "domain of content."

Let's look at the assessment of customer satisfaction to demonstrate what kind of evidence should be examined. The domain or universe of content refers to all possible items that could be included in the customer satisfaction questionnaire. If we define our universe of content as those items that reflect satisfaction with the service provided, the questionnaire developed should have items representative of this defined universe. The goal of content validity is to have a set of items that best represents the universe; these items will compose our final questionnaire.

Examples of items appropriate for assessing customer satisfaction with service are "I am not happy with the way I was treated" or "The service was pleasant." These items are representative of what people would say if they were either dissatisfied or satisfied with the service they received. On the other hand, items that seem inappropriate for assessing customer satisfaction with service are "I am happy with the product" or "I am happy with the price I paid." These seem to be related to customers' attitudes toward the product received and the price of the service or product, rather than customer satisfaction with the service.

Content-related evidence involves the judgment of people familiar with the purpose of the questionnaire. These people determine the correspondence between the content domain and the items of the measure. The critical incidents approach outlined in Chapter 2 is designed to ensure that the defined universe of important customer requirements is represented by the items in the customer satisfaction questionnaire.

Criterion-Related Strategy

Criterion-related strategy is concerned with examining the systematic relationship (usually in the form of a correlation coefficient) between scores on a given scale and other scores it should predict.

Again, I will use the customer satisfaction example to help illustrate a criterion-related strategy. You might be interested in how well the perception of various dimensions of quality predicts the extent to which people endorse the particular service (for example, telling friends about it). These two constructs are conceptually different. The former focuses on customers' perceptions of the product's quality characteristics. The latter focuses on a particular behavior that may be predicted by people's level of satisfaction. The correlation between the measures of perceptions of quality and endorsement behavior represents a systematic relationship between these two variables. We would expect to find some dimensions of quality (as perceived by the customer) to be related to endorsement behavior with that product. The higher the quality, the more frequent the endorsements.

Construct-Related Strategy

In the field of psychology, a construct can be defined as an attribute or characteristic inferred from research (Guion 1965). Construct-related evidence is derived from both previous validity strategies (content and criterion) and focuses on examining relationships between many variables. It is desirable to demonstrate two things when examining the correlations between measures. The first is that the scale correlates with variables with which it should correlate. This is termed *convergent validity*. The second is that the scale does not correlate with things with which it should not correlate. This is termed *discriminant validity* (Campbell and Fiske 1959). We can establish evidence of convergent and discriminant validity by correlating test scores designed to measure the same thing and correlating test scores designed to measure different things, respectively.

Another approach in obtaining construct-related evidence is through the use of a multitrait-multimethod (MTMM) matrix (Campbell and Fiske 1959). The MTMM approach requires the measurement of multiple constructs (or traits) through multiple measurement devices (or methods). The MTMM matrix is the correlation matrix of these constructs measured by different methods. The MTMM approach helps us determine the extent to which the correlations between constructs are due to the constructs (traits) being measured versus the methods being used to measure them. Various patterns of correlations in the MTMM matrix indicate the extent to which the underlying constructs are being measured. We want to see high correlations between the measures of the same construct using different measurement instruments (evidence of convergent validity). We also want to see relatively low correlations—lower than the convergent validities—between the measures of different constructs using the same measurement instrument (evidence of discriminant validity).

Construct-related evidence also can be provided by examining the correlation between a given variable and other variables. The variable of interest is embedded in a theoretical framework. This framework can be theoretically derived and helps to define the meaning of the constructs being measured. This framework can tell us that this variable should correlate with certain variables and not with others. Using our previous example in discussing criterion-related strategies, the constructs *perception of quality* and *customer satisfaction* should be embedded into the theoretical framework of customer satisfaction. We would expect a measure of perceived quality to be related to a measure of customer satisfaction if we believe that the perceived quality of a product leads to customer satisfaction. However, we would not expect a relationship between customer satisfaction and, say, shoe size, since there is no theoretical reason why these two should be related. If we did find a relationship between these two variables, it could suggest that our measure of customer satisfaction is actually a poor measure. (It is possible, however, that the theoretical framework of customer satisfaction should be changed to include shoe size.)

Summary

Validity refers to the extent to which inferences from scores are meaningful. There are three methods of providing evidence for validity of scores on a customer satisfaction questionnaire. A content-related strategy focuses on the sample of items in the questionnaire and how well they represent the entire domain of customer satisfaction items. A criterion-related strategy focuses on statistical relationships between measures and whether scores predict what they should predict. A construct-related strategy is composed of the two former strategies and is more of a theory-driven method. It specifies to what the measure should and should not relate.

Chapter Summary

This chapter discussed measurement issues of reliability and validity. Reliability refers to the degree to which observed scores obtained from a questionnaire are systematically related to some underlying true scores (the degree to which observed scores are free from random error). Reliability of scales is especially important when studying the relationship between variables. Low reliability decreases the observed correlation between two variables. Thus, if reliability of either or both measures is low, incorrect conclusions about the relationship between the variables are likely. Although reliability is an important characteristic of a questionnaire, we must also concern ourselves with the meaning of the scores. We must ensure that the observed score represents the dimension we intend to measure. Validity refers to the degree to which we can make these types of inferences.

CHAPTER 4

Customer Satisfaction Questionnaire Construction

Item Generation, Response Format, and Item Selection

This chapter will give you some practical guidelines to follow when developing customer satisfaction questionnaires. In addition to reiterating the significance of customer requirements and satisfaction items, I will include new information on characteristics of good items, scaling procedures, and item selection. Finally, I will present a process for questionnaire construction integrating this information.

Customer satisfaction questionnaires are constructed in four phases: (1) Determining questions (items) to be used in the questionnaire, (2) Selecting the response format, (3) Writing the introduction to the questionnaire, and (4) Determining the content of the final questionnaire (selecting items from the initial set of satisfaction items which will compose your measure).

Determining Questions or Items

Let's start with an example of an organization that would like to develop a customer satisfaction questionnaire. Suppose that the organization, in an attempt to gauge how well it services its customers, includes these requests in its questionnaire.

1. Please rate the availability of the service.

2. Please rate the responsiveness of the staff.

3. Please rate the professionalism of the staff.

These three requests were obviously designed to measure three customer requirements: availability of service, responsiveness of service, and professionalism of service.

Although these customer requirements may be meaningful and valid service characteristics, there are problems with the requests. There is ambiguity in the phrases; *availability* and *responsiveness* might be interpreted differently by different people. As a result, responses to these questions will reflect this ambiguity. To illustrate how different people may have differing definitions for the same word, I asked 10 people to tell me the meaning of *some* using a number. Their answers ranged from *three* to *seven*.

Similarly, if you ask your customers to indicate how satisfied they are with the availability of service they received, they may have different definitions of the word *availability* and thus are thinking of different things when they respond. Subsequently, it would be difficult to interpret customers' responses. To avoid this problem, a customer satisfaction questionnaire should use more specific statements that would leave less room for varying interpretations. Some statements that could more clearly describe *availability* include

1. The merchant was available to schedule me at a good time.

2. I could get an appointment with the merchant at a time I desired.

3. My appointment was at a convenient time.

Availability is now defined more precisely in terms of scheduling and appointment time. Thus, responses to each of these items are more definitive than responses to the previous items. In addition, all three of these items still reflect the customer requirement of availability of service.

When we use more specific statements, the questionnaire provides specific feedback concerning organizational and staff performance. For example, the questionnaire in the first example with its use of the term *availability* may indicate that customers are not satisfied with the availability of service. Knowing that the customers are not satisfied, however, does little to help the organization pinpoint how to accomplish improvements. If the organization used more specific items (as in the second example), it would know precisely how to increase customers' level of satisfaction with the customer requirement of availability of service.

In summary, when developing questionnaires to assess customer satisfaction with a given product or service, we must ensure that our questions are not ambiguous. Using specific statements in questionnaires will enhance the information gained, because responses from customers mean the same thing across customers (no differing definitions) and responses will provide more specific feedback on ways to improve the service or product.

Satisfaction Items Revisited

We would like the questions in our questionnaire to be specific. The next step would be to determine what questions or statements to include. Recall that, in Chapter 2, the critical incident technique includes the creation of satisfaction items. These can be used as items in the questionnaire. Satisfaction items related to the banking industry from Figure 2.1 are presented in Figure 4.1.

Satisfaction items can also provide indirect help by aiding the generation of new items for the questionnaire. This process entails rewriting the

---

1. I waited a short period of time before I was helped.

2. The service started promptly when I arrived.

3. The teller handled transactions in a short period of time.

4. The teller took a long time to complete my transaction.

5. The financial consultant was available to schedule me at a good time.

6. My appointment with the financial consultant was at a convenient time.

7. The teller talked to me in a pleasant way.

8. The teller was very personable.

9. The teller carefully listened to me when I was requesting a transaction.

10. The teller knew how to handle the transactions.

11. The quality of the way the teller treated me was high.

12. The way the teller treated me met my expectations.

13. I am satisfied with the way the merchant treated me.

Figure 4.1. Satisfaction items from Figure 2.1.

satisfaction items so that they reflect a neutral statement (neither positive nor negative) rather than a declarative statement. These items, however, are still specific in their content. These items (using the banking industry) appear in Figure 4.2.

The items, either satisfaction items or items generated from them, are specific enough to be of value for feedback purposes. Instead of indicating only that customers are satisfied or dissatisfied with the level of professionalism of the service, these items can specify exactly why customers are satisfied or dissatisfied (items 7 through 10). In addition to studying the specific feedback these satisfaction items offer, we can calculate a general index of the professionalism customer requirement by combining the responses of items 7 to 10. We can also calculate indices for other quality dimensions or customer requirements using specific satisfaction items: responsiveness (items 1 and 2), speed of transaction (items 3 and 4), availability (items 5 and 6), and overall satisfaction with service (items 11

---

1. Period of time waited before I was helped

2. Promptness of service when I arrived

3. Length of time of the transaction

4. Time to complete my transaction

5. Availability of financial consultant to schedule me for an appointment

6. Convenience of my appointment with the financial consultant

7. Way in which the teller talked to me

8. Way in which the teller conducted the transaction

9. Way in which the teller listened to me when I was requesting a transaction

10. Knowledge of teller in handling the transactions

11. The quality of the way the teller treated me

12. Overall quality of the visit

13. The way I was treated

Figure 4.2. New items generated from original satisfaction items.

through 13). We can then determine the reliability of these summary scores using the reliability estimate formulae in Chapter 3.

The quality dimension development process also resulted in statements that could be included in the questionnaire. Recall that these statements also describe specific instances of the service or product that defined their respective quality dimensions. These statements are similar to the satisfaction items that result from the critical incident approach. Consequently, these statements can also be used directly in the customer satisfaction questionnaire.

Characteristics of Good Items

Writing items for the questionnaire can be difficult. It is important that items possess certain characteristics. They should appear relevant to what you are trying to measure, assessing customer requirements established earlier in the process. Items that do not appear to measure anything relevant to the service or product might confuse the respondent, especially if the instructions indicate that the questionnaire is designed to assess the quality of the service or product.

Items should also be concise. Items that are too long can make the questionnaire too long and difficult to read. Discard superfluous words. An example of a long item is

> *The service person seemed to act in a very personable manner to me when I asked for service.*

A concise item reflecting the same content would be

> *The service person was very personable.*

Items should be unambiguous. The respondent should be able to understand precisely what the items are asking. Any ambiguity in the items can lead to equivocal responses. Try to avoid items that are vague and imprecise. For example, an item that might be ambiguous is

> *The transaction with the service provider was good.*

This item does not reflect precisely why the service was good. Some respondents might interpret the item as assessing the promptness of the transaction, while others might think it assesses the service provider's professionalism. To avoid this confusion, we can write two items.

> *The transaction took a short period of time.*
> *The service provider talked to me in a pleasant way.*

Each of these items reflects two unambiguous thoughts, each representing one customer requirement.

A good item will contain only one thought. That is, the item should ask only one question. If an item asks more than one question, the respondent may be confused if he or she wants to respond affirmatively to one part of the question and negatively to the other part. A positive response to this type of item would indicate that the respondent agrees to both parts of the item. A negative response might indicate either that the respondent disagrees with one part of the item or that the respondent disagrees with both parts of the item. An example of a poor item is

> *The provider listened to me and took a short time to handle the transaction.*

This item contains two parts, one dealing with how the provider listened to the customer and the other on whether the provider handled the transaction in a short amount of time. This item can be divided into two separate items.

> *The provider listened to me.*
> *The provider took a short time to handle the transaction.*

The fifth characteristic of a good item is that it should not contain a double negative. An example of an item with a double negative is

> *The clerk was never not there when he or she was needed.*

A better way to write this item is

> *The clerk was there when he or she was needed.*

In summary, a good item should appear relevant, be concise and unambiguous, contain only one thought, and not contain double negatives. Items with these characteristics offer respondents clear and simple questions to which to respond. They lead to a questionnaire that is easy to read and complete.

Although the items are an important part of the questionnaire, the response format of the items can also influence the quality of the responses obtained. The following section discusses response formats.

Response Formats

The second step of scale construction will be to select a response format for the questionnaire. A response format determines how customers can respond to the items on the questionnaire. The choice of a response format is an extremely important step in the development process since the response format determines how the data from the questionnaire can be used.

There are several possible response formats or scaling methods for questionnaires. These scaling methods include Thurstone's method of equal-appearing intervals (Thurstone 1929), Guttman's scalogram approach (Guttman 1950), and the Likert scaling method (Likert 1932), to name a few. Questionnaire development using either the Thurstone or Guttman approach is more laborious than the Likert method. In addition, scales developed using the Likert method yield higher reliability coefficients with fewer items than scales developed using the Thurstone method (Edwards and Kenney 1946). Therefore, for the sake of simplicity and utility, I will not present the Thurstone or Guttman approaches. I will limit this discussion of response formats to two approaches: the checklist format and the Likert-type format. Several books discuss the other types of scaling procedures not presented here (Dawes 1972; Fishbein 1967; and Reckase 1990).

Checklist Format

The quality of a service or product can be quantified by the number of positive things said about it. The more positive things said about a service (or the fewer negative things said about it), the better the service. For each item in the questionnaire, the customers will be allowed to respond either "yes" or "no." Customers are asked to respond "yes" if the satisfaction item reflects the service or product they received and "no" if the item does not reflect the service or product they received. An example of a checklist format is included in Figure 4.3. The checklist format should be used only when the satisfaction items are being used as the items in the questionnaire. The benefit of the checklist method is the ease with which customers can respond to the items. Customers can easily indicate whether or not the item describes the service they received.

Likert-Type Format

The quality of the service or product can also be indexed by the strength of response toward each satisfaction item. The Likert-type format is designed to allow customers to respond in varying degrees to each item that describes the service or product. For example, although two customers may say that the item describes the service, one customer may want to indicate the item especially describes the service more so than does the other customer.

Please indicate whether or not each statement describes the service you received. Check "Yes" if the statement describes the service or "No" if the statement does not describe the service.

	Yes	No
1. I could get an appointment with the merchant at a time I desired.	_____	_____
2. The merchant was available to schedule me at a good time.	_____	_____
3. My appointment was at a convenient time for me.	_____	_____
4. The merchant was quick to respond when I arrived for my appointment.	_____	_____
5. The merchant immediately helped me when I entered the premises.	_____	_____
6. My appointment started promptly at the scheduled time.	_____	_____

Figure 4.3. Example questionnaire using a checklist response format.

To allow customers to respond in varying degrees to each item, a Likert-type response format can be used. R. A. Likert (1932) developed a scaling procedure in which the scale represents a bipolar continuum. The low end represents a negative response while the high end represents a positive response. Some Likert-type formats appear in Figure 4.4. Each represents a bipolar continuum.

We can use these response formats for a particular type of item. The first response format in Figure 4.4 (the agree to disagree continuum) is used with satisfaction items. Recall that satisfaction items are declarative items that reflect specific good or bad aspects of the service or product. The response scale, therefore, should reflect whether the satisfaction item describes the service. Customers respond to each item in terms of how well that particular item describes the service they received. The quality of the service is then indexed by the extent to which the items describe the service received. An example of a questionnaire using this rating format appears in Figure 4.5.

The second and third response formats in Figure 4.4 (dissatisfied-satisfied or poor-good continua) can be used for items like those found in Figure 4.2. Although these items still reflect specific aspects of the service, they are rather neutral. The response scale, therefore, should reflect the

Strongly Disagree	Disagree	Neither Agree nor Disagree	Agree	Strongly Agree
1	2	3	4	5
Very Dissatisfied	Dissatisfied	Neither Satisfied nor Dissatisfied	Satisfied	Very Satisfied
1	2	3	4	5
Very Poor	Poor	Neither Poor nor Good	Good	Very Good
1	2	3	4	5

Figure 4.4. Examples of Likert-type response formats.

Please indicate the extent to which you agree or disagree with the following statements about the service you received from [company name]. Circle the appropriate number using the scale below.

> 1—I Strongly Disagree with this statement (SD).
> 2—I Disagree with this statement (D).
> 3—I Neither agree nor disagree with this statement (N).
> 4—I Agree with this statement (A).
> 5—I Strongly Agree with this statement (SA).

	SD	D	N	A	SA
1. I could get an appointment with the merchant at a time I desired.	1	2	3	4	5
2. The merchant was available to schedule me at a good time.	1	2	3	4	5
3. My appointment was at a convenient time for me.	1	2	3	4	5
4. The merchant was quick to respond when I arrived for my appointment.	1	2	3	4	5
5. The merchant immediately helped me when I entered the premises.	1	2	3	4	5
6. My appointment started promptly at the scheduled time.	1	2	3	4	5

Figure 4.5. Questionnaire using a Likert-type response format.

degree to which the items (aspects of service) are satisfying (or good) versus dissatisfying (or poor). The quality of the service is indexed by the degree to which people say they are satisfied with the service or the degree to which the service is rated as good. Examples of questionnaires using these rating formats appear in Figures 4.6 and 4.7.

Advantage of Likert-Type Format
The advantage of using the Likert-type format rather than the checklist format is reflected in the variability of scores that result from the scale.

Please indicate the extent to which you are satisfied or dissatisfied with the following aspects of the service you received from [company name]. Circle the appropriate number using the scale below

    1—I am Very Dissatisfied with this aspect (VD).
    2—I am Dissatisfied with this aspect (D).
    3—I am Neither satisfied nor dissatisfied with this aspect (N).
    4—I am Satisfied with this aspect (S).
    5—I am Very Satisfied with this aspect (VS).

	VD	D	N	S	VS
1. Appointment time with the merchant	1	2	3	4	5
2. Availability of merchant to schedule me at a good time	1	2	3	4	5
3. Convenience of my appointment	1	2	3	4	5
4. Responsiveness of the merchant when I arrived for my appointment	1	2	3	4	5
5. Promptness of the start time of my appointment	1	2	3	4	5

Figure 4.6. Questionnaire using a Likert-type response format of the satisfaction continuum.

With the quality dimension represented in our questionnaire, we allow customers to express the degree of their opinion in the service or product they received rather than restricting them to a "yes" or "no" answer. From a statistical perspective, scales with two response options have less reliability than scales with five response options (Lissitz and Green 1975). In addition, reliability seems to level off after five scale points, suggesting minimal incremental utility of using more than five scale points.

In addition, using the Likert-type format will still allow you to determine the percentage of positive and negative responses for a given item. You may do this by combining the responses on the ends of the scale (for example, combining Strongly Disagree with Disagree and combining

Please rate the extent to which the aspect of the service from [company name] was good or bad. Circle the appropriate number using the scale below.

        1—Aspect of service was Very Poor (VP).
        2—Aspect of service was Poor (P).
        3—Aspect of service was Neither poor nor good (N).
        4—Aspect of service was Good (G).
        5—Aspect of service was Very Good (VG).

	VP	P	N	G	VG
1. Appointment time with the merchant	1	2	3	4	5
2. Availability of merchant to schedule me at a good time	1	2	3	4	5
3. Convenience of my appointment	1	2	3	4	5
4. Responsiveness of the merchant when I arrived for my appointment	1	2	3	4	5
5. Promptness of the start time of my appointment	1	2	3	4	5

Figure 4.7. Questionnaire using a Likert-type response format of the goodness continuum.

Strongly Agree with Agree). A response of 1 or 2 is now considered to be a response of 1, a response of 3 is considered to be a response of 2, and a response of 4 or 5 is now considered to be response of 3. We have transformed our five-point scale into a three-point scale. A score of 1 represents a negative response, while a score of 3 represents a positive response. This transformation, therefore, creates somewhat of a checklist format.

Introductions to Customer Satisfaction Questionnaires

The next step is to write the introduction to the questionnaire. The introduction should be brief. It should explain the purpose of the questionnaire and provide instructions for completing the questionnaire.

Also, you might explain how the data will be used. Keep this in simple terms that are easily understandable. Usually the questionnaire is designed to assess the customers' level of satisfaction. In some circumstances, however, a questionnaire may be designed for a special research project. To the extent that the customers' knowledge of the purpose of the project does not influence their responses, you might explain the purpose of the project in the instructions. Inclusion of the purpose could increase customers' perceptions that their response is highly valued in obtaining information about the project, thus making them more likely to complete the questionnaire.

The introduction should tell how to complete the items and explain the scale to be used. It is imperative that these instructions match the type of response format in the questionnaire. When you use the agree-disagree continuum as the response format, the instructions should ask respondents to indicate the extent to which they agree or disagree with the statements in the questionnaire. When you use the satisfaction continuum as the response format, the instructions should ask respondents to indicate the extent to which they are satisfied.

I have been asked why some of the items in the questionnaires seem redundant. Customers may become irritated because they feel they are answering the same question over and over again. Therefore, you might want to include the reason for the similarity of some items. State that the questionnaire was designed to include multiple items so that you obtain a more accurate assessment of your customers' opinion. The inclusion of this point might not be necessary if the items in the questionnaire are not highly similar to each other. You might want to pilot test the questionnaire to see if respondents comment about the apparent redundancy of items.

An example of an introduction for a questionnaire using the agree-disagree continuum is

> To better serve you, we would like to know your opinion of the quality of our service at [name of company or department]. You recently received service from our company [or department]. Please indicate the extent to which you agree or disagree with the following statements about the service you received from the staff. Circle the appropriate number using the scale

below. Some statements are similar to one another to ensure that we accurately determine your opinion concerning our service.

1—I Strongly Disagree with this statement (SD).
2—I Disagree with this statement (D).
3—I Neither agree nor disagree with this statement (N).
4—I Agree with this statement (A).
5—I Strongly Agree with this statement (SA).

This introduction includes the purpose of the questionnaire and instructions for completing the questions. Also, the introduction explains the purpose of using multiple items which are similar to each other.

Item Selection

Step four in the questionnaire construction process requires selecting the items to be used in the final questionnaire. Item selection might be warranted if the critical incidents technique resulted in a large number of satisfaction items. For example, if the critical incidents technique resulted in four quality dimensions each containing 10 items, it might not be practical to use all these items since it would be difficult to get customers to complete a 40-item questionnaire. In this situation, we might want to select the best items from the original set to create a smaller, yet equally effective, customer satisfaction questionnaire. If the ratio of satisfaction items to quality dimensions is small (2:1 or less), we might not want to conduct any item selection procedure. Excluding items from an already small set could result in a customer satisfaction questionnaire with low reliability.

I will present two methods of item selection that will help you select the satisfaction items to include in the customer satisfaction questionnaire. The first method is based on human judgment, and the second is based on mathematical indices.

Judgmental Item Selection

One way to select items is to use your best judgment. For your final customer satisfaction questionnaire, try to include items that best represent customers' requirements. The most critical element of this process is examining the similarity of items within a given quality dimension or customer requirement. Because the goal is to select items that best represent a particular dimension (customer satisfaction or various dimensions of customer requirements), these items should be somewhat similar to each other. If the items obtained from the critical incidents technique are all good, however, selecting the best items might be rather difficult.

One way to select the best satisfaction items—those that clearly reflect the quality dimension—is to have two people independently select a specified number of satisfaction items. Those chosen by both people will be retained. If there is low agreement, it is possible that all satisfaction items are equally good indicators of the underlying quality dimension; as a result, people cannot make a distinction between the items, and the low agreement is due to chance factors.

If there is no agreement in selected items, another method is to use a random selection process. If all the satisfaction items are judged to be equally good indicators of the quality dimensions, then any randomly selected set of satisfaction items from the original list will be a representative sample of items from the entire list. Another method is to select either every odd or every even numbered satisfaction item from the full list.

Mathematical Item Selection

Another method of selecting items is to administer all items generated from the critical incidents approach to some actual customers. After these customers complete the questionnaire, conduct item analysis on the data. Item analysis is a catch-all phrase that includes such processes as correlational analysis and factor analysis. You may conduct these statistical techniques to select the best items (those that have equal means and are highly interrelated). These statistical procedures require the help of an expert in questionnaire development. The following section of this chapter illustrates one approach that can be used in item selection.

Statistical procedures such as these will allow you to select which items to retain for your final measure of customer satisfaction. Although this approach is more complex than judgmental item selection, you achieve the invaluable payback of knowing your final questionnaire is statistically reliable; items retained as a result of the item analysis will be, by design, mathematically sound. The general goal in the selection of items is to retain items that differentiate between customers who are dissatisfied and those who are satisfied and drop items that do not. That is, the items should be able to discriminate between varying levels of customer satisfaction. Items on which highly satisfied and highly dissatisfied customers score the same are not very useful. Item analysis will allow us to identify those items that can discriminate between varying levels of satisfaction.

Item-total correlations. Item-total correlations are correlations between an item and the overall dimension score to which that item belongs (not including the one item being correlated). For example, if we had three items, each measuring the same quality dimension, we would calculate three item-total correlations: (1) Item 1 correlated with the composite of items 2 and 3, (2) Item 2 correlated with the composite of items 1 and 3, and (3) Item 3 correlated with the composite of items 1 and 2. This type of correlation will tell you the extent to which each item is linked to the overall dimension score with which it should be highly linked. The criterion for a cutoff for a correlation coefficient varies depending on the purpose of the measure being developed. When developing a general type of measure, you would use less stringent criteria compared to a measure designed to assess a more specific attitude (Likert 1932). An important requirement is that the overall score of the measure be reliable.

As an example, we might have five items we want to combine into an overall score of professionalism. We must ensure that combining the five items makes sense. If all the items are designed to measure the same dimension (perception of professionalism), then all items for that dimension should be positively related to each other, and we would expect to see high item-total correlations. Let's say we used the questionnaire on 100 customers and calculated five item-total correlation coefficients, one for each item. The results of a hypothetical item-total correlation analysis appear in Figure 4.8. We see that item 3 is not highly correlated with a composite of the remaining four items and might be dropped from the questionnaire. The remaining items show relatively high item-total correlations with the composite score of the remaining items. The results suggest that it would make sense to combine items 1, 2, 4, and 5 to obtain an overall score of professionalism.

The low correlation between item 3 and the remaining items could be due to several things. One possibility of why an item demonstrates a low correlation with its subscale might be that it is poorly written. For example,

Overall score (minus item being correlated)	
Item 1	$r = .67$
Item 2	$r = .55$
Item 3	$r = .23$
Item 4	$r = .59$
Item 5	$r = .77$

Figure 4.8. Hypothetical results of item-total correlations of items designed to measure perception of professionalism.

it could include two thoughts rather than one. Therefore, some respondents might want to respond favorably to one part of the item and unfavorably to the other part of the item. The item may have to be rewritten to reflect only one thought or may have to be divided into two separate items.

Another possibility is that a particular item measures some other customer requirement than what was originally thought. For the previous example, we could calculate a correlation between item 3 and the other customer requirements. If item 3 does show a high correlation with another customer requirement, perhaps it should not be dropped from the questionnaire but, instead, included in the summary score for that particular customer requirement to which it is highly linked.

Another possibility is that the item represents a different customer requirement than those included in the questionnaire. An item may not correlate highly with any of the customer requirements. It could be that we failed to establish an important customer requirement in our clustering of critical incidents. This correlational approach could address such errors of omission. When this situation arises, perhaps we could write more items to reflect the content of that particular item. Subsequently, we could re-administer the revised questionnaire (with the new items) to conduct additional item analysis. If the new items are representative of that lone item, then that lone item should now correlate highly with the new items, thus forming a new customer requirement scale.

Group differences. Another mathematical item selection strategy employs the comparison of two groups of respondents (Likert 1932). This procedure is also conducted after respondents have completed the questionnaire. Within each subscale (for example, availability or timeliness), we select two groups of people, each group representing the extreme of the attitude measured by a particular scale. Usually, the top and bottom 10 percent are selected, based on their overall score for the particular subscale. Next, for each group, we calculate means for each item. Then we calculate a difference score for each item, subtracting the mean of the lower extreme group from the mean of the higher extreme group.

For each item we obtain a difference score. This difference score reflects how much a particular item was able to discriminate between the two groups on an attitude the item was designed to measure. The higher the difference score, the higher the discrimination. If an item does not differentiate between the two groups, then we would obtain a difference score of 0. These items are dropped from the questionnaire. For items that are positively phrased (higher score means higher level of the attitude), we select items that have a large positive difference score. For those items that are negatively phrased (higher score means lower level of the attitude), we select items that have a large negative difference score.

The indices used in the item-total correlation procedure (item-total correlation) and the group differences procedure (difference score) have been shown to be highly correlated (Likert 1932). This suggests that both procedures will result in similar outcomes with respect to the inclusion of items in the final form of the questionnaire.

Factor analysis. Another statistical technique of item selection, often used in conjunction with item-total correlations, is factor analysis. This technique (see Appendix K) will demonstrate which items are more highly related to the underlying dimension they are designed to measure.

Factor analysis is a highly specialized form of analysis. It is beyond the scope of this book to provide you with exact procedures for the selection of items. However, here are some general guidelines. It is essential that items within each scale load on a single factor if the items are to be used in a composite score. When an item loads highly on a different factor than the one for which it was intended, this suggests that the item might best be combined with items with which it is highly related. When an item does not load highly on any factor, this suggests that the item does not discriminate between high and low groups on the attitudes that are measured with the items in the current questionnaire.

An advantage of using factor analysis is the identification of underlying constructs (customer requirements) being measured by the items in the questionnaire. Also, factor analysis allows us to determine which customer requirement each item is measuring. A disadvantage of factor analysis is that it requires a large number of respondents to complete questionnaires if the results are to be reliable. The number of respondents should be five to 10 times the number of items in the questionnaire. For example, if the questionnaire contains 20 items, the factor analysis should be conducted using the responses of 100 to 200 people.

Factor analysis has been used in applied research. For example, Parasuraman, Zeithaml, and Berry (1988) used factor analysis in developing a service quality questionnaire. The goal of the research was to develop a reliable scale that assesses various components of service quality. The authors present the results of the exploratory factor analysis of responses to 97 items.

On the basis of the factor analysis, the authors selected items that were good indicators of underlying dimensions. They also presented the results of the factor analysis, which included the number of factors as well as the factor pattern matrix (after rotation). This article presents an excellent example of the use of factor analysis in developing customer satisfaction questionnaires.

Mathematical item selection is usually used in the initial stages of questionnaire development. Even if you use the judgmental item selection process, you may conduct item analysis on the retained items (after customers have completed them) to determine if the items chosen constitute a reliable scale. Figure 4.9 presents the chronological use of item analysis in the selection of items when using either the mathematical item selection or the judgmental item selection process.

Chapter Summary

Items in the customer satisfaction questionnaire should be relevant, concise, and unambiguous. They should also be written clearly to reflect only

Judgmental Item Selection	Mathematical Item Selection
1. Select small set of items using judgmental criteria or random selection.	1. Place all satisfaction items in the questionnaire.
2. Place this set of satisfaction items in the questionnaire.	2. Use questionnaire on customers.
3. Use questionnaire on customers.	3. Conduct item analysis to determine which items to retain for final questionnaire (need sufficient sample size of approximately five people per item if factor analysis will be used).
4. Conduct item analysis to determine if these items measure quality dimensions.	4. Examine outcome of item analysis and select good items for final version of questionnaire.
5. Examine outcome of item analysis to retain good items.	5. Use final version of the questionnaire.
6. Results may indicate entire questionnaire revision (if items do not measure the underlying dimensions).	

Figure 4.9. The use of item analysis in judgmental item selection and mathematical item selection.

one thought and avoid double negatives. Also, the introduction provides the purpose of the questionnaire as well as instructions for completing it.

This chapter presented two response formats that can be used in questionnaires. A checklist format allows customers to indicate whether a particular item represents the service or product. A Likert-type format allows customers to further distinguish their response beyond what is allowed by the checklist format. The choice between these two types of formats depends on the type of data desired from the questionnaire.

Steps	Important Issues
1. Generate items for questionnaire.	• Select items from satisfaction item list.
	• Write items based on satisfaction items.
2. Ensure items are written appropriately.	• Items should appear relevant to what you are trying to measure.
	• Items should be concise.
	• Items should be unambiguous.
	• Items should contain only one thought (items ask only one question).
	• Items should not contain double negatives.
3. Select response format for items.	• Checklist format.
	• Likert-type format.
4. Write introduction to questionnaire.	• State the purpose of the questionnaire.
	• State instructions on how to complete the questionnaire.
5. Select representative sample of items.	• Items within each quality dimension should be similar in content to each other.
a. Could use judgmental item selection to select items	• Use multiple judges to select the items.
b. Could use mathematical item selection to select items	• Use item-total correlations or group differences approach in selecting items.
	• Could also use factor analysis
6. Evaluate the retained items.	• Calculate reliability of the scales within questionnaire using split-half method or Cronbach's estimate.

Figure 4.10. Guidelines in the development of questionnaires.

Also, this chapter outlined two procedures used when selecting items for the customer satisfaction questionnaire. The judgmental procedure can be useful when the initial items are all good items. If you are using the mathematical approach, consult somebody conversant in these mathematical procedures when you attempt to select items. Mathematical item selection is designed to select items that are statistically sound.

Figure 4.10 outlines the general steps to follow in questionnaire development. Each step is accompanied by various methods that are used for each step as well as other important issues to consider. This figure is designed to summarize and highlight the important points in the chapter and can be used as a checklist when developing the questionnaire.

CHAPTER 5

Sampling Methods

Sometimes it is not possible to administer surveys to all your customers. For some organizations that have tens of thousands of customers, they may not have the resources to conduct a large-scale project. In fact, it may not be necessary to survey all of the clients in order to get a reliable picture regarding all the customers' level of satisfaction. This chapter will cover topics related to sampling. These topics include methods of sampling, methods of determining sample size, determining confidence levels, and methods of increasing response rates to written surveys.

Statistical Sampling

We always make judgments about a large group of "things" based on our observations on a smaller subset of those "things." For example, we talk to a few of our customers to get an idea of the quality of the service we provide to all of our customers. In quality improvement organizations, people check a group of products to determine if there are any major problems with the entire lot of products. To determine the quality of coffee beans from a roaster, the test taster tastes a small handful taken from that roaster. When preparing a stew, the chef might taste a small spoonful from the pot in which the stew is cooking to determine if the entire pot is ready. In all these examples, the people have drawn conclusions about the entire group of things (such as all the soup or all the coffee beans) from a small subset of those things (for example, a spoonful of soup or a handful of beans). We typically refer to the large group as the *population* and the small subset of that group as the *sample* (see Appendix F for a more detailed description of the characteristics of populations and samples).

When conducting a customer satisfaction survey, we typically cannot administer the customer survey to the entire customer base. We may not have the financial resources to measure all of our customers' perceptions, or we may need the results of the survey immediately, which would preclude the time-consuming task of measuring all customers' attitudes. In these and other cases, we administer the customer survey to a smaller set of customers, a sample of customers. The method of selecting a sample from the larger population is referred to as *sampling*.

A major goal in sampling is to ensure that the results of the client satisfaction questionnaire are representative of the larger population of customers. This chapter will cover various methods of statistical sampling that will help you determine your sampling plan. It is assumed that readers have a basic knowledge of statistics. For a quick review of statistics, readers are referred to the appendices before reading this chapter. A goal of this chapter is to help readers gain a better understanding of the intricacies of sampling methods. After reading this chapter, readers should be able to conduct simple statistical sampling.

Types of Sampling: Census, Judgment, and Statistical

We are the owners of a newspaper and we would like to know the satisfaction level of our customers, the readers of our newspaper. The first thing we need to do is determine the population of our customers. The determination of our population was done, in part, early on in our questionnaire development phase. We tailored the questionnaire with a specific customer base in mind. Using sampling terminology to define our population of customers, a question to ask ourselves is, "To whom do we want the customer survey results to generalize?" To generalize the results to the population, we must first ensure that the sample of respondents of our survey is representative of that larger population. In our newspaper study, all readers of our newspaper are our population. To determine the customers' satisfaction levels from a sample of readers, we could take one of three general approaches to obtain a sample from this population. The three broad sampling approaches are: census, judgment, and statistical.

Census Sampling

One approach is to gather information from all of our readers. This is referred to as *census sampling* and is essentially sampling all of the possible cases in our population. In this case, we know the sample is representative of the population because the sample *is* the population. A census approach can be used in various circumstances. For instance, due to the nature of the product, the company might want input from all of its customers. For example, if we are a manufacturer of a new and specialized surgical device, we might want feedback from all of our customers (surgeons) who use our product. We may view each customer as a useful source of critical information, critical enough to warrant census sampling. We may also use census sampling when our population is small enough where sampling a small subset is not needed. Manufacturers of an expensive bone-cutting device may have only a few customers (say, 100) that use these devices. In this case, a census approach to sampling would be feasible. Finally, we may have a case in which all the information regarding our customers is on the computer. Because computers are used to analyze our data, we could easily include all customers in the analysis. The major drawback to using census sampling is the high cost associated with measuring all cases in the population.

Judgmental Sampling

Another approach to sampling would be to use our judgment in the selection of the customers we measure. Using our example of the newspaper publisher, we might want to select our sample from our population based on readers' age to ensure all age categories are represented in our sample. In addition, to ensure that both genders are represented in our sample, we may be mindful of the gender of our readers in our selection of our sample. The inclusion of the cases from the population into the sample is based solely on the discretion of the person conducting the sampling procedure. The use of judgmental sampling is useful in case studies where one or few cases are needed to illustrate major points of the researcher. The business consultant Tom Peters uses this method. He illustrates his theories with a few companies. One major drawback to using judgmental sampling is that you are unable to generalize to a population. The conclusions of such case studies can be used as a great starting point for understanding business processes. Making generalizations to the population, however, is another matter. A statistical approach to sampling is a better approach if you would like to make strong conclusions regarding the population.

Statistical Sampling

The third approach in determining our sample is based on statistical probability. In this case, we rely on mere chance to determine who is selected in our sample. The major characteristics of statistically chosen samples over judgmentally chosen samples are: (1) We use random selection in the inclusion of the cases into the sample, (2) We can statistically determine an appropriate sample size, and (3) We can statistically determine the probability that our sample is not representative of the population.

A major advantage of using the statistical sampling approach over judgmental sampling is that you are able to generalize your results to the population from which the sample was drawn. Although the person who is conducting the sampling might think that his or her judgment in selecting a sample is not flawed, it is difficult to convince others of the representativeness of the final sample to the entire population. The person creating the sample might have certain biases (of which he or she is not aware) that influence the selection of cases into the sample.

At a certain level, the results of a customer survey tell us the satisfaction level of the sample of customers. At another level, we hope that the results tell us about the satisfaction level of the entire population of customers. If the sample is somehow not representative of the population of customers, we may have wasted our time in conducting such a survey. The possible effect of judgmental sampling on the outcome of a study is quite apparent. For example, if the results of the customer satisfaction survey determine bonuses for particular offices, the office manager for a particular office might administer the customer survey to those customers he thinks are satisfied. The conclusions based on such a sample might not reflect the true level of satisfaction of all the customers. In this case, this sample is referred to as a *biased sample*. A biased sample is a sample that is not representative of the population. Statistical sampling is a method that increases the chances that the sample is representative of the population.

Table 5.1 contains the three sampling methods just explained. Their definition and important points to consider are presented in the table. The use of census and judgmental sampling are not commonly conducted due to their relatively high cost and lack of generalizability, respectively. Statistical sampling is a very useful method of gathering data and providing useful information about the population. The next section will focus on different types of statistical sampling methods. These are simple random sampling, stratified sampling, and cluster sampling.

Table 5.1. Sampling methods.

Method	Definition	Important Points
Census	Select all cases from the population	• Sample is representative of the population because it *is* the population
		• Could be used when feedback from all customers is important
		• Could be used if all data are easily accessible (data are already on computer)
		• Cost may be high
Judgment	Select subset of cases based on discretion of person creating the sample	• Degree to which results from sample can generalize to population is questionable
		• Easy approach
Statistical	Select subset of cases based on chance	• Can calculate probability that our sample is not representative of the population
		• Can generalize results to the population

Simple random sampling. This method of sampling is the simplest approach in determining the cases to be included in the sample. In simple random sampling, a random sample is selected in such a way that every case in the population has an equal chance of being included in the sample. We may be interested in the overall satisfaction level of all of the readers (subscribers and those buying the paper at a newsstand) of our newspaper but want to survey only 100 customers. To obtain a random sample from our population of customers, we first need a list of all our readers ($N = 9000$). Next, we randomly select 100 readers as our sample and measure their level of satisfaction with the newspaper. From this sample, we make generalizations about the satisfaction level of the entire customer base (the population).

Stratified sampling. Stratified sampling refers to the approach in which the population is divided into two or more groups (strata) and simple random sampling is conducted within each group. When determining the various strata to be used in the study, it is important that the various strata are mutually exclusive. That is, membership in one of the stratum precludes membership in the other strata.

For stratified sampling, each stratum is treated as if it were a separate population. From each of these strata, cases are selected to be included into the sample. For example, we may divide the population of readers into various strata based on such variables as annual income of reader, gender of reader, and location of reader. Looking at the annual income of readers, we might divide our population into the following five strata.

- $20,000 or less
- Greater than $20,000 and less than $40,000
- Greater than $40,000 and less than $60,000
- Greater than $60,000 and less than $80,000
- Greater than $80,000

For the gender of the reader, the identification of the two strata is apparent.

- Female
- Male

For the location of the reader, we might identify five districts (strata) where our newspapers are distributed.

- Wallingford
- Eastside
- Ballard
- West Seattle
- Auburn

When using a stratified random sampling procedure, we would first divide the population of customers into the strata that were identified. Using the gender strata, we would first divide the population into the two respective groups or strata (male versus female). From each group or stratum, the readers would be randomly selected. Using the districts strata, we would first divide the readers into the five respective groups (Wallingford, Eastside, Ballard, West Seattle, and Auburn). Next, from each of these five groups, we would randomly select the readers. It is also possible to overlap the variables and create more strata. For example, we could take gender and district variables and create a 10-level strata. As is seen in Table 5.2., we would have 10 different strata, each defined by a particular district and gender. Using stratified sampling for these strata, we would first divide the population into these 10 different strata (for example, Wallingford/Female, Wallingford/Male), and conduct simple random sampling within each of the 10 strata.

Table 5.2. Strata for stratified sampling.

	Districts				
Gender	Wallingford	Eastside	Ballard	West Seattle	Auburn
Female					
Male					

There are some advantages of using a stratified sampling method over a simple random sampling.

1. We can obtain a better precision with the same overall sample size or obtain the same level of precision with a smaller sample sign.

2. We can obtain estimates of customer satisfaction levels for each stratum. This is particularly good when we want to make comparisons across different strata. Although we can make comparisons across different groups even if we use simple random sampling, stratified random sampling ensures that we have enough customers within each stratum to make these comparisons meaningful and useful.

3. We can focus on a particular stratum in which we are interested. We might be very interested in our male, Wallingford readers to determine why male readership is so low in that district.

Under what conditions would we want to conduct stratified random sampling? The division of the population into various strata might be useful if we believe that there are differences in these various strata and if one of the stratum contains a relatively smaller number of cases compared to the other strata. For example, the content of our newspaper might be aimed at people involved in childrearing. Typically, these types of newspapers have more female readers than male. We might want to see if the female readers are more satisfied with our newspaper than our male readers. Given that we have a limited number of males who read our paper, a simple random selection of readers from the entire population might lead to only a few males in our sample and, consequently, lead to a poor estimate of the satisfaction level of the entire population of male readers. To obtain a better estimate of the level of satisfaction of male readers, we could first divide our population into two strata, male and female, and randomly select a given number of males from our male stratum to ensure we have a high number of males in our final overall sample. Consequently, this method would lead to a more powerful comparison between the two genders on levels of customer satisfaction.

Cluster sampling. The previous two sampling methods involved creating samples by selecting individual cases (customers) to be included in the sample. Cluster sampling, on the other hand, is a sampling approach in which the selection process is conducted at the group level rather than the individual level. These "groups" are groups of customers. For example, the group of customers may represent different store locations. That is, the individual cases within the population are grouped or clustered into larger groups. These groups, in turn, are the level at which random selection is conducted. Such groupings or clusters might include office location, product line, or physician specialty. Therefore, the random selection process would result in a small subset of offices, products, or type of physician, respectively.

For example, we might have 200,000 customers throughout our 200-office location. These 200 offices would constitute our clusters. In cluster sampling, we would think of our 200 offices as our population and then randomly select our clusters to form our sample from this 200-office population. We could randomly select, say, 40 offices (clusters) to be included in our sample. We would use the customer surveys from these 40 offices in our statistical analysis.

If the clusters are large (for example, there are many cases within the clusters), it is possible to conduct random sampling from the selected clusters. Within each of the selected clusters, we would conduct a random sampling of the individual cases. This is referred to as *two-stage cluster sampling*. In our previous example, even though we have only 40 offices as a result of our cluster sampling procedure, each of these clusters may be quite large. On the average, each office has surveys on 1000 clients. Consequently, we would have 40,000 customer surveys in our sample. If this number is too large to handle, we could conduct random sampling from these 40,000 clients to obtain a smaller sample.

Summary

We have covered three different types of sampling methods: simple random sampling, stratified random sampling, and cluster sampling. These methods are presented in Table 5.3. For random sampling, each customer has an equal chance of being selected from the overall sample. In stratified random sampling, the population is divided into clusters or groups and random sampling is conducted within each stratum or group. Each customer within each group has an equal chance of being selected. In cluster sampling, random sampling is conducted at the group level. Each group, rather than each customer, has an equal chance of being selected.

Table 5.3. Statistical sampling methods.

Method	Definition	Steps	Important Points
Simple random	Each customer has an equal chance of being selected	• Obtain list of all customers (population) • Randomly select customers from this list	• Simple method • Assume there is some variability in the characteristic being measured
Stratified	Within each stratum, each customer has an equal chance of being selected	• Divide customers into strata (or groups) • Conduct simple random selection within each group	• Each level of the groupings must be mutually exclusive from the others • Each stratum should be treated as if it was a population • Can obtain better precision with same sample size • Obtain estimates for each stratum • Can target specific strata to ensure they are included in the final overall sample
Cluster	Each cluster (or group) has an equal chance of being selected	• Customers are already "naturally" clustered into groups • Conduct simple random sampling of the clusters	• Clusters must already be formed • Can conduct random sampling within the selected clusters

The next part of the chapter will cover the determination of sample size. Toward this end, we need an understanding of statistics, parameters, and sampling error. Although these concepts are discussed in Appendix F, they will be presented here to assist in your understanding of the determination of sample sizes.

Sample Size and Sampling Error

Recall that statistical sampling leads to a sample of cases that were randomly drawn from the population. As a result of statistical sampling, we end up with a sample from which we can make generalizations about the population. Numbers calculated from the sample are referred to as *statistics*. Numbers calculated from the entire population are referred to as *parameters*. Statistics are denoted by the following symbols: The mean is $\bar{x}$, the variance is s^2, and the standard deviation is s. Parameters are usually denoted by Greek symbol. The population mean is μ, the variance is (σ^2, and the standard deviation is σ. We use statistics as estimators of the parameters. For example, we can measure the level of customer satisfaction from the sample and conclude, based on this sample, the level of satisfaction of the population.

So, in terms of generalizing from the sample of customers to the population of customers, we use the statistics calculated from the sample as estimators for the parameters calculated from the population of customers.

Sampling Error

Suppose we have a customer base of 500 customers (population). It would be possible to draw random samples of some size from this population. For illustrative purposes, let's set our sample size to equal 10. For each sample we select from this population, we calculate the mean level of satisfaction. This statistic (the sample mean of customer satisfaction) would be our estimator of the parameter (the population mean of customer satisfaction). If we randomly select a sample of size 10 many times, we would probably get different results each time we calculate the mean of that particular sample. This variation from sample to sample is referred to as *sampling error*. In any given sample, the satisfaction level of the 10 customers would be a little bit higher or lower than the satisfaction level for all 500 customers. This type of error is expected to occur and is considered to be random.

Let's look at an example to illustrate the concept of sampling error. For the sake of argument, let's say the level of satisfaction of our population of customers might be 4.5 (of course, we might never know this but it really helps me out in explaining this concept to you). In our company, we have several teams working on the measurement of customer satisfaction, each team responsible for measuring the satisfaction level of 10 customers. In one randomly selected sample of 10 customers, Team A finds the level of customer satisfaction to be 4.0. Team B finds that the level of customer satisfaction for its 10 randomly selected customers to be 4.7. Yet another team, Team C, finds that its randomly selected sample of 10 customers results in a satisfaction level of 4.9. Are each of the teams wrong? No, of course not. The error in the estimation of the true population parameter of 4.5 is expected and is a result of the use of a sample.

Standard Error of the Mean

In the previous example, we observed sampling error; the means of the different samples varied from sample to sample. Because we do not know the exact population mean, we cannot calculate the exact amount of error associated with any one sample mean. We can determine, however, the degree of error we would expect for any given sample size. I know this all sounds magical but it is really quite simple. In theory, we could randomly select an infinite number of samples of size 10 and calculate the mean. As a result of this process, we would get an infinite number of means (each based on a sample size of 10). Next, we could plot these means to form a distribution. This distribution of sample means is, in turn, described by a mean and a standard deviation. This distribution of means is referred to as a *sampling distribution of the mean*. The mean of this sampling distribution would be our best estimate of the population mean and the standard deviation of this distribution would be our standard error of the mean (sem). The sem would be the degree of error we would expect in our sample mean. OK. That was not the simple method. As you might have guessed, it is impossible to randomly select an infinite number of samples in order to calculate the standard error of the mean. The simple method of determining the standard error of the mean involves a simple formula. The standard error of the mean can be calculated if we know the population standard deviation. The formula for the standard error of the mean is

$$\text{Standard error of the mean} = \sigma/\sqrt{n}$$

where n is the sample size and σ is the population standard deviation. If we do not know σ, we can calculate the standard error of the mean using the sample standard deviation as an estimate of the population standard deviation.

The sem essentially is a measure of the degree of sampling error. From this formula, you can see the relationship between the sem (sampling error) and sample size. As sample size increases, sampling error decreases.

The relationship between sampling error and sample size is quite intuitive. (I always hated when my statistics professor said that phrase in class, but now I understand what he was saying.) It is quite clear if we look at an example we used earlier. From our population of 1,000,000 customers, we randomly select five customers and calculate the mean satisfaction level. We place that sample of customers back into the population and randomly select another sample of five customers. We do this again and again. Do you think the sampling distribution of these means would reflect wide variability? You bet. We know that we need more customers to get a good estimate of the population mean.

Now, from our population of 1,000,000 customers we randomly select 500 customers and calculate the mean satisfaction level. We place that sample of customers back into the population and randomly select another sample of 500 customers. We do this again and again. Do you think the sampling distribution of these sample means would reflect wide variability? Probably not.

Let's use numbers now to illustrate this point. Let's say we calculate the sample standard deviation (to be used as our estimate of our population standard deviation) and it equals 1.01. Now, using our formula for the sem, we can calculate the sem for various sample sizes. In our former case with the sample size of five, the sem would be .45 ($1.01/\sqrt{5}$). In the latter case with the sample size of 500, the sem would be .045 ($1.01/\sqrt{500}$). The larger the sample size, the smaller the sem (sampling error).

Calculating Sample Size

Statistical sampling helps us ensure that we can make generalizations from our sample to the population from which the sample was drawn. An important characteristic regarding our sample is the degree of precision of our generalizations. We can define precision as the degree of sampling error (the amount our sample statistics vary from the population parameter). The greater the sampling error, the less precision we have in our estimate of the population parameter. We can use our knowledge of sampling error to help us calculate the precision of our estimate of the population parameter. Additionally, we can use our knowledge of sampling error (and its relationship to sample size) to help us determine the sample size we need for a given level of precision of our estimate.

When considering the determination of the sample size (n), we must consider three variables.

- Standard deviation of the characteristic being measured (s)

- Confidence level (t)

- Tolerable error (TE)

Standard deviation reflects the degree of variability of the characteristic being measured. We denote this value with an s.

The *confidence level* reflects the degree of confidence we have that the sample statistic we obtain from our sample is close to the population parameter. The degree of confidence is operationalized by a t-value (found in any statistics textbook). If a 95 percent confidence level is desired, we can set t to equal roughly 2.0.

Table 5.4 lists some t-values for some commonly used confidence levels.

These t-values are used to calculate the *confidence interval*. The confidence interval describes the interval that surrounds the sample statistic. The confidence interval is calculated by first multiplying the sem by the t-value. Next, this value is subtracted from the mean (estimate) to get the lower bound of the confidence interval and added to the mean to get the upper bound of the confidence interval. The formula for the confidence interval is

$$\text{Confidence interval} = \bar{x} \pm (s/\sqrt{n})\, t$$

Table 5.4. *t*-values for commonly used confidence levels.

Confidence level (as a percent)	*t*-value
50	0.6745
80	1.282
90	1.645
95	1.960 (2.0)
98	2.326
99	2.578
99.5	2.810

For example, we could conduct a survey on a sample of 300 customers and calculate a mean of 4.5 and a standard error of .04. To calculate a 95 percent confidence level, we would multiply .04 by 2.0. The lower confidence interval would be 4.42 and the upper confidence interval would be 4.58.

So, how do you interpret these results? Someone could hand you a report with a confidence interval of 4.5 and 4.9 with a 95 percent confidence level using a sample size of 300. What does that mean? If you were to conduct this sort of study 100 times, the results of each of these 100 studies would result in slightly different confidence intervals (perhaps 4.4 to 4.8 or 4.45 to 4.85). Based on statistical theory, given a 95 percent confidence interval, out of the 100 studies you could conduct, 95 studies would result in a confidence interval that would encompass the true population mean.

Tolerable error reflects the desired level of precision. Tolerable error is essentially the sampling error at a specified level of confidence.

Next, we will use this information to determine the appropriate sample size to attain a given level of confidence and tolerable error. To calculate the needed sample size, the survey team sets two factors: the confidence level and the amount of tolerable error. The standard deviation of the characteristic being measured is estimated with existing data.

Let's look again at the formula for the sem: $s/\sqrt{n}$. Recall that the tolerable error is the degree of sampling error given a specified level of confidence. Therefore, the formula for tolerable error is very similar to the formula for the sem.

$$\text{Tolerable error} = \text{TE} = (t \times s)/\sqrt{n}$$

We add the *t*-value in the formula to specify a given level of confidence. Given the other values of the equation remain the same, the greater the confidence we want, the greater the tolerable error must be.

Given this formula, we can now solve for the sample size, *n*. This results in the following formula.

$$n = (t^2 \times s^2)/\text{TE}^2$$

So, we see how these variables are related to sample size (*n*). As your desired level of confidence increases (*t*), sample size must increase. If the variability of the characteristic increases (*s*), the sample size increases. If tolerable error (TE) decreases, sample size increases.

Let's look at a real example. For a major insurance company, we want to determine the needed sample size for a given level of confidence (*t*) and a given level of tolerable error (TE). The survey team wanted to have a confidence level of 95 percent (*t* = 2.0) and a tolerable error (TE) = .20. (Using a five-point scale as our response format, this amount of error was acceptable.) Using previous survey research conducted at this insurance company and other survey research, we have found that *s* for survey items, on the average, equals 1.0.

Given the formula to calculate sample size, we solve for *n* and see that we need a sample size of $100 = (2^2 \times 1.0^2)/.20^2$ to obtain a tolerable error of .20 with a 95 percent confidence level.

Next, we set up different scenarios given a level of tolerable error at a 95 percent confidence level. Table 5.5 contains this information.

Summary

From basic formula, we were able to determine sample size for a given level of precision. When conducting customer surveys, we need to ensure that our results from our sample of customers are good estimates of our population parameters. By using these formulae, we can determine a satisfactory level of precision. These formula are useful when planning your customer satisfaction survey. Before any surveys have been administered,

Table 5.5. Tolerable error at a 95 percent confidence level.

If $s = 1.0$	
TE	**n**
.20	100
.30	44
.40	25
.50	16

we could estimate the number of surveys we need. This would greatly help us in the budgeting process of conducting our customer satisfaction study (for example, printing costs, mailing costs, labor hours). We would have the financial numbers in hand to help us convince management of the cost/benefit of conducting a customer survey.

Random Selection Procedures

The three sampling procedures discussed previously involve a method of random selection, each in a slightly different form. The difference among the various sampling procedures (random, stratified, and cluster) is reflected in the unit that is selected. In the simple random sampling procedure, the unit of selection is the individual customer from the entire population. In the stratified sampling procedure, the unit of selection is the individual customer from each stratum. In the cluster sampling procedure, the unit of selection is not the individual customer but is the group of customers. In each of the sampling procedures, random selection procedures are used to select the units.

Next, we will cover two types of random selection procedures. These two types of random selection procedures are: systematic selection with a random start and random number sampling.

Systematic Selection with a Random Start

In this procedure, the selection procedure is conducted by selecting the sample based on a fixed interval between the sampling units (typically the customer) after establishing a random starting point. The fixed interval is calculated by dividing the population size by the sample size. The random start point is typically determined by selecting a random number (usually with a computer) that is between 1 and the sampling interval.

For example, we may want to sample 100 of our customers from our population of 14,210 customers. First, we need the list of 14,210 customers in some form, either on computer or in some format where they can be counted by hand. Next, we divide 100 into 14,210 to obtain our sampling interval. This is calculated to be 142.1. Rounding down to the nearest whole number, our sampling interval is 142. Next, we establish a random starting point by randomly selecting a number between 1 and 142, inclusive. This is done by arbitrarily picking a number from Appendix L. If our random starting point was calculated to be 90, we would first survey customer 90 and then survey every 142nd customer thereafter. We would survey customer 90, 232, 375, 517, and so on until we reach our criteria of 100 customers.

Random Number Sampling

The next method of random selection procedures is best illustrated by an example. Say we have 20,000 customers and we want to obtain a random sample consisting of 100 customers. The chance of selecting one person from the population would be 1 in 200 (or .5 percent). We could select these customers by placing each of their names onto a separate sheet a paper and placing those 20,000 sheets of paper into a barrel and blindly selecting 100 sheets. With this method, each person has an equal chance of being selected. (Actually, the chance of being selected increases slightly if we do not replace the customer back into the population.)

If the population is small enough, this paper-in-a-barrel method would be possible. With large populations, however, this method is not practical. Instead, we would use a computer program that would randomly select 100 customers from a list of the population of customers (given that the list is on a computer).

Another method would be to use a random number table. Let's say we have 200 customers and we want to sample 100 of them. You should assign each customer a number ranging from 1 to 200. Next, use a random number table to determine which customer is selected into the sample. A random number table is presented in Appendix L. You should note that the numbers in this random number table have five digits. Since we are interested in 200 customers, we need to look at only the first digits in each of the five-digit random numbers. First, look away from the random number table and arbitrarily put your finger somewhere on the table. This is your starting point. Let's say your finger falls on the number 06476 (column 7, row 4). The three-digit number is 64. So, we would select customer 64 to be included in our sample. Go to the next number in the table (70782). Since the first three digits of this number are larger than 200, we go on down until we find a number in which the first three digits are 200 or less (12159). So, customer 121 is selected into the sample. Once a number has been used in the selection, all subsequent encounters of that number are ignored. This procedure is done until 100 customers have been selected for the sample.

As is very evident even in this simplistic example, the random number table method is not practical when our population is very large (thousands) or our sample is large. Typically, the selection of a sample is conducted with the aid of a computer. This method of the random number table is useful, nonetheless, to illustrate the concept that goes behind the random selection of a sample from the population.

Table 5.6 summarizes the two random selection procedures. The specific steps for each selection procedure are presented in this table.

Summary

The various sampling methods and random selection procedures just discussed illustrate the importance of the representativeness of the sample when making generalizations about the population. As we can see, the precision with which we can make our estimation of the population parameters is dependent, in part, on the results of the sampling methods. The next section will cover the effect of response rates on the sampling process and will cover various methods of increasing response rates.

Response Rates

When conducting a customer survey, it is unlikely that all customers will return a completed survey. For our purposes, response rate is defined as

Table 5.6. Random selection procedures.

Method	Definition	Steps
Systematic selection with a random start	Selection procedure is conducted by selecting the sample based on a fixed interval between the sampling units after establishing a random starting point	• Acquire complete list of the unit (typically customers) • Divide sample size into population size to obtain interval (z) • Establish random starting point to select unit • Select every zth unit from the list
Random number sampling	Random number table (or comparable computer program) used to select customers	• Assign all units (typically customer) a unique number • Use random number table to select unit into the sample

the percent of returned, completed surveys of all the surveys that were administered. For example, if we mail out 1000 surveys and only 300 written surveys are returned, we have a response rate of 30 percent. For written, mail surveys, response rates can be very low. Due to apathy, interest level, and other various factors, customers may not complete a survey. A low response rate does affect the outcome of the sampling procedure. We saw earlier in this chapter the relationship between sample size and tolerable error. Here are the formula again.

$$n = (t^2 \times s^2)/\text{TE}^2$$

$$\text{Tolerable error} = \text{TE} = (t \times s)/\sqrt{n}$$

If a survey team is relying on a given number of surveys to establish a given level of precision, a low response rate from customers will lead to a wider confidence interval. Recall that the confidence level and tolerable error are affected by the sample size. As sample size decreases, the confidence interval increases and tolerable error increases.

Consequently, when planning our sampling procedures, we must take into account the response rate. To obtain a given sample size, in the end our sampling procedure will require administering more customer surveys than we will ultimately need for analysis. For example, we may have concluded that we need a sample size of 200 for a given level of confidence. If we expect a response rate of 30 percent for our survey, how many surveys should we administer (mail)? The formula to calculate the distribution sample size is

$$\text{Distribution size} = \text{Needed sample size/Response rate}$$

where distribution size is the number of surveys we should administer; needed sample size is the sample size we determined we needed for a given level of confidence and tolerable error; and response rate is the actual or expected number of returned surveys from our satisfaction study.

For our example, we would need to administer about 670 surveys (200/.30) to our customers. This size of a distribution of customer surveys would help us ensure that we have enough customers in our final sample to maintain a given level of confidence and tolerable error that were established earlier in the sampling process.

Establishing Response Rates

The key factor in the previous equation is the response rate. Our distribution sample size is dependent on this factor. Response rates can vary from study to study. In my experience, I have seen response rates as low as 7 percent and as high as 50 percent. We really have little control on establishing our response rate. We can, however, estimate what our response rate will be for our study. We could determine if a survey was conducted in the past and use that information to see what our response rate will be for our study. Another method would be to conduct a literature search in our specific industry to determine what other researchers have found regarding response rates of similar customer groups. If these methods are not feasible, it is always possible to conduct our satisfaction survey and monitor the response rates throughout the process and adjust our mailing list (increase the distribution list size) to obtain more customers in our final sample.

The factors that tend to affect the response rates are related to the ease with which the subjects can return the surveys. Basically, if the return process is made simple for customers, the response rate will go up. Some research regarding the factors that affect response rates for mail surveys are presented next.

Methods of Increasing Response Rates of Mail Surveys

Although we mail out a given number of customer surveys, we invariably will get only a portion mailed back to us. Here are some conclusions regarding methods to increase response rates in mail surveys. The following methods have been shown to increase response rates of mail surveys.

• Repeated contacts in the form of preliminary notification and follow-ups. If it is possible, the customers should receive warning that they will be part of a satisfaction survey. Once the customers are included in the sample, they should be notified with follow-up contacts requesting completion of their surveys.

• Appeals. Customers want to know how their input will be used and whether their opinions are making a difference in the organization. Informing the recipients of mail surveys about the use of their information will increase response rates. In the survey, tell your customers why their opinions are valued and how the information will be used throughout the company.

• Inclusion of a return envelope. If your customer survey is multiple pages long, you should include an envelope for the return of the survey. Relying on the customer to provide his or her own envelope adds to the difficulty of returning the survey. The cost spent on envelopes might be less than the cost of mailing out more customer surveys if the response rate is low. Additionally, some companies format the survey in such a way that allows the survey itself to be mailed back to the organization. The organization prints the return address on one side of the survey so that customers only have to fold the survey to expose the return address and drop it in a mailbox.

• Postage. Providing postage for the return of the mail survey increases the chances that the recipient will return the survey. Again, making the return process easier for customers by providing postage increases the likelihood that they will return the survey.

• Monetary incentives. Providing incentive in the form of monetary reward has been shown to increase response rates to mail surveys. Each customer who returns a survey could be given a small monetary token. In addition, a monetary incentive could be in the form of a lottery. From all customers who returned a survey, one is randomly chosen to receive a monetary reward for completion of the survey. Some companies have informed customers that the company would donate a certain amount of money to a given charity for every returned survey. While monetary incentives work, other studies have shown that nonmonetary incentives do not increase response rates.

• First-rate outgoing postage. Research has shown that the outgoing postage has an effect on the response rates. First-rate postage has been shown to increase the response rates of mail surveys. This first-rate postage may indicate to the recipient of the survey the importance of the survey; companies wouldn't use first-rate postage if the results were not important to them.

• Sponsorship. Finally, research has shown that mail surveys are more likely to be returned if the study is sponsored by a third party. Typically, this third party could be a survey research firm or a university. The sponsoring organization, acting as an independent party, might lend credibility to the entire survey process. The customers may feel that their responses will be treated with more care and honesty from an unbiased party who is organizing the data.

Summary

The use of these methods to increase response rates does not guarantee that all surveys will be returned. The use of these methods, however, does increase your chances that the surveys will be returned. The extent to which these methods are used might depend on your resources. Some companies might not be able to provide monetary incentives to customers or might not be able to provide first-rate outgoing postage. Although these methods are presented separately, some of these methods might be used in conjunction with the other methods. The more methods you can use to increase response rates, the better. At a minimum, if you are conducting a survey, you should provide postage and a means for which to have the surveys returned.

Using Customer Satisfaction Questionnaires

This chapter will present five examples of customer satisfaction questionnaires and outline some specific things you can do with data derived from them. I will demonstrate how you can present and summarize data, as well as determine which of the customer requirements is most important in determining customer satisfaction. Also, I will demonstrate how the data can be applied to traditional quality improvement methodologies, including control charting techniques.

Examples of Customer Satisfaction Questionnaires

Previous chapters outlined some guidelines and issues to address when developing customer satisfaction questionnaires. This section will present five customer satisfaction questionnaires: one based on the results of the quality dimension development process applied to the software industry, another based on the general quality dimensions applied to a facilities organization within a company, and three based on the results of the critical incidents applied to the banking and automobile industries and the internal statistical department in Chapter 2. These will allow you to see the structure of a questionnaire, designed on the basis of the guidelines presented in earlier chapters.

Software Quality

The response format for each questionnaire is the Likert-type format using the agree-disagree continuum. (The checklist format could have been used also.) The questionnaire for the software industry appears in Figure 6.1. Although there are 20 items in the questionnaire, this questionnaire was designed to represent 10 dimensions of software quality.

To better serve you, we would like to know your opinion of the quality of our software. Please indicate the extent to which you agree or disagree with the following statements about the software [name of software]. Circle the appropriate number using the scale below. Some of the statements are similar to one another to ensure that we accurately determine your opinion concerning the software.

       1—I Strongly Disagree with this statement (SD).
       2—I Disagree with this statement (D).
       3—I Neither agree nor disagree with this statement (N).
       4—I Agree with this statement (A).
       5—I Strongly Agree with this statement (SA).

	SD	D	N	A	SA
1. I am able to complete my job with this software.	1	2	3	4	5
2. The software meets my specifications in getting my job done.	1	2	3	4	5
3. I am able to perform functions with precision.	1	2	3	4	5
4. The software allows me to perform functions accurately.	1	2	3	4	5
5. I was able to learn about the output from programs in a short amount of time.	1	2	3	4	5
6. The output of the programs is easy to understand.	1	2	3	4	5

Figure 6.1. Example of a customer satisfaction questionnaire for the software industry.

	SD	D	N	A	SA
7. Fixing an error in the operational program is easy.	1	2	3	4	5
8. Locating an error in the operational program is easy.	1	2	3	4	5
9. The testing of the program required a short amount of time.	1	2	3	4	5
10. Testing the program to ensure it performed functions was easy.	1	2	3	4	5
11. Transferring the program between different hardware configurations is easy.	1	2	3	4	5
12. I am able to transfer programs between different software environments with little problem.	1	2	3	4	5
13. Coupling one system to another is easy.	1	2	3	4	5
14. The software allows for simple coupling between systems.	1	2	3	4	5
15. Communicating between software components is simple.	1	2	3	4	5
16. I am able to communicate between software components easily.	1	2	3	4	5
17. I am able to modify the operational program with little effort.	1	2	3	4	5
18. Changing the operational program is easy to do.	1	2	3	4	5
19. I am very happy with the software.	1	2	3	4	5
20. The software meets my expectations.	1	2	3	4	5

Additional comments:

Figure 6.1. *Continued.*

Therefore, we could conceivably derive 10 scores, each score representing the quality for a particular dimension. The dimensions and their items are

1. Correctness (items 1 and 2)
2. Reliability (items 3 and 4)
3. Usability (items 5 and 6)
4. Maintainability (items 7 and 8)
5. Testability (items 9 and 10)
6. Portability (items 11 and 12)
7. Interoperability (items 13 and 14)
8. Intra-operability (items 15 and 16)
9. Flexibility (items 17 and 18)
10. Overall satisfaction (items 19 and 20)

Additional analysis (factor analysis) might reveal a smaller subset of dimensions after customers complete the questionnaire. Customers may not be able to distinguish between nine separate dimensions of software quality.

Facilities Department

The next questionnaire is presented in Figure 6.2. This example illustrates the use of customer satisfaction questionnaires for internal customers (customers within the same company as the provider). The questionnaire was based on the general service quality dimensions presented by Kennedy and Young (1989). The items reflect each of the quality dimensions. The quality dimensions and their respective items are

1. Availability of service (items 1 through 3)
2. Responsiveness of service (items 4 through 6)
3. Timeliness of service (items 7 through 9)
4. Professionalism of service (items 10 through 12)
5. Overall satisfaction with service (items 13 through 15)
6. Overall satisfaction with product (items 16 through 18)

To better serve you, we would like to know your opinion of the quality of our services and products. You recently received help from Facilities department. Please indicate the extent to which you agree or disagree with the following statements about the service you received from the staff of Facilities. Circle the appropriate number using the scale below. Some of the statements are similar to one another to ensure that we accurately determine your opinion concerning our service.

      1—I Strongly Disagree with this statement (SD).
      2—I Disagree with this statement (D).
      3—I Neither agree nor disagree with this statement (N).
      4—I Agree with this statement (A).
      5—I Strongly Agree with this statement (SA).

	SD	D	N	A	SA
1. I could get help from Facilities when I needed.	1	2	3	4	5
2. The Facilities staff was there when they were needed.	1	2	3	4	5
3. I could arrange convenient meeting times with the staff.	1	2	3	4	5
4. Facilities was quick to respond when I asked for help.	1	2	3	4	5
5. Facilities immediately helped me if needed.	1	2	3	4	5
6. I waited a short period of time to get help after I asked for it.	1	2	3	4	5
7. Facilities completed the job when expected.	1	2	3	4	5
8. Facilities did not meet my deadline(s).	1	2	3	4	5
9. Facilities staff finished their responsibilities within the stated time frame.	1	2	3	4	5
10. The staff conducted themselves in a professional manner.	1	2	3	4	5

Figure 6.2. Example of a customer satisfaction questionnaire for a facilities organization.

	SD	D	N	A	SA
11. The staff was courteous.	1	2	3	4	5
12. The staff cared about what I had to say.	1	2	3	4	5
13. The quality of the way Facilities treated me is high.	1	2	3	4	5
14. The way Facilities treated me met my expectations.	1	2	3	4	5
15. I am satisfied with the way Facilities treated me.	1	2	3	4	5
16. The quality of the final job Facilities provided is high.	1	2	3	4	5
17. The job met my expectations.	1	2	3	4	5
18. I am satisfied with the job that Facilities provided.	1	2	3	4	5
Additional Comments:					

Figure 6.2. *Continued.*

Although this questionnaire might represent a comprehensive examination of the general service quality dimensions, there still may be other quality dimensions specific to any one facilities organization that should be included in the questionnaire. Therefore, more items might be needed to more fully represent the entire range of possible quality dimensions.

Banking Industry

The next questionnaire is presented in Figure 6.3 and represents the banking industry. One of its statements has a negative connotation (item 4). It is possible that some items in any questionnaire will be phrased negatively. Due to this "negativity," a score of 5 for this statement reflects poor service while a score of 1 reflects good service. Therefore, adding the scores from this statement (item 4) to scores from item 3 would be incorrect. Due to

To better serve you, we would like to know your opinion of the quality of our services and products. Please indicate the extent to which you agree or disagree with the following statements about the service you received from [company name]. Circle the appropriate number using the scale below. Some of the statements are similar to one another to ensure that we accurately determine your opinion concerning our service.

> 1—I Strongly Disagree with this statement (SD).
> 2—I Disagree with this statement (D).
> 3—I Neither agree nor disagree with this statement (N).
> 4—I Agree with this statement (A).
> 5—I Strongly Agree with this statement (SA).

	SD	D	N	A	SA
1. I waited a short period of time before I was helped.	1	2	3	4	5
2. The service started immediately when I arrived.	1	2	3	4	5
3. The teller handled transactions in a short period of time.	1	2	3	4	5
4. The teller took a long time to complete my transaction.	1	2	3	4	5
5. The financial consultant was available to schedule me at a good time.	1	2	3	4	5
6. My appointment with the financial consultant was at a convenient time.	1	2	3	4	5
7. The teller talked to me in a pleasant way.	1	2	3	4	5
8. The teller was very personable.	1	2	3	4	5
9. The teller carefully listened to me when I was requesting a transaction.	1	2	3	4	5
10. The teller knew how to handle the transactions.	1	2	3	4	5
11. The quality of the way the teller treated me was high.	1	2	3	4	5

Figure 6.3. Example of a customer satisfaction questionnaire for the banking industry.

	SD	D	N	A	SA
12. The way the teller treated me met my expectations.	1	2	3	4	5
13. I am satisfied with the way the teller treated me.	1	2	3	4	5
Additional comments:					

Figure 6.3. *Continued.*

the negativity of item 4, we would reverse the scores for this statement so that a score of 1 on the original scale becomes 5, 2 on the original scale becomes 4, 4 on the original scale becomes 2, and 1 on the original scale becomes 5. Once we have completed the transformation, averaging the response of items 3 and 4 is appropriate.

You could conceivably derive 13 scores for each customer based on this questionnaire (one score for each of the 13 items). This questionnaire, however, was designed to assess four quality dimensions and one dimension labeled *overall customer satisfaction*. Therefore, some items would be combined to get measures of customers' perception of various quality dimensions. The dimensions and their corresponding items are

1. Responsiveness of service (items 1 and 2)
2. Speed of transaction (items 3 and 4)
3. Availability of service (items 5 and 6)
4. Professionalism (items 7 through 10)
5. Overall satisfaction with service (items 11 through 13)

Automobile Industry

The next customer satisfaction questionnaire is presented in Figure 6.4 and represents the automobile industry. The introduction to this questionnaire is addressed to the person who just drove a particular car. This demonstrates a particular use of customer satisfaction questionnaires: the

We would like to know your opinion of the quality of the automobile you just drove. Please indicate the extent to which you agree or disagree with the following statements. Circle the appropriate number using the scale below. Some of the statements are similar to one another to ensure that we accurately determine your opinion concerning the automobile.

1—I Strongly Disagree with this statement (SD).
2—I Disagree with this statement (D).
3—I Neither agree nor disagree with this statement (N).
4—I Agree with this statement (A).
5—I Strongly Agree with this statement (SA).

	SD	D	N	A	SA
1. The seating position was very comfortable.	1	2	3	4	5
2. The visibility through the window was good.					
3. The inside of the car was noisy.	1	2	3	4	5
4. The instrumentation panel was simple to understand.	1	2	3	4	5
5. The instrumentation panel was clearly visible from the driving seat.	1	2	3	4	5
6. The car stopped smoothly when I applied the brakes.	1	2	3	4	5
7. The car vibrated at high speeds.	1	2	3	4	5
8. The car handled corners well.	1	2	3	4	5
9. I enjoyed driving the car.	1	2	3	4	5
10. I liked the overall driving experience of the car.	1	2	3	4	5
11. The drive was excellent.	1	2	3	4	5

Additional comments:

Figure 6.4. Example of a customer satisfaction questionnaire for the automobile industry.

comparison of cars from different automobile manufacturers. This questionnaire might be used by an independent customer research group conducting a study comparing different cars. The full experimental design of the study would be complex and will not be presented here. The general design of the study, however, would be to allow customers to drive all the cars being studied. After each drive, the person completes the questionnaire to indicate his or her perception of the car's quality. Subsequently, the data can be used to make direct comparisons between the automobiles.

Again, scores derived from this questionnaire should reflect dimensions being measured by the various items. The dimensions and their corresponding items are

1. Interior quality (items 1 through 3)
2. Instrumentation (items 4 and 5)
3. Drivability (items 6 through 8)
4. Overall satisfaction with auto (items 9 through 11)

Statistical Support Department

The questionnaire for the statistical support department is presented in Figure 6.5. This questionnaire would likely be distributed to customers after the completion of a project. The customer would answer the questionnaire with respect to that particular project. This questionnaire was designed to assess five customer requirements as well as overall customer satisfaction.

1. Statistical support (items 1 through 3)
2. Enthusiasm (items 4 and 5)
3. Final written report (items 6 and 7)
4. Responsiveness (items 8 and 9)
5. Project management (items 10 and 11)
6. Overall satisfaction with service (items 12 and 13)

Uses of Customer Satisfaction Questionnaires

Next, I will present four uses of customer satisfaction questionnaires: (1) Summarizing data with descriptive statistics, (2) Determining the most

To better serve you, we would like to know your opinion of the quality of our services and products. You recently received help from the statistical support department. Please indicate the extent to which you agree or disagree with the following statements about the service you received from the staff. Circle the appropriate number using the scale below. Some of the statements are similar to one another to ensure that we accurately determine your opinion concerning our service.

1—I Strongly Disagree with this statement (SD).
2—I Disagree with this statement (D).
3—I Neither agree nor disagree with this statement (N).
4—I Agree with this statement (A).
5—I Strongly Agree with this statement (SA).

	SD	D	N	A	SA
1. The staff person explained the statistical tests in understandable words.	1	2	3	4	5
2. The statistical analyses were thorough.	1	2	3	4	5
3. The staff understood my software requirements.	1	2	3	4	5
4. The staff person was always willing to help.	1	2	3	4	5
5. The staff person went out of his or her way to help.	1	2	3	4	5
6. The written report was sufficiently detailed.	1	2	3	4	5
7. The written report contained what I needed.	1	2	3	4	5
8. The staff person completed the job quickly.	1	2	3	4	5
9. The staff person finished the project in the stated time frame.	1	2	3	4	5
10. The staff person planned out the entire project through its completion.	1	2	3	4	5

Figure 6.5. Example of a customer satisfaction questionnaire for an internal statistical support department.

	SD	D	N	A	SA
11. The staff person understood how much time the project required.	1	2	3	4	5
12. I am satisfied with the service I received.	1	2	3	4	5
13. The quality of the service met my expectations.	1	2	3	4	5
Additional comments:					

Figure 6.5. *Continued.*

important customer requirement, (3) Control chart techniques to track the quality of the product or service over time, and (4) The comparison of customer satisfaction between companies.

Summary Indices

The presentation of the data is an important issue. The quality of the data obtained from the customer satisfaction questionnaire depends on the way in which the data are summarized and presented. A reliable questionnaire will be of little practical use if the data cannot be understood. This part of the chapter will present some summary indices of a sample of data and will demonstrate how data can be presented.

One way to summarize the data is to use summary indices that describe important aspects of the data. Summary indices that describe a sample of data are called *statistics* (Appendix E).

The statistics that summarize the elements in a data set reflect the central tendency of the data and the dispersion of the data. Three statistics are the *arithmetic average* or *mean*, the *variance*, and the *standard deviation*. The mean indicates the central tendency of data, while the latter two describe the spread of the data. The formula for the arithmetic average is $(\Sigma x_i)/n$. The Σ notation (called *sigma*) indicates summation of the variables, and n equals the number of elements in the data set. For the present

equation, sigma indicates that all the observations going into the calculation of the mean will be added together. This sum is then divided by the
number of observations. The resulting number is the mean. The equation
for the mean can also be expressed as

$$\bar{x} = \frac{x_1 + x_2 + \ldots + x_n}{n}$$

where n equals the number of elements in the data set.

The formula for the variance is

$$s^2 = \frac{\sum_{i=1}^{n}(x_1 - \bar{x})^2}{n - 1}$$

where n equals the number of elements in the sample.

The sample standard deviation, which is also a measure of variability,
is the square root of the sample variance.

Presentation of Data

I will use a hypothetical example to illustrate how data can be presented.
A company used a customer satisfaction questionnaire to gauge the level
of service it provided. This questionnaire was designed to measure several
customer requirements and overall customer satisfaction. A portion of
these items appears in Figure 6.6. Items 1 through 3 measure availability of
service, items 4 through 6 measure responsiveness of service, and items 7
through 9 measure overall customer satisfaction.

The company solicited responses from customers. Data for 20 customers are presented in Table 6.1. It is apparent, even from this small
set of data, that examination of the raw data does not reveal much information. The table looks like a series of unrelated numbers. We need to
summarize the data in a clear, concise format to help us interpret the
important findings. To do so, we have calculated the average and standard
deviation for each item.

Also, summary scores for the two customer requirement categories
are calculated, as well as a summary score for overall customer satisfaction. These scores are the average of the items within that given dimension. These summary scores can provide a more general measure of

Please indicate the extent to which you agree or disagree with the following statements concerning the service you received. Please circle your response for each question using the following scale.

       1—I Strongly Disagree with this statement (SD).
       2—I Disagree with this statement (D).
       3—I Neither agree nor disagree with this statement (N).
       4—I Agree with this statement (A).
       5—I Strongly Agree with this statement (SA).

	SD	D	N	A	SA
1. I could get an appointment with the merchant at a time I desired.	1	2	3	4	5
2. The merchant was available to schedule me at a good time.	1	2	3	4	5
3. My appointment was at a convenient time for me.	1	2	3	4	5
4. The merchant was quick to respond when I arrived for my appointment.	1	2	3	4	5
5. The merchant immediately helped me when I entered the premises.	1	2	3	4	5
6. My appointment started promptly at the scheduled time.	1	2	3	4	5
7. The quality of the way the merchant treated me was high.	1	2	3	4	5
8. The way the merchant treated me met my expectations.	1	2	3	4	5
9. Overall, I am satisfied with the service.	1	2	3	4	5

Figure 6.6. Example of satisfaction items measuring two customer requirements and overall customer satisfaction.

Table 6.1. Example data from 20 customers responding to a customer satisfaction questionnaire.

				Satisfaction items					
Customer	1	2	3	4	5	6	7	8	9
1	5	4	5	3	4	4	3	4	3
2	3	2	3	5	4	5	4	4	4
3	4	5	5	3	2	2	3	3	4
4	3	2	3	4	3	4	4	5	4
5	3	3	3	4	4	4	3	3	3
6	4	4	5	4	5	4	4	5	4
7	3	4	2	4	3	3	3	2	3
8	5	4	5	4	4	4	5	4	5
9	3	2	3	4	3	4	4	4	3
10	3	4	3	4	4	4	3	4	3
11	5	5	5	5	5	5	5	5	5
12	4	4	4	3	3	4	4	4	4
13	4	4	5	5	5	4	4	4	5
14	2	2	3	4	4	5	3	3	2
15	4	5	5	4	4	3	4	3	3
16	5	4	5	5	5	5	4	4	4
17	3	4	3	5	4	4	4	4	4
18	3	2	4	3	3	4	2	2	2
19	5	4	3	4	5	4	3	3	4
20	3	3	3	4	3	3	4	4	4
Mean =	3.70	3.55	3.83	4.05	3.85	3.95	3.65	3.70	3.65
Standard deviation =	0.92	1.05	1.04	0.69	0.88	0.76	0.75	0.87	0.88

Summary scores for customer requirements (reliability estimates in parentheses)

	Availability of service (.85)	*Responsiveness of service* (.81)	*Overall satisfaction* (.88)
Mean =	3.70	3.95	3.67
Standard deviation =	.88	.66	.74

service quality and are particularly useful for presentations to upper management. We have calculated reliability estimates (Cronbach's alpha estimate) for each dimension. These estimates are essential because they indicate the quality of the summary scores.

Summary

It is important that data from questionnaires be summarized in an understandable format. Often, the mean and standard deviations are used to summarize information in the data set. Summary scores for each dimension can provide general measures of the quality of the service or product.

Identify Important Customer Requirements

Suppose our service organization has developed a customer satisfaction questionnaire that assesses five quality dimensions and overall customer satisfaction, and we solicit responses from our customers. Also, suppose that the questionnaire results indicate that the average score for the five quality dimensions and overall customer satisfaction are roughly the same. In addition, our supervisor has given us the resources to increase service quality. Given this information, on which of the five quality dimensions should we apply the resources?

For this situation (and possibly for all situations), examining the satisfaction level for each dimension would be of little use, since the satisfaction levels are (or could be) the same across all dimensions. A better method would be to determine which quality dimension is most highly related to overall customer satisfaction. If our goal is to increase overall customer satisfaction, we should direct resources toward those dimensions that would increase overall customer satisfaction.

To determine which dimensions are closely linked with overall customer satisfaction, we could determine the extent to which each dimension is correlated with overall customer satisfaction. One way to determine which quality dimension is most important would be simply to ask customers the extent to which each quality dimension is important in making them satisfied with the service. For example, customers could rate the importance of each quality dimension in their satisfaction. For each dimension, we would calculate an average score of these ratings. This average would indicate the level of importance of that particular dimension in satisfying the customers.

Research on human judgment, however, suggests that people are poor judges as to what information they think they use. A statistical model is better at predicting outcomes compared to judgmental models. One statistical approach is correlation analysis (see Appendix J).

After customers complete the customer satisfaction questionnaire, we would calculate scores for each quality dimension. Therefore, each customer would get a score on each of the quality dimensions represented on the customer satisfaction questionnaire, as well as a score for overall satisfaction.

After calculating scores, the next step would be to correlate each quality dimension with the overall satisfaction score. The correlations between each of the quality dimensions and overall customer satisfaction scores reflect the importance of each quality dimension in predicting overall customer satisfaction. The higher the correlation, the more important the quality dimension is in satisfying customers.

Here is an illustration of this method using quality dimensions associated with the banking industry. Suppose I calculated the correlations between each of the quality dimensions and overall customer satisfaction and found them to be $r = .50$ for responsiveness of service, $r = .15$ for speed of transaction, $r = .25$ for availability of service, and $r = .40$ for professionalism. These results reveal that both responsiveness and professionalism are important in determining overall customer satisfaction. As a result, resources would probably have their greatest effect on overall customer satisfaction if applied in these two areas.

Determination of important quality dimensions does not have to be confined to a single point in time. Even though current results indicate the most important quality dimensions are responsiveness and professionalism, other quality dimensions may come to the fore later. The relative ordering of customers' requirements or expectations may change over time. Thus, a continual determination of important customer requirements is necessary. Also, it is important to consider the effect of reliability on the correlation between variables (see Chapter 3). Recall that a statistically nonsignificant correlation between two variables might result from the unreliability of the scales. Therefore, you must determine the reliability of the scales.

Summary

Recall that all of the quality dimensions being assessed by the customer satisfaction questionnaire are, by design, important to customers. It is beneficial to understand which of these quality dimensions is most highly linked with overall customer satisfaction. This information is necessary when determining where to direct company resources. The best method is to collect data with the questionnaire and determine, through correlational analysis, the most important quality dimensions.

Interpretation of the correlations is reserved for those knowledgeable in statistics. Factors such as restriction in range of scores and collinearity of quality dimensions should be considered when determining which quality characteristic is most important in determining overall customer satisfaction. Also, calculation of correlation coefficients is only one way of determining the important dimensions. Another approach involves multiple regression analysis, which is a more sophisticated method of determining relationships between variables. For interested readers, several statistics textbooks include these topics (Neter, Wasserman, and Kutner 1985; Pedhazur 1982).

Once we have identified these important quality dimensions, the next step is to track their level of quality. This is often done with the help of control charts. Next, I will present an overview of control chart techniques and discuss specific uses of these charts. A more comprehensive discussion of control charts and statistical process control methodologies is available elsewhere (Montgomery 1985).

Control Charts

Control charts represent various ways data can be charted. An example of a control chart appears in Figure 6.7. The control chart is a visual display of the overall service or product quality. In addition, control charts can display each of the quality characteristics. The ordinate (vertical axis) of the control chart represents the measurement of the overall quality dimension of a particular quality dimension. The abscissa (horizontal axis) represents either the sample number or time. The control chart includes a center line representing the average value of the quality dimensions over the entire

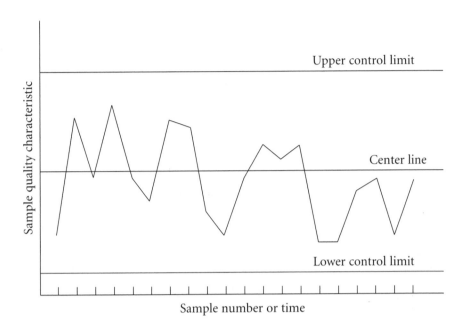

Figure 6.7. Example of a control chart.

range of samples. The chart also contains an upper control limit (UCL) and lower control limit (LCL) that run parallel with the center line.

There are general formulae for the control chart's center line, UCL, and LCL. Let's use Q to represent the sample statistic of the quality characteristic we are measuring. Let's indicate the mean of Q as $\bar{x}_Q$ and the variance of Q as $s^2_{(Q)}$. With these labels, the general formulae for the control charts are

$$\text{UCL} = \bar{x}_Q + k\sqrt{s^2_{(Q)}}$$
$$\text{Center line} = \bar{x}_Q$$
$$\text{LCL} = \bar{x}_Q - k\sqrt{s^2_{(Q)}}$$

where k represents a constant used to determine the distance of the UCL and LCL from the center line. It is standard that k equal 3.0; therefore, 3 will be used in the remaining equations.

Interpretation of the Control Chart

Control charts can monitor the business processes that generate the data in the chart. Each data point in the control chart indicates how the process is running at a given time. Over time, because of natural variability inherent in the process, we expect that not all data points will fall on the center line. This natural variability is due to random causes referred to as *uncontrollable factors*. Under these conditions, we expect the data points will fall somewhere between the UCL and the LCL. When this pattern occurs, the process is said to be *in statistical control*.

There are additional sources of variability that will influence the output of the process. The variability from these other sources is usually larger than the natural variability and is due to events that represent a potential problem in the process when they occur. The sources of this extreme variability are referred to as *assignable causes*. Their presence is indicated by a data point falling outside the control limits (either above the UCL or below the LCL). When this pattern occurs, the process is said to be *out of control*. Using control charts helps us remove the source of this type of variability. Specific uses of control charts will be presented in examples later in the chapter.

Types of Data

Quality dimension data can be categorized as *attribute data* and *variable data*. Attribute data are usually categorical. Measurements of quality characteristics are classified as either conforming to specifications or not conforming to specifications and divide occurrences into nondefective or defective categories, respectively.

Variable data are numerical. We can apply a unit of measurement (for example, inches or minutes) to quality characteristics. Not only can we determine the number of nonconforming occurrences, we can also determine the degree to which an occurrence is not conforming to specifications.

The type of data that is gathered is often a function of the process being measured or the measurement tool used. As will be apparent later, data from customer satisfaction questionnaires can be used as either categorical data or variable data. We can apply either of the two types of data (attribute or variable) to control charts. Next, I will present some ways in which we can apply data from customer satisfaction questionnaires to control chart techniques.

Control Charts for Attribute Data

Recall that we can allocate attribute data into categories (for example, categories of defective and nondefective). Two attribute control charts that apply are the *p* chart and the *c* chart.

The *p* Chart

Quality of a service could be evident in the percentage of people who volunteer at least one negative response. A decrease in the percentage of these people indicates an increase in the quality of service. For any given sample of customers completing our questionnaire, we can calculate the percentage of people who gave at least one negative response. In a sense, this percentage represents the number of defects in our sample. The formula for this percentage is

$$p_i = D_i / n_i$$

where D_i is the number of people who gave at least one negative response for a given sample (*i*) and n_i is the sample size.

The percentage, *p*, is calculated for every sample. Given that the sample size is constant, we can create the control chart using the average of all *p*s. The formula for the UCL, center line, and LCL are

$$UCL = \bar{p} + 3\sqrt{\frac{\bar{p}(1 - \bar{p})}{n}}$$

$$Center\ line = \bar{p}$$

$$LCL = \bar{p} - 3\sqrt{\frac{\bar{p}(1 - \bar{p})}{n}}$$

Example of the *p* Chart

Using the customer satisfaction questionnaire for the banking industry (see Figure 6.3), we would like to determine the percentage of customers who give at least one negative response about service they received from banking personnel. The bank is experiencing a high number of complaints related to banking personnel. A negative response occurs when the customer indicates he or she either disagreed or strongly disagreed to a positively phrased satisfaction item (for example, questions 2 and 3) or agreed or strongly agreed to a negative satisfaction item (for example, question 4). Data collected over 20 weeks appear in Table 6.2. Sample size for each of the 20 samples is 50.

The calculations of the UCL, center line, and LCL are

$$\text{UCL} = .213 + 3(.0579) = .3867$$

$$\text{Center line} = .213$$

$$\text{LCL} = .213 - 3(.0579) = .0393$$

Table 6.2. Data for the p control chart example (note $n = 50$).

Sample	Number of customers who gave at least one negative response (D_i)	Percentage of customers who gave at least one negative response (p_i)
1	5	.10
2	20	.40
3	15	.30
4	16	.32
5	10	.20
6	8	.16
7	15	.30
8	20	.40
9	7	.14
10	2	.04
11	10	.20
12	13	.26
13	20	.40
14	13	.26
15	4	.08
16	4	.08
17	9	.18
18	11	.22
19	5	.10
20	6	.12
	total = 213	$\bar{p} = .213$

The resulting control chart appears in Figure 6.8. The plotted numbers for each sample represent the percentage of people who gave at least one negative response on the customer satisfaction questionnaire. The control chart indicates that several points lie outside the control points. This could indicate that an event (assignable cause) occurred during the week in which those points fell outside the UCL. Perhaps during those weeks new staff members were being trained on the job or some employees resigned, leaving the bank understaffed. If we can identify assignable causes for these points, we should exclude these samples when calculating the control limits and center line. We do this because the control limits and center line are calculated to reflect how the process typically functions. If no assignable causes are apparent, then the current control limits and center line are appropriate.

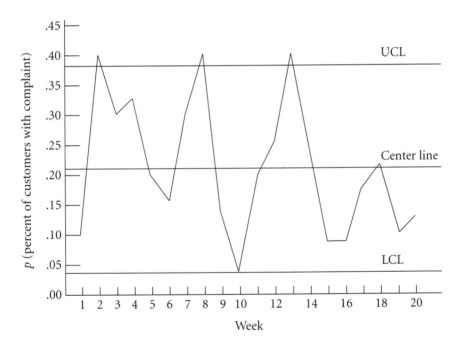

Figure 6.8. The *p* control chart using data from Table 6.2.

The c Chart

The *p* chart allowed us to display the percentage of customers who gave at least one negative response. We may, however, want to get an indication of how many negative responses there were among a given sample of customers. A customer may have many negative responses about the service he or she received. The *c* chart is a way of graphing this type of data, where *c* is the total number of negative responses indicated by the customers. The formula for the UCL, center line, and LCL are

$$UCL = \bar{c} + 3\sqrt{\bar{c}}$$
$$Center\ line = \bar{c}$$
$$LCL = \bar{c} - 3\sqrt{\bar{c}}$$

where *c* is the number of negative responses per sample.

Example of the c Chart

I will use the banking example again to illustrate the *c* chart. We would now like to monitor the total number of negative responses from customers. We collect data for 20 weeks (see Table 6.3). After examining the data, we decide to create a control chart. The control limits and the center line are calculated to be

$$UCL = 31.61$$
$$Center\ line = 18.65$$
$$LCL = 5.69$$

The *c* control chart is presented in Figure 6.9. The figure demonstrates that no points fall outside the control limits, suggesting that the process is in control. This indicates that the average number of negative responses per sample is approximately 19. Even though the process is in statistical control, the data indicate a high number of negative responses from customers. Changing this situation warrants a change in the banking personnel's contact with customers. This type of process change requires action from management and might include additional training for banking personnel, providing more tellers, or increasing the number of banking windows.

Table 6.3. Data for the c control chart example (note $n = 50$).

Sample (week)	Number of negative responses (c_i)	Average number of negative responses per person (u_i)	Percentage of negative responses out of all possible responses [$p_i(tot)$]
1	15	.30	.023
2	20	.40	.038
3	14	.28	.022
4	25	.50	.038
5	24	.48	.037
6	18	.36	.028
7	26	.52	.040
8	28	.56	.043
9	15	.30	.023
10	8	.16	.012
11	17	.34	.026
12	20	.40	.038
13	28	.56	.043
14	21	.42	.032
15	13	.26	.020
16	16	.32	.025
17	18	.36	.028
18	22	.44	.034
19	10	.20	.015
20	15	.30	.023
	$\bar{c} = 18.65$	$\bar{u} = .373$	$\bar{p}(tot) = .029$

Additional data presented in Table 6.3 illustrate other methods of control charting based on the original information for the c control chart. The two additional variables, u and $p(tot)$, are calculated from c. The u variable reflects the average number of negative responses per person and is calculated by dividing c by the number of customers per sample. For our example, the variable u will be calculated by dividing c by 50. We can

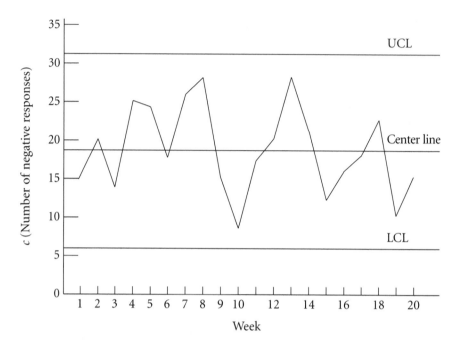

Figure 6.9. The *c* control chart using data from Table 6.3.

also plot this variable in a control chart called the *u* chart. The formulae for the control limits and the center line are

$$UCL = \bar{u} + 3\sqrt{\frac{\bar{u}}{n}}$$

$$\text{Center line} = \bar{u}$$

$$LCL = \bar{u} - 3\sqrt{\frac{\bar{u}}{n}}$$

where *u* is the average number of negative responses per person for a given sample and *n* is the number of customers per sample.

Also, *p(tot)* reflects the percent of negative responses out of all the possible responses for a given sample. Since our questionnaire had 13 questions, we calculate *p(tot)* by dividing *u* by 13. Again, the *p(tot)* variable can be incorporated into a control chart with its corresponding control limits and center line. The formulae are

$$UCL = \bar{p}(tot) + 3\sqrt{\frac{\bar{p}(tot)(1 - \bar{p}(tot))}{n(tot)}}$$

$$Center\ line = \bar{p}(tot)$$

$$LCL = \bar{p}(tot) - 3\sqrt{\frac{\bar{p}(tot)(1 - \bar{p}(tot))}{n(tot)}}$$

where $p(tot)$ represents the percentage of negative responses for a given sample and $n(tot)$ represents the total possible number of responses for a given sample ($n(tot)$ = number of items × sample size).

It is important to note that the variables c and u might be misinterpreted, either indicating a product/service problem that does not actually exist or indicating no problem when a problem actually exists. It should be apparent that the number of negative responses from customers depends on the number of items on the questionnaire. A high number of questionnaire items creates a greater potential for negative responses.

For example, c (the number of negative responses) may equal 40 for a sample of 50 people responding to a 100-item questionnaire, while c equals 20 for a sample of 50 people responding to a two-item questionnaire. By using the c chart or u chart, we might conclude that customers from the first sample are more dissatisfied than customers from the second sample, since the number of negative responses is larger in the first sample. A closer look indicates that this conclusion is not warranted.

We should look at the number of possible responses that could have been made by the sample. For the first sample, 5000 negative responses are possible (100 items × 50 customers). For the second sample, 100 negative responses are possible (two items × 50 customers). In the first sample, negative responses constitute .8 percent of all possible responses, while in the second sample negative responses make up 20 percent of all possible responses.

Therefore, when using the c and u chart, we must consider the number of items on the questionnaire when making conclusions. One way to avoid this problem is to use the $p(tot)$ chart, since it takes into account the number of items on the questionnaire.

Summary

Customer satisfaction questionnaires can provide attribute data that we can subsequently incorporate into control charts for attribute data. There are several types of control charts used with attribute type data. The p chart monitors the percentage of customers who give at least one negative response to the customer satisfaction questionnaire. The c chart monitors the total number of negative responses. From the c chart data, we can calculate other statistics (u and $p(tot)$) with corresponding control charts. Although we can apply data from customer satisfaction questionnaires to attribute control charts, the data are probably best suited for variable control charts.

Control Charts for Variable Data

Recall that variable data represent measurements of quality characteristics. We can develop customer satisfaction questionnaires that provide scores reflecting units of measurement: the higher the score, the higher the quality of the service or product.

Because variable data are quantified in units of measurement, the distribution of scores can be represented by two statistics: the average and the standard deviation. The average represents the center of the distribution, and the standard deviation represents the variability of scores around the average. The larger the standard deviation, the wider the variability. In quality improvement efforts, it is customary to control both the average of the quality characteristics and the variability. Control of the average is accomplished with a control chart for means, the $\bar{x}$ chart. Control of the variability of the process can be accomplished with a control chart for the standard deviation, the s chart.

The $\bar{x}$ and s Control Charts

The $\bar{x}$ chart plots the means of a quality characteristic for each sample, while the s chart plots the standard deviations of the quality characteristic for each sample. For a given sample, we calculate the mean of the quality characteristic by adding the scores for the quality characteristic and dividing by the sample size, n. The formula for sample average was presented earlier. If we have a sample that consists of three observations where $x_1 = 5$, $x_2 = 4$, and $x_3 = 2$, then the mean for this sample equals

$$\bar{x} = (5 + 4 + 2)/3 = 3.67$$

We can also calculate the average value of the sample averages. If we have a number of samples, it is possible to calculate averages for each sample and obtain an average of the sample averages. The formula for this overall average is

$$\bar{\bar{x}} = \frac{\bar{x}_1 + \bar{x}_2 + \ldots + \bar{x}_m}{m}$$

where m equals the number of samples.

This overall sample average provides the center line for the control chart. Also, recall that the distribution for each of the samples can be represented by an index of variability called the *sample standard deviation*. To calculate the standard deviation, we will first calculate the sample variance. The formula for the sample variance was presented earlier in the chapter. After calculating the sample variance, we can calculate the standard deviation by taking the square root of this variance. Again, if we have multiple samples, we can calculate a sample standard deviation for each sample.

We can now calculate the average standard deviation for all the samples. This formula is

$$\bar{s} = \frac{1}{m}\Sigma s_1$$

where m equals the number of samples, and Σs_1 is the sum of all sample standard deviations.

We calculate the UCL and LCL for the $\bar{x}$ chart using the average standard deviation. The calculation of the control limits also involves a constant, c_4, that depends on the sample size. A full explanation of this constant is presented in Montgomery (1996) and will not be discussed here. The upper and lower control limits for the s chart also depend upon two constants, B_4 and B_3, respectively. These constants are also discussed in Montgomery (1996).

Knowing the sample averages and the average standard deviation, we can now calculate the parameters for the $\bar{x}$ chart. The formulae for the center line and upper and lower control limits are

$$\text{UCL} = \bar{\bar{x}} + \frac{3\bar{s}}{c_4\sqrt{n}}$$

$$\text{Center line} = \bar{\bar{x}}$$

$$\text{LCL} = \bar{\bar{x}} - \frac{3\bar{s}}{c_4\sqrt{n}}$$

where n equals the sample size.

The formulae for the parameters of the s chart are

$$\text{UCL} = B_4\bar{s}$$

$$\text{Center line} = \bar{s}$$

$$\text{LCL} = B_3\bar{s}$$

Example of $\bar{x}$ and s Charts

A bank would like to determine its customers' level of satisfaction. The bank collects data over 20 weeks using the customer satisfaction questionnaire in Figure 6.3. Each week the bank collects data from 25 customers. The bank decides that, of the four quality characteristics, the most important is the speed of transaction dimension (items 3 and 4). As a result, the bank examines only this dimension. The data appear in Table 6.4.

The center line and the upper and lower control limits for the $\bar{x}$ chart are

$$\text{UCL} = 3.739$$

$$\text{Center line} = 3.03$$

$$\text{LCL} = 2.321$$

where the constant for the UCL and LCL are $c_4 = .9896$.

Table 6.4. Data for the $\bar{x}$ and s control chart example (note $n = 25$).

Sample	Score for speed of transaction dimension (average of items 3 and 4)	Sample standard deviation for speed of transaction dimension
1	2.5	1.20
2	3.0	1.10
3	3.4	1.15
4	3.2	1.22
5	3.7	1.10
6	3.0	1.00
7	2.7	1.21
8	3.2	1.15
9	3.2	1.10
10	3.4	1.20
11	3.0	1.25
12	2.9	1.18
13	2.8	1.20
14	3.1	1.15
15	3.6	1.18
16	3.2	1.23
17	2.9	1.20
18	2.9	1.17
19	2.4	1.21
20	2.5	1.20
	total = 60.6	total = 23.4

The center line and the upper and lower control limits for the s chart are

$$\text{UCL} = 1.679$$
$$\text{Center line} = 1.17$$
$$\text{LCL} = 0.661$$

where the constants for the UCL and LCL are $B_4 = 1.435$ and $B_3 = .565$. The control charts appear in Figure 6.10.

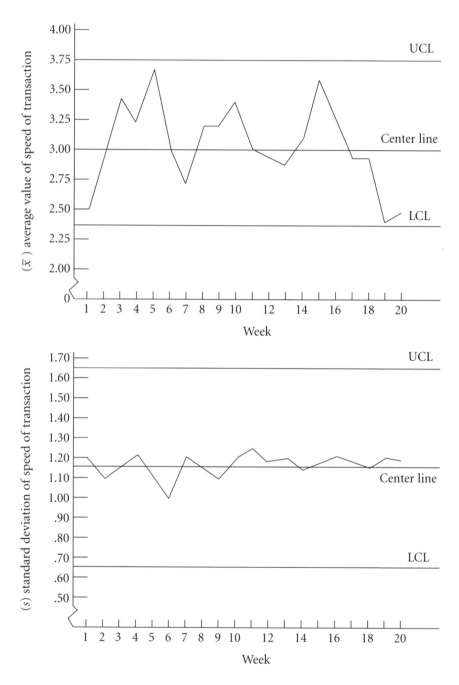

Figure 6.10. The $\bar{x}$ and s control chart using the data from Table 6.4.

These two control charts indicate that the process is in statistical control. The $\bar{x}$ chart, however, indicates that there is considerable room for improvement. Since the scores can range from 1 to 5, the average score of 3.03 indicates that customers' perception of the quality of speed of transaction can be improved. Management intervention in the process will improve the average.

Once management implements changes, we can calculate differences between pre- and post-interventions and conduct statistical tests to see if these differences are substantial. The mathematical formula for testing differences in data is available in various statistics textbooks (Loftus and Loftus 1988).

Charting and presenting the data can provide a feedback mechanism for employees who are in direct contact with the customers and who may directly influence customers' perceptions. Charting techniques such as these have been effective in increasing organizational productivity (Pritchard, et al. 1988). In addition, goal setting, used in conjunction with this feedback method, can increase performance even more (Locke, et al. 1981).

Organizational Comparisons

Not only can customer satisfaction data be used to make comparisons within a single organization across time, it can also be used to make comparisons between organizations (see Appendices F through I). Comparisons between organizations can help identify areas for improvement for organizations with lower satisfaction scores on certain dimensions. An organization can determine dimensions on which it is poorly serving its customers and determine how other companies serve their customers on that particular dimension.

Organizations can also compare satisfaction with products. For example, some automobile manufacturers are designing their cars to make the driver "feel" better. A direct comparison between these cars and other cars could determine if these automobiles do, in fact, make the driver feel better. In fact, the comparison could use the customer satisfaction questionnaire in Figure 6.4.

Organizations making comparisons with other organizations would be taking some risk, since their scores may indicate that they are the lowest among all organizations in the comparison. However, the Baldrige

Award dictates that companies make these comparisons. With these types of data, organizations that score low will identify the dimensions on which they should focus their resources. Better organizational decisions based on actual data will allow these organizations to make improvements in appropriate areas.

Determine Effectiveness of Intervention Programs

Companies spend millions of dollars on intervention programs designed to increase the quality of their services and products. Intervention often takes the form of formal employee training programs as well as new business processes to facilitate work flow. In either case, customer satisfaction questionnaires can determine the effectiveness of these programs (see Appendices F through I).

Training Programs

Companies implement employee training programs to enable employees to fulfill their job duties. A company might have determined through a customer satisfaction questionnaire that its customers are not satisfied with the service they received. The company might, therefore, implement a program to improve employees' communication and interpersonal skills in hopes that this will lead to better employee-customer interactions.

The company might determine the effectiveness of such a training program by comparing customer satisfaction results before and after training. If customer satisfaction scores are higher after training than before, this provides evidence of the program's effectiveness. Statistical analyses will determine if differences are meaningful. There are various methods for determining the effectiveness of intervention programs (Campbell and Stanley 1966).

Benchmarking

Benchmarking is the search for an industry's best practices that lead to excellent performance. Camp (1989) outlined a process of benchmarking that includes identifying premier companies and determining their business practices. Once a company identifies these superior business practices, it may incorporate them into its own practices or change existing processes to conform to the ones identified. This change is designed to increase the organization's effectiveness in meeting its customers' requirements.

It is important to determine if these changes have, in fact, led to increases in performance. Customer satisfaction questionnaires can index the effectiveness of this benchmarking process in changing customers' perceptions. This is done by examining the difference between customer satisfaction before and after benchmarking has been implemented.

Additional Questions

Other questions might also be included in a customer satisfaction questionnaire. Some could solicit information about the time the customer received the service. This might reveal if differences in customer perception are due to factors present only at certain times of the day. A question about the location of the service might provide useful information. For instance, a bank could determine if certain branches are better than others at satisfying customers. Once identified, successful business processes from one location can be adopted by another. Also, a question asking for information on the type of product might determine if certain products are more appealing than others.

Additional questions could be included to obtain more information for comparisons. Companies should carefully choose questions that represent variables that would provide potentially rich information. Questions should have a specified purpose. If certain patterns are suspected (differences between branches, time of day, and so on), an additional question could help substantiate such predictions and lead to insights about possible improvements.

Chapter Summary

The utility of customer satisfaction questionnaires is dependent, in part, on the use of the data. This chapter covered effective presentation of data. It also demonstrated other uses for customer satisfaction questionnaires: determining the quality dimensions of the product or service that strongly predict overall customer satisfaction, monitoring business processes over time, making organizational comparisons, and determining effectiveness of intervention programs. Figure 6.11 summarizes these uses.

Uses	Important Issues
1. Present current standing of customer satisfaction.	• Present means and standard deviations of specific items as well as overall scores of each dimension
2. Identify important customer requirements.	• Use correlational analysis relating customer requirements to overall satisfaction scores
3. Monitor satisfaction levels over time.	• Use control charting techniques
	• Control chart method depends on the type of response format you select (checklist–attribute data versus Likert-type–variable data)
	• Types of control charts include p chart, c chart, u chart, x chart, and s chart
4. Provide organizational comparisons.	• Comparisons should be made on companies using the same questionnaire
	• An independent research firm could conduct comparisons
5. Determine program effectiveness.	• Evaluate effect of training programs
	• Conduct benchmarking studies

Figure 6.11. Uses of customer satisfaction questionnaires.

CHAPTER 7

Examples of Customer Satisfaction Questionnaires

This chapter presents specific examples of customer satisfaction questionnaire development and use in three service industries: dental, newspaper, and a coffee shop. It is always easy to talk about using guidelines when developing surveys in the abstract and quite another thing when one has to put these guidelines to practice. You will see that the survey process is quite different from company to company. These differences in the survey process from company to company are due to various factors that affect the ease with which a particular company is able to subscribe to the guidelines outlined in this book. For example, you will see that some companies were not able to conduct a sampling plan, while others were confined to using general items in their questionnaires. Although each of these examples is very different than the rest, the usefulness of obtaining customer satisfaction data is demonstrated in each example.

Dental Patient Satisfaction

A large insurance company, House of Teeth Insurance, Inc., that provides dental insurance developed a patient satisfaction survey to determine the patients' perceptions regarding the quality of the care they received from the dentists on their provider list. Additionally, this patient survey was to allow the insurance company to obtain feedback regarding the quality of the insurance it provided its customers. The survey team consisted of the director of marketing and two external consultants who specialized in survey development.

Questionnaire Development

The survey team examined the previous patient satisfaction survey to determine what content should be included in the new survey. The team inspected the items and also analyzed some existing data to determine if there were any factors that could be identified in a factor analysis of the data. Figure 7.1 includes some of the old items.

In addition to examining the previous survey, the survey team reviewed current literature on the measurement of dental patient satisfaction. The review of these types of studies might lead to the inclusion of important quality factors that may have been missed in their previous survey. This literature review covered recent articles in scientific, peer-reviewed journals. Some journal articles used in this literature review, and their conclusions, are included in Figure 7.2. As can be see in this figure, the researchers have found various factors that define the quality of dental care. There are some researchers who have found more dental patient satisfaction factors than other. There is even some overlap with respect to what some of the researchers found. In any case, these articles provided useful information regarding the content of the questionnaire the survey team wanted to develop.

With the information from the existing survey as well as the results from the review of the literature covering dental patient satisfaction, the

---

1. My dentist's office was clean and orderly.

2. I feel the wait time to schedule a dental appointment at my dentist's office was reasonable.

3. The insurance personnel did not seem to be concerned about my well-being.

4. The insurance personnel I spoke with on the toll-free telephone line were courteous.

Figure 7.1. Items from the previous dental patient satisfaction survey.

Authors	Quality Factors
Andrus and Buchheister (1985)	• Technical competence • Interpersonal skills
Factor analysis was used to determine the quality dimensions	• Office organization • Financial considerations
Koslowsky, Bailit, and Valluzzo (1974)	• Technical competence • Dentist personality • Office organization • Financial considerations
Davies and Ware (1981)	• Access • Availability convenience
They used principal components—not recommended when looking at underlying constructs. However, they report it supported their five-facet hypothesis. Scale reliabilities ranged from .52–.81. There are single-item scales.	• Cost • Pain • Quality
Chapko, Bergner, Green Beach, Milgrom, and Skalabrin (1985)	• Dentist-patient relations • Technical quality of care • Access
Scale reliabilities range from .46 to .79. Some are single-item scales. The interscale correlations are low but the low reliabilities may have attenuated these correlations; thus, the scale measures fewer facets of dental patient satisfaction.	• Patient waiting time • Cost • Facilities • Availability • Continuity • Pain • Auxiliaries performing expanded duties • Staff-patient relations • Staff technical quality of care • Office atmosphere

Figure 7.2. Facets of dental patient satisfaction.

survey team developed the new dental patient satisfaction survey. The goal of the survey team was to develop a survey that

1. Was short

2. Comprehensively covered the important quality factors determined in the literature review

3. Provided specific feedback to the dentists

4. Included items that assessed patients' satisfaction with the company's insurance policy

The process of developing the survey was one of compromise. On the one hand, the survey team wanted to ensure that the survey was a reliable instrument, which meant including multiple items in the scale. However, the team wanted a survey instrument that was short enough to facilitate the patients' completion of it. With these goals in mind, the survey team developed the customer satisfaction questionnaire presented in Figure 7.3.

Sampling Plan

The survey team decided to allow each patient the opportunity to provide feedback regarding the quality of dental care and insurance quality. Consequently, a sampling plan on the administration of the survey was not needed. However, because each doctor was to be given feedback regarding his or her quality, sample size of returned surveys was examined to determine what sample size was needed to ensure a given level of confidence for a specific level of tolerable error. That is, the survey team wanted to ensure that the results for any one doctor were reliable. The survey team decided to use a 95 percent confidence level and a tolerable error of .20. That is, the criteria of a 95 percent confidence level with a tolerable error of .20 was to be attained before a given doctor received results for his or her quality of care. The appropriate sample size was determined that would satisfy these criteria.

Because some doctors were used more frequently than other doctors, the frequency with which they received feedback results varied accordingly. Given a constant response rate across doctors, we would expect doctors with a higher patient load to receive more frequent feedback because the confidence interval (CI) of 95 percent and a tolerable error of .20 would be reached more quickly compared to doctors with a lower patient load.

House of Teeth Insurance, Inc., is concerned about your satisfaction as our customer. We are striving to provide the best dental plan available. Please take a few moments to answer the following questions, as they relate to your dental office visit and the insurance plan benefits. Please return the completed survey within the next 10 days. Thank you.

	Strongly Agree	Agree	Neutral	Disagree	Strongly Disagree	Not Applicable
1. I was able to schedule an appointment at a good time.	☐	☐	☐	☐	☐	☐
2. The dental office is inconsiderate of my time.	☐	☐	☐	☐	☐	☐
3. The front office staff was courteous.	☐	☐	☐	☐	☐	☐
4. The front office staff was helpful in explaining my insurance dental benefits.	☐	☐	☐	☐	☐	☐
5. I was treated poorly because I had insurance benefits coverage.	☐	☐	☐	☐	☐	☐
6. The dentist treated me fairly.	☐	☐	☐	☐	☐	☐
7. The office was clean.	☐	☐	☐	☐	☐	☐
8. The office uses outdated equipment.	☐	☐	☐	☐	☐	☐
9. The dental office used sterilized instruments.	☐	☐	☐	☐	☐	☐
10. Gloves, masks, and glasses were used by the staff during dental procedures.	☐	☐	☐	☐	☐	☐
11. The dentist/staff told me how much the dental work would cost before beginning the treatment.	☐	☐	☐	☐	☐	☐
12. The dentist/staff explained the treatment procedures with me.	☐	☐	☐	☐	☐	☐
13. The treatment prescribed was inappropriate for my needs.	☐	☐	☐	☐	☐	☐
14. The dental work done for me was top quality.	☐	☐	☐	☐	☐	☐
15. The dentist reduced my discomfort during the dental treatment.	☐	☐	☐	☐	☐	☐
16. The hygienist was rough during my teeth cleaning appointment.	☐	☐	☐	☐	☐	☐

Figure 7.3. Dental patient satisfaction survey.

	Strongly Agree	Agree	Neutral	Disagree	Strongly Disagree	Not Applicable
17. There were plenty of available dental offices on the insurance list from which to choose.	☐	☐	☐	☐	☐	☐
18. The offices on the insurance list require me to travel a long distance.	☐	☐	☐	☐	☐	☐
19. I received superior benefit coverage under the insurance plan.	☐	☐	☐	☐	☐	☐
20. The information I received from the insurance company fully explained my dental benefits.	☐	☐	☐	☐	☐	☐

	1 week	2 weeks	3 weeks	4 weeks	4+ weeks	N/A
21. How long did you have to wait to schedule an appointment?.	☐	☐	☐	☐	☐	☐

	5 min	10 min	15 min	20 min	20+ min	N/A
22. How long did you have to wait in the dentist's waiting room before seeing your dentist?	☐	☐	☐	☐	☐	☐

	Yes	No	Not sure			
23. I would recommend this office to a friend or relative.	☐	☐	☐			
24. I would recommend the insurance dental plan to a friend or relative.	☐	☐	☐			

	Very Satisfied	Satisfied	Neutral	Dissatisfied	Very Dissatisfied	
25. Overall, how satisfied were you with the dental office visit.	☐	☐	☐	☐	☐	
26. Overall, how satisfied were you with the insurance dental benefits plan.	☐	☐	☐	☐	☐	

Figure 7.3. *Continued.*

The survey team used the standard formula for estimating sample size to guide them in their survey plan.

$$n = (t^2 \times s^2)/e^2$$

Where n equals the sample size, t equals the level of confidence, s equals the standard deviation, and e equals tolerable error.

Recall that this formula allows us to determine what our sample size should be for our desired level of confidence and tolerable error with a specific standard deviation. For the House of Teeth Insurance, Inc. Dental Health Satisfaction Survey, we have set $t = 2.0$ (95 percent confidence interval), and $e = .20$. Using previous survey research conducted at House of Teeth Insurance, Inc. and other survey research, we have found that s for survey items, on the average, equals 1.0. If we want tolerable error to equal .20 (in the same unit of measurement as the scale being used), sample size would need to equal 100. In other words, we need a sample size of 100 to obtain a 95 percent confidence interval with a .20 level of tolerable error.

We must also take into consideration the idea of response rates. We saw that we need a sample size of 100 to ensure the specified level of confidence and tolerable error. Due to low response rates, we will have to mail out more than 100 surveys to ensure we have 100 returned surveys in the end. Specifically, if we have a history of a 10 percent response rate, we would need to mail out 1000 surveys to ensure that we would get 100 surveys returned. Several hypothetical examples were presented to the survey team and are presented in Table 7.1.

Given these factors, the survey team decided to take the following approach regarding feedback provision to a given dental clinic. First, the team decided that clinics with a large patient base would require larger samples for feedback. Although sampling error is not associated with the size of the population, the dentists of larger clinics may perceive the data

Table 7.1. Number of surveys needed to be mailed (mailout) for a 95 percent confidence interval, standard deviation of 1.0, and varying degrees of tolerable error.

Tolerable error	Sample size	Mailout (25% response rate)	Mailout (40% response rate)
.20	100	400	250
.30	44	176	110
.40	25	100	63
.50	16	64	40

Note: If s is less than 1.0, then the sample size (n) given would result in a smaller level of tolerable error.

as more valid if the data are based on larger sample sizes. Thus, the distribution of the survey for larger clinics (those clinics with sample sizes greater than 300) will be set at a given number (Mailout = 176, so $n = 44$ and tolerable error =.30). For smaller clinics, sample size will be set to obtain an acceptable level of tolerable error. However, due to the small client base and low response rates, the desired sample sizes may not be reached within a given quarter. Thus, feedback would have to be delayed until an acceptable level of tolerable error is obtained for a given office. This would result in feedback being conducted only twice per year rather than four times per year.

Survey Administration

The administration of the survey was conducted through mail. After the patient received treatment, the patient was mailed the customer satisfaction survey. The completion and return of the survey was voluntary. To improve the response rate, postage was provided on the client satisfaction survey. Additionally, the customers were told that, for every survey they returned, House of Teeth Insurance, Inc. would donate $1 to a charity of the patient's choosing. Due to the large sample size of this survey process, the surveys were created so that the responses could be electronically scanned into the computer. This procedure greatly reduced time and money for manually inputting the data.

Survey Results

The survey results presented in Figure 7.4 represent a one-quarter period. In this particular quarter, the company received 14,062 completed patient satisfaction surveys.

Items in the survey were coded for numerical analysis. The coding scheme was conducted so that higher scores represented higher levels of customer satisfaction. For positively phrased items (such as "The front office staff was courteous" or "The office was clean"), the following coding was used on positively phrased items: Strongly Agree = 5, Agree = 4, Neutral = 3, Disagree = 2, Strongly Disagree = 1. For negatively phrased items (such as "The office used outdated equipment" or "The treatment prescribed was inappropriate for my needs"), the following coding scheme was used: Strongly Agree = 1, Agree = 2, Neutral = 3, Disagree = 4, Strongly

	Percentage of respondents						
	SA	A	N	D	SD	Mean	StD
1. I was able to schedule an appointment at a good time.	44.7	38.7	6.8	5.3	4.6	4.14	1.06
2. The dental office is inconsiderate of my time.	10.2	11.6	9.4	29.4	39.4	3.76	1.35
3. The front office staff was courteous.	48.0	40.9	7.0	2.4	1.7	4.31	.84
4. The front office staff was helpful in explaining my insurance dental benefits.	25.9	37.7	23.7	8.1	4.6	3.72	1.07
5. I was treated poorly because I had insurance benefits coverage.	4.5	5.1	10.6	32.3	47.5	4.13	1.08
6. I was treated fairly by the dentist.	44.7	41.1	7.4	3.6	3.2	4.21	.95
7. The office was clean.	50.6	41.9	4.8	2.0	1.6	4.37	.80
8. The office uses outdated equipment.	4.7	7.3	14.5	35.8	37.7	3.94	1.11
9. The dental office used sterilized instruments.	38.7	49.4	9.6	1.3	1.0	4.24	.75
10. Gloves, masks, and glasses were used by the staff during dental procedures.	51.4	43.3	2.4	2.1	.8	4.42	.72
11. The dentist/staff told me how much the dental work would cost before beginning the treatment.	29.1	38.4	12.4	14.2	5.9	3.71	1.19
12. The dentist/staff explained the treatment procedures with me.	34.6	46.9	9.5	6.2	2.9	4.04	.97
13. The treatment prescribed was inappropriate for my needs.	5.9	8.7	10.3	35.3	39.9	3.95	1.17
14. The dental work done for me was top quality.	34.0	40.7	15.3	5.9	4.1	3.95	1.05
15. The dentist tried to reduce my discomfort during the dental treatment.	36.0	44.4	13.1	4.0	2.6	4.07	.94
16. The hygienist was rough during my teeth cleaning appointment.	4.3	6.8	11.1	38.9	38.9	4.01	1.08
17. There were plenty of available dental offices on the insurance list from which to choose.	10.4	27.3	20.4	21.6	20.3	2.86	1.30
18. The offices on the insurance list require me to travel a long distance.	7.6	12.5	17.3	39.7	22.9	3.58	1.19
19. I received superior benefit coverage under the insurance plan.	21.8	41.0	21.9	9.1	6.2	3.63	1.11
20. The information I received from the insurance company fully explained my dental benefits.	21.2	56.4	14.5	5.6	2.3	3.89	.88

Figure 7.4. Descriptive statistics for each item in the patient satisfaction survey.

	1 week	2 weeks	3 weeks	4 weeks	4+ weeks	Mean	StD
21. How long did you have to wait to schedule an appointment?	32.0	25.2	14.0	9.8	19.0	3.42	1.49
	5 min	10 min	15 min	20 min	20+ min	Mean	StD
22. How long did you have to wait in the dentist's waiting room before seeing your dentist?	29.1	31.9	19.3	7.8	10.9	3.62	1.28
	Yes	No	Not sure				
23. I would recommend this office to a friend or relative.	69.6	16.9	13.5			2.22	1.21
24. I would recommend the insurance dental plan to a friend or relative.	68.3	11.1	20.6			2.26	1.13
	VS	S	N	D	SD	Mean	StD
25. Overall, how satisfied were you with the dental office visit.	46.1	33.5	8.6	6.5	5.3	4.08	1.13
26. Overall, how satisfied were you with the insurance dental benefits plan.	31.7	45.7	13.4	6.5	2.7	3.97	.98

Figure 7.4. *Continued.*

Disagree = 5. For the scheduling availability and wait time items (questions 21 and 22), items were coded such that a shorter wait time reflected a higher score (5—higher scores indicate higher levels of satisfaction) and a longer wait time reflected a lower score (1—lower scores indicate lower levels of satisfaction). For the recommend/not recommend items (items 23 and 24), the following coding scheme was used: Yes = 3, Not sure = 1, No = 0.).

To get a general idea of the satisfaction of the patients, the survey team calculated the statistics (mean and the standard deviation) for each item in the survey. The results of this analysis are presented in Figure 7.4.

As we can see from the survey results, the responses vary from unfavorable to favorable. On the average, however, most of the items have a favorable response; many items with a five-point scale have an average response above 4.0.

Factor Analysis of the Client Satisfaction Survey

Although we have 26 items in the survey, we might be able to combine the responses into smaller categories. The statistical method to determine if this is appropriate is factor analysis (see Appendix K). The factor analysis tells us if we are able to combine some of the items in our scale to obtain subscale scores. For example, rather than thinking that items 3 and 4 measure two distinct quality factors, they might be combined to obtain a score that we could call *dentist office professionalism*. Additionally, items 8, 9, and 10 might be combined to obtain a score we would call *equipment quality*. Factor analysis is a method that would allow us to see if combining these items is appropriate.

I factor analyzed items 1 through 20. The results of the factor analysis are presented in the factor pattern matrix located in Table 7.2. The elements in the factor pattern matrix tell us how well each item is related to

Table 7.2. Rotated factor pattern matrix of the 26 items in the dental patient satisfaction survey.

	Factor 1	Factor 2	Factor 3	Factor 4
Q1	**.40**	.33	.16	.23
Q2	.08	**.43**	.07	.06
Q3	**.51**	.35	.22	.15
Q4	**.66**	.25	.15	.15
Q5	.28	**.62**	.14	.17
Q6	**.44**	**.45**	.37	.17
Q7	.26	.31	**.56**	.12
Q8	.07	**.45**	.39	.12
Q9	.27	.23	**.61**	.17
Q10	.27	.14	**.59**	.14
Q11	**.57**	.05	.24	.08
Q12	**.58**	.24	.40	.13
Q13	.15	**.51**	.20	.13
Q14	**.45**	**.44**	**.44**	.23
Q15	**.44**	.32	**.40**	.16
Q16	.19	**.40**	.22	.14
Q17	.12	.04	.10	**.58**
Q18	−.03	.19	.08	**.43**
Q19	.35	.25	.17	**.47**
Q20	.30	.07	.09	**.43**

the underlying dimension. Although this particular factor pattern matrix is not as clear as we would like, it still provides some useful information. Some items clearly load on a single factor (such as items 1, 2, 3, and 4). These items clearly measure only one underlying thing. Some items, however, do not load clearly onto only one factor. For example, items 6, 14, and 15 load on more than one factor, suggesting that these items measure more than one underlying thing.

From this rotated factor pattern matrix, we see that there are four underlying factors. These factors with their corresponding items are

1. Interpersonal skills (1, 3, 4, 11, 12)

2. Technical competence (2, 5, 8, 13, 16)

3. Sterilization of office (7, 9, 10)

4. Insurance quality (items 17, 18, 19, 20)

The survey team labeled these factors based on the items that loaded onto these factors. It is possible that other people would come up with different labels for these same factors. The actual labels are not important; what is important is that we understand that some items are measuring the same thing and that it is possible to obtain summary scores based on the responses to these items. Based on the factor analysis, subscale scores were calculated for each of the four factors using the items that represented the factors. These subscale scores were calculated by averaging the items within each factor. Due to the content of items 6, 14, and 15, these items were included in the interpersonal skills subscale score.

We can now present the results at a more general level. Additionally, an estimate of reliability (internal consistency) can be calculated for each of the subscales derived from the factor analysis. The descriptive statistics for the subscales are presented in Table 7.3.

Correlational analysis. Next, we can use the data to determine which of the four factors of dental satisfaction (technical competence, interpersonal skills, sterilization of office, or insurance quality) is correlated with some of the other items in the customer satisfaction survey. The insurance company would be interested in knowing which of these four factors best predicts overall satisfaction with the dental office visit (question 25) or the

Table 7.3. Descriptive statistics for subscale scores for the patient satisfaction survey.

Variable	Mean	StD	Cases
Interpersonal skills	4.03	.73	14062
Technical competence	3.94	.81	13976
Sterilization of office	4.34	.62	14056
Insurance quality	3.50	.78	14053

Note: StD = standard deviation

extent to which the patient makes recommendations about the dentist's office (question 23) or insurance plan (question 24). One method to determine the relative predictive power of each subscale is to examine the correlation coefficients of each subscale with the remaining items in the customer satisfaction questionnaire. This correlation matrix is presented in Table 7.4. Included in the correlation matrix are the reliability estimates (Cronbach's alpha) for each of the four subscales.

From Table 7.4, we find that the overall satisfaction rating of the insurance plan (question 26) was most highly related to the insurance quality subscale. That is, patients who said they were satisfied overall with the insurance plan also indicated that there were plenty of offices from which to choose, they didn't have to travel long distances to get to the dentist's office, they thought they received superior benefits, and their benefits were fully explained to them. Also, we see that the interpersonal skills subscale was the best predictor of overall satisfaction with the dental office visit (question 25), wait time for scheduling an appointment (question 21), wait time in the dentist's waiting room (question 22), and whether the patient would recommend the dentist's office to a friend or relative (question 23). Finally, we see that the insurance quality subscale was the best predictor of whether or not the patient would recommend the insurance plan to a friend or relative (question 24).

Regression analysis. From the correlational analysis, we found that the interpersonal skills factor was a good factor at predicting some important

Table 7.4. Correlations among the subscales and the remaining items in the patient satisfaction questionnaire.

	1	2	3	4	5	6	7	8	9	10
1. Interpersonal	(.87)									
2. Technical	.57	(.69)								
3. Sterilization	.66	.49	(.75)							
4. Insurance	.48	.35	.38	(.60)						
5. Q21	.38	.22	.20	.23	—					
6. Q22	.43	.37	.31	.25	.27	—				
7. Q23	.66	.51	.48	.39	.27	.40	—			
8. Q24	.38	.30	.28	.48	.18	.21	.48	—		
9. Q25	.78	.57	.57	.45	.31	.45	.77	.45	—	
10. Q26	.44	.33	.34	.58	.19	.24	.41	.66	.52	—

Note: All correlations significant at the .01 level. Reliability estimates (Cronbach's alpha) is located in diagonal. Reliability estimates cannot be calculated for single-item measures. *N* ranges from 11662 to 14062; Interpersonal = Interpersonal skills; Technical = Technical competence; Sterilization = Sterilization of office; Insurance = Insurance quality.

customer behaviors and attitudes (questions 23 and 25). The correlations of the three other subscales with these same customer behaviors and attitudes are also quite high and might still be important in the understanding of customer satisfaction and behavior. A more powerful approach at determining which of the four subscales best predicts the other variables is through a statistical method called *regression analysis* (see Appendix J).

The specific type of regression analysis conducted here is referred to as *stepwise regression analysis*. For these analyses, the predictor variables were the four subscales. A total of four stepwise regression analyses were conducted, one for each of the outcome variables. This form of regression analysis allows you to see the unique contribution of all four subscales in predicting a given outcome variable. The results of the stepwise regression analysis are presented in Table 7.5.

Table 7.5. Stepwise regression analysis of the dental patient satisfaction questionnaire.

	Subscale	ΔR^2	p
Question 23	Interpersonal skills	.4339	.01
(recommend office)	Technical competence	.0274	.01
	Insurance quality	.0049	.01
	Sterilization of office	.0007	.01
	Total for four variables in the equation	.4669	.01
Question 24	Insurance quality	.2299	.01
(recommend plan)	Interpersonal skills	.0308	.01
	Technical competence	.0038	.01
	Total for three variables in the equation	.2645	.01
Question 25	Interpersonal skills	.6065	.01
(office satisfaction)	Technical competence	.0257	.01
	Insurance quality	.0060	.01
	Sterilization of office	.0013	.01
	Total for four variables in the equation	.6395	.01
Question 26	Insurance quality	.3348	.01
(insurance satisfaction)	Interpersonal skills	.0357	.01
	Technical competence	.0027	.01
	Sterilization of office	.0002	.05
	Total for four variables in the equation	.3734	.01

Note: $N = 14062$, ΔR^2 = percent of variance accounted for at each step in the analysis.

As we can see from the results of the stepwise regression analysis, all of the subscales uniquely contribute in the explanation of the customer satisfaction and customer recommendation variables. However, a degree of caution must be noted. Due to the large sample size, even small effect sizes are statistically significant. The ΔR^2 shows us the effect size of the given subscale. We see that, after the first subscale has been entered into the equation, not much more of the variance can be explained by the remaining subscales. It is best to examine not only the significance of the effect but the actual effect size (R^2) when interpreting the results. For example, many of the subscales, even though statistically significant, explain less than .5 percent of the variance in the outcome variables.

Some interesting findings can still be seen from the results. We found that interpersonal skills and technical competence are both important predictors of customer satisfaction of and customer recommendation for dentist's office. Additionally, insurance quality as well as interpersonal skills are both important predictors of customer satisfaction of and customer recommendation for the insurance plan. Interpersonal skills of the office staff is related to two areas: office quality and insurance quality. Consequently, the insurance company's resources might be best served if they are focused on increasing the interpersonal skills of the dental office staff. Increases in interpersonal skills scores might be reflected in increases in customer satisfaction scores for both the dental office as well as insurance quality.

Summary

The development and use of the dental patient satisfaction questionnaire was very labor intensive. The importance of providing reliable and valid information to the dentist's office warranted an in-depth review of current literature of dental patient satisfaction research. It was important that the survey team members not miss important quality dimensions in their development of the survey. Additionally, the customer satisfaction survey allowed customers to rate the quality of the insurance program. We saw that the dental patient satisfaction survey provided very useful information regarding the factors that were highly related to customer recommendation behavior. Additionally, the results of the survey provided two very useful pieces of information. On the one hand, the results of the survey allowed the insurance provider to monitor the quality of its insurance benefits. On the other hand, the survey allowed the insurance company to monitor the quality of the dentists in its provider network and, subsequently, provide feedback to them in order for them to ensure a high degree of customer satisfaction.

Reader Survey

Our next customer survey example is on a much smaller scale than our dental patient satisfaction example. A small newspaper publisher publishes a monthly newspaper *(The Parent)* for parents. The newspaper contains articles and information about children and is marketed to parents. The purpose of the reader survey was to provide the publisher information regarding readers' demographics, lifestyles, and shopping habits. Such questions included, but were not limited to, the extent of computer use, other newspapers that are read, and recreational activities. Additionally, the publisher of *The Parent* wanted to get a general sense of the customer satisfaction level of the newspaper.

Questionnaire Development

The survey team consisted of the owner of the publishing company and a survey consultant. The survey from the previous year was used as a starting point for the new survey. Questions were modified and additional questions were added. The survey instructions and a partial list of the questions are included in Figure 7.5.

Administration of the Survey

The administration of the reader survey was conducted through the newspaper itself. The reader survey was printed on one side of a single page in the newspaper. After completion of the survey, the reader was instructed to send the survey to an independent consulting firm that was responsible for data management and analysis. The reader was to provide his or her own stamp and envelope to return the survey. To increase response rates, the readers who turned in completed surveys were entered into a drawing to win a gift certificate. Because all readers had the opportunity to complete the survey, no sampling plan was developed.

Results

A total of 201 readers completed the reader survey. The results of the survey are presented in Figure 7.6.

From the standard deviations in Figure 7.6, we could calculate the standard error of the mean for each item. The standard error for each

Please take a few moments to complete this survey. Your participation will help us to serve you better. Please return your completed survey by January 24 to enter a drawing to win a $100 gift certificate from one of our advertisers.

1. Are you: ☐ Male ☐ Female

2. What is your age?
   ☐ Under 18   ☐ 30–34   ☐ 45–49
   ☐ 18–24   ☐ 35–39   ☐ 50–54
   ☐ 25–29   ☐ 40–44   ☐ 55 or older

3. What is your marital status? ☐ Married ☐ Single (never married)
   ☐ Divorced/separated/widowed

4. Are you currently employed full or part time?
   ☐ Employed full time, that is, 30 hours or more a week.
   ☐ Not employed
   ☐ Employed part time, that is, less than 30 hours per week

5. What was your total household income, before taxes, in 1994? Please include all family members' incomes from all sources.
   ☐ Less than $20,000   ☐ $40,000–$49,999   ☐ $100,000–$149,999   ☐ $300,000 or more
   ☐ $20,000–$29,999   ☐ $50,000–$74,999   ☐ $150,000–$199,999
   ☐ $30,000–$39,999   ☐ $75,000–$99,999   ☐ $200,000–$299,999

6. What is the highest level of education that you have attained? (Please check only one.)
   ☐ Some high school or less   ☐ Graduated four-year college
   ☐ Graduated high school   ☐ Postgraduate study without degree
   ☐ Attended college less than one year   ☐ Master's degree
   ☐ Attended college 1–3 years   ☐ Doctoral degree

7. Please select the category that best describes your type of employment. (Please check only one.)
   ☐ Full-time parent   ☐ Professional health care related
   ☐ Technical/administration/   ☐ Educator
      Sales/service   ☐ Executive/management
   ☐ Not employed   ☐ Other (please specify): _____

8. How frequently do you read a copy of *The Parent*?
   ☐ Monthly   ☐ Every other month   ☐ Less than every other month

9. Does your spouse read *The Parent*? ☐ Yes ☐ No

10. Including yourself, how many adults usually read or look through your copy of *The Parent*? (check one)
    ☐ 1   ☐ 2   ☐ 3   ☐ 4   ☐ 5   ☐ 6 or more

11. Please estimate how much time you spend reading *The Parent*.
    ☐ About 15 minutes   ☐ About 45 minutes   ☐ More than 1 hour
    ☐ About 30 minutes   ☐ About 1 hour

Customer Satisfaction Survey—Please indicate how much you agree with each of the following statements concerning *The Parent*.

	Strongly Disagree	Disagree	Neutral	Agree	Strongly Agree
1. Overall, I am satisfied with the quality of the articles in *The Parent*.	☐	☐	☐	☐	☐
2. The articles in *The Parent* are informative.	☐	☐	☐	☐	☐
3. I enjoy reading *The Parent*.	☐	☐	☐	☐	☐

Figure 7.5. *The Parent* reader survey.

1. Are you: Male   Female

	Percent
Male	3.0
Female	97.0

2. What is your age?

	Percent
Under 18 years	.5
18–24 years	3.5
25–29 years	15.7
30–34 years	20.2
35–39 years	30.3
40–44 years	20.7
45–49 years	6.1
50–54 years	1.5
55 or older	1.5

3. What is your marital status?

	Percent
Married	85.4
Divorced/separated/widowed	9.0
Single (never married)	5.5

4. Are you currently employed full or part time?

	Percent
Employed full time	34.5
Not employed	37.6
Employed part time	27.9

5. What is your total household income?

	Percent
Less than $20,000	10.6
$20,000–$29,999	5.0
$30,000–$39,999	12.8
$40,000–$49,999	16.1
$50,000–$74,999	28.3
$75,000–$99,999	15.6
$100,000–$149,999	9.4
$150,000–$199,999	.6
$200,000–$299,999	1.7
$300,000 or more	0.0

6. What is the highest level of education that you have attained?

	Percent
Some high school or less	.5
Graduated high school	2.1
Attended college less than one year	6.8
Attended college 1–3 years	19.5
Graduated four-year college	33.2
Postgraduate study without degree	12.1
Master's degree	21.6
Doctoral degree	4.2

7. Please select the category that best describes your type of employment.

	Percent
Full-time parent	37.5
Technical/administration/ sales/service	18.8
Not employed	6.8
Professional health care related	10.8
Educator	14.8
Executive/management	7.4
Other (please specify):	4.0

8. How frequently do you read a copy of *The Parent*?

	Percent
Monthly	74.1
Every other month	18.9
Less than every other month	7.0

9. Does your spouse read *The Parent*?

	Percent
Yes	21.0
No	79.0

10. Including yourself, how many adults usually read or look through your copy of *The Parent*?(check one)

	Percent
1	67.7
2	24.7
3	6.6
4	.5
5	.0
6 or more	.5

11. Please estimate how much time you spend reading *The Parent*.

	Percent
About 15 minutes	11.2
About 30 minutes	32.5
About 45 minutes	21.3
About 1 hour	21.8
More than 1 hour	13.2

		Percentage of respondents					
	SA	A	N	D	SD	Mean	StD
1. Overall, I am satisfied with the quality of the articles in *The Parent*.	1.5	0.5	9.0	64.3	24.6	4.10	0.69
2. The articles in *The Parent* are informative.	1.5	1.0	7.5	63.2	26.9	4.13	0.71
3. I enjoy reading *The Parent*.	1.5	1.0	2.6	53.6	41.3	4.32	0.72

Note: StD = standard deviation

Figure 7.6. Descriptive statistics of the reader survey.

mean is calculated to be .05. Consequently, the 95 percent confidence interval for each mean is:

Question 1   CI = 4.10 ± 2 × .05;   CI = 4.00 < X < 4.20

Question 2   CI = 4.13 ± 2 × .05;   CI = 4.03 < X < 4.23

Question 3   CI = 4.31 ± 2 × .05;   CI = 4.21 < X < 4.41

From these results, we see that we can be fairly certain that our observed means using our sample of 201 customers are good estimates of the population mean (all our customers). We have a fairly tight confidence interval around our estimate of each of the means. In addition, we are fairly confident that each of our population means for each item all fall above 4.00 (satisfied), indicating that our customers are generally satisfied with the newspaper.

Overall Newspaper Satisfaction Score

The correlation among the three customer satisfaction questionnaires range from .74 to .78, suggesting that the items may be measuring one underlying construct. Therefore, an overall satisfaction score was calculated by averaging the three customer satisfaction items. The internal consistency estimate (Cronbach's alpha) for this overall satisfaction score is .91. This high reliability estimate for the three-item scale also suggests that these items measure one underlying construct. The descriptive statistics for this overall satisfaction score are presented in Table 7.6.

Next, we can use this overall satisfaction score to make some comparisons with some of our other variables in our reader survey. For example, we might find that readers who spend more time reading *The Parent* are more satisfied with the newspaper. Other variables can be examined to determine their relationship with overall customer satisfaction. We will

Table 7.6. Descriptive statistics for the overall newspaper satisfaction score.

	Mean	Standard deviation	Minimum value	Maximum value	Number of cases
Overall satisfaction	4.18	.65	1.00	5.00	201

use analysis of variance (ANOVA) to test these possibilities (see Appendix I). The results of the analyses are presented in Table 7.7. Note that not all of the variables from the survey are used in the ANOVAs; this is based on the fact that many of the variables had a limited number of responses for certain categories (such as questions 1, 2, 3, and 10). Conducting such analysis using these variables would not lead to reliable results.

Based on the ANOVAs presented in Table 7.7, we found that there are significant differences using the overall satisfaction score for some of the

Table 7.7. ANOVA using the overall newspaper satisfaction score.

Question 4. Are you currently employed full or part time?

Source	df	Sum of squares	Mean squares	F ratio	F prob.
Between groups	2	2.28	1.14	2.76	.07
Within groups	194	80.22	.41		
Total	196	82.50			

Question 6. What is the highest level of education that you have attained?

Source	df	Sum of squares	Mean squares	F ratio	F prob.
Between groups	7	5.10	.73	1.75	.10
Within groups	182	75.89	.42		
Total	189	80.99			

Question 7. Please select the category which best describes your type of employment.

Source	df	Sum of squares	Mean squares	F ratio	F prob.
Between groups	6	5.16	.86	1.98	.07
Within groups	169	73.58	.44		
Total		175	78.74		

Question 8. How frequently do you read a copy of *The Parent*?

Source	df	Sum of squares	Mean squares	F ratio	F prob.
Between groups	2	.54	.27	.64	.53
Within groups	198	83.37	.42		
Total	200	83.91			

Table 7.7. *Continued.*

Question 9. Does your spouse read *The Parent*?

Source	df	Sum of squares	Mean squares	F ratio	F prob.
Between groups	1	1.51	1.51	4.03	.05
Within groups	184	69.07	.38		
Total	185	70.58			

Means for overall satisfaction score:

Yes = 4.36[a]   No = 4.14[a]

Question 11. Please estimate how much time you spend reading *The Parent*.

Source	df	Sum of squares	Mean squares	F ratio	F prob.
Between groups	4	6.12	1.53	3.85	.00
Within groups	192	76.27	.40		
Total	196	82.39			

Means for overall satisfaction score:

	About 15 minutes	About 30 minutes	About 45 minutes	About 1 hour	More than 1 hour
Means:	3.83[ab]	4.11	4.18	4.38[b]	4.41[a]

Note: Within each ANOVA, means with common superscripts are significantly different from each other.

reader variables. Readers who report their spouse read *The Parent* also report higher levels of overall customer satisfaction compared to readers who indicate their spouse does not read *The Parent*. Readers who are more satisfied with *The Parent* also indicate they spend more time reading that newspaper compared to readers who are less satisfied with *The Parent*. We can see that some of the results approach statistical significance. It is possible that, with additional survey data, the observed difference for these results would have become statistically significant.

Summary

The reader survey was designed to allow the publisher to obtain information regarding reader behavior, reader demographics, and customer satisfaction.

The survey team was able to demonstrate that, even with relatively small samples sizes, it is possible to obtain a high degree of confidence with a small level of tolerable error. Also, the survey team showed that overall customer satisfaction was related to some of the reader's behavior (such as time spent reading the newspaper and whether spouse reads the newspaper—recommendation behavior). This information might be useful when establishing advertising rates for the newspaper. Comparative information of these scores with competitors could establish a pricing structure in which scores on the satisfaction scale dictate cost of advertising in a given newspaper. If satisfaction scores are related to reader behavior (such as time spent reading the newspaper or spouse more likely to read the newspaper), then an advertiser would want to advertise in a newspaper where readers are highly satisfied and, consequently, are more likely being exposed to the advertisements in the newspaper.

Coffee Shop

The next customer satisfaction survey example involves a company that owns coffee shops, Wake Up, Inc. The company wanted to determine the quality of the products and services it provided to its customers in order to increase levels of customer satisfaction. The primary customer group consists of customers who purchase products on the premises of the various locations. The company provides different coffee drinks and foods.

The survey team consisted of the president of Wake Up, Inc. as well as other corporate representatives of the company: marketing, operations, quality, and research. The goal of the survey process was to allow the company to obtain reliable, valid information while maintaining a simple, short survey instrument.

Questionnaire Development

The survey team used a preliminary survey to determine what kinds of factors are important in defining the quality dimensions of its products and services. Specifically, the survey team wanted to know what factors the customers use when deciding which coffee house they would use. In this preliminary survey, customers were asked to rate the quality of the service they received on many different quality factors. Additionally, the customers were asked to rank the top four quality factors they use when selecting a coffee house. These factors used in the preliminary survey were developed based on the expertise of the survey team members. A total of 100 people were surveyed in this process. Table 7.8 contains the results of this initial survey.

From Table 7.8, the survey team concluded several things. First, based on the results from the rating portion of the survey (top part of the survey), they saw that clients were less satisfied with the following quality dimensions.

- Wait time
- Barista friendliness
- Food quality
- Price
- Coffee drink flavor

Second, based on the results from the ranking portion of the survey (bottom part of the survey), the survey team saw that, of the 12 possible factors, five of the factors were checked frequently as important issues. These factors were

- Wait time
- Barista friendliness
- Food quality
- Coffee drink flavor
- Location

The goal of the survey process was to obtain reliable and valid information from the customers regarding important quality dimensions of the services and products. With this survey, the company hoped to be able to monitor the levels of customer satisfaction and see improvement over time in satisfaction scores. Although the preliminary survey could be used as the final survey form as the survey of choice, its length precluded its final use. The long survey would result in a lower response rate than a shorter survey. Additionally, many of the factors that the survey team thought would define the company's products and services were not

Table 7.8. Results from the preliminary survey.

Thank you for visiting Wake Up, Inc. To better serve you, we would like your input regarding our products and services. Please take some time to complete the following survey. For each question, indicate your response using the scale below. If the questions do not apply to you, circle NA (Not Applicable). Feel free to make any additional comments.

	1 Very Dissatisfied	2 Dissatisfied	3 Neither Satisfied nor Dissatisfied	4 Satisfied	5 Very Satisfied	NA Not Applicable	
1. Merchandise	0	0	14	45	41	0	4.27
2. Wait time	0	14	27	36	18	0	3.62
3. Food quality	0	0	14	55	32	0	4.18
4. Coffee drink flavor	0	0	5	68	27	0	4.23
5. Barista friendliness	0	5	18	55	18	0	3.90
6. Barista responsiveness	0	0	0	45	55	0	4.52
7. Barista knowledge	0	0	5	41	45	0	4.45
8. Barista attire	0	0	5	18	77	0	4.73
9. Cleanliness of store	0	0	0	41	59	0	4.59
10. Price	0	0	18	55	18	0	4.00
11. Overall service quality	0	0	9	50	41	0	4.32
12. Overall product quality	0	0	5	55	41	0	4.36

What factors are important to you when selecting a coffee house? Please check the top four (4) most important dimensions from the list below.

	Percent
1. Barista friendliness	86
2. Price	23
3. Barista knowledge	27
4. Wait time	73
5. Coffee drink flavor	95
6. Location	45
7. Food quality	68
8. Special products	0
9. Jazz shows	0
10. Coffee publication	0
11. Reputation	5
12. Other:	9

ranked by the customers. Furthermore, customers gave high marks on many of the dimensions; including these types of items in a survey would add minimal utility above a more brief questionnaire that included important factors. As a result, the survey team decided to select only "important" factors for the final version of the questionnaire. The determination of these "important" factors was based on the results of the preliminary survey and the input of the survey team. Two additional questions were included to obtain overall ratings of service quality and product quality. The final survey instrument included the questions located in Figure 7.7.

Please send us feedback on this report. For each of the following six questions, indicate your response using the scale below. If the questions do not apply to you, circle NA (Not Applicable). Feel free to make additional comments.

Name: _____

Address: _____

_____

Date of service: _____

	Very Dissatisfied	Dissatisfied	Neither Satisfied nor Dissatisfied	Satisfied	Very Satisfied	Not Applicable
1. Wait time	1	2	3	4	5	NA
2. Barista friendliness	1	2	3	4	5	NA
3. Coffee drink flavor	1	2	3	4	5	NA
4. Food quality	1	2	3	4	5	NA
5. Overall service quality	1	2	3	4	5	NA
6. Overall product quality	1	2	3	4	5	NA

Comments: _____

Figure 7.7. Wake Up, Inc. client satisfaction survey.

Administration of the Survey

A sampling approach to the distribution of the survey was not conducted. Client satisfaction cards were placed at the area where the purchase transaction took place. The client satisfaction survey was printed on a 3 × 5-inch business reply mail card. The method of administration of the survey cards may not result in a random sample of customers. It is up to the customers to decide whether they will pick up the survey card and complete it. This method of administration, however, offered an easy method to collect customer information. Once the customers completed the survey card, the customers were to mail the cards to the corporate office of Wake Up, Inc. Once on-site, each card was read by the president of Wake Up, Inc. If scores were considered low (scores of 1s and 2s), a letter was written to the customer with an apology. Next, the data from each survey card were input in a computer database. Data management and analysis were conducted on the premises of the company.

Results

The results of the customer satisfaction survey are presented here. The results cover the first three quarters of 1995. The response rate for the customer survey was around 5 percent resulting in a total of 985 completed surveys. The percentage of responses for each response option, and the means and standard deviations for each item, are presented in Table 7.9.

Table 7.9. Descriptive statistics (percentages, means, standard deviation, standard error of the mean) for each item.

Percentage								
	VD	D	N	S	VS	Mean	SD[1]	SE[2]
1. Wait time	3.0	5.2	14.3	28.8	48.7	4.15	1.04	.03
2. Barista friendliness	0.2	1.0	7.9	38.3	52.5	4.42	0.70	.02
3. Coffee drink flavor	0.7	1.3	6.5	38.7	52.8	4.42	0.73	.02
4. Food quality	0.9	1.9	8.0	34.7	54.6	4.40	0.79	.03
5. Overall service quality	1.0	1.8	7.3	37.2	52.7	4.39	0.78	.02
6. Overall product quality	0.7	2.4	6.5	35.6	54.9	4.42	0.77	.02

Note: N = 985; SD[1] = standard deviation; SE[2] = standard error of the mean

From Table 7.9, we see that, overall, the scores for the satisfaction survey are generally positive, almost all above 4.0 (Satisfied). Because of an adequate sample size, there is not much sampling error associated with these survey results. Given a 95 percent confidence level, we can calculate the confidence interval for each item. They are

Wait time	$CI = 4.15 \pm 2 \times .03;\ CI = 4.09 < X < 4.21$
Barista friendliness	$CI = 4.42 \pm 2 \times .02;\ CI = 4.38 < X < 4.46$
Coffee drink flavor	$CI = 4.42 \pm 2 \times .02;\ CI = 4.38 < X < 4.46$
Food quality	$CI = 4.40 \pm 2 \times .03;\ CI = 4.34 < X < 4.46$
Overall service quality	$CI = 4.39 \pm 2 \times .02;\ CI = 4.35 < X < 4.43$
Overall product quality	$CI = 4.42 \pm 2 \times .02;\ CI = 4.38 < X < 4.46$

A next step would be to determine which quality factors are highly related to the general measures of service quality and product quality. This is conducted by examining the correlations among the items in the customer satisfaction measure. Correlations among the items in the client satisfaction survey are reported in Table 7.10.

As we can see, all items are somewhat correlated with each other. We see that wait time correlated more highly with service quality than with product quality. Additionally, if among the four factors measured in the survey, barista friendliness is correlated the highest (but just slightly

Table 7.10. Correlations among the items in the client satisfaction questionnaire.

	Q1	Q2	Q3	Q4	Q5
Q1: Wait time					
Q2: Barista friendliness	.4780				
Q3: Coffee drink flavor	.4366	.7676			
Q4: Food quality	.4126	.7263	.8269		
Q5: Service quality	.6539	.6893	.6723	.6724	
Q6: Product quality	.4720	.7474	.8078	.8294	.7589

Note: N = 898 to 917. All correlations significant at the .001 level.

more) with service quality compared to the rest. Additionally, of these same four, food quality and coffee drink flavor are correlated the highest with product quality compared to the other two variables. These findings suggest that a good way to increase service quality is to focus on issues related to the friendliness of the staff. Higher levels of satisfaction with the staff might lead to higher levels of satisfaction with the overall satisfaction with the service. To increase satisfaction levels related to product quality, however, our efforts might best be focused on factors that directly affect the quality of the tangible products (such as food quality and coffee drink flavor). To study all of these four factors' effects on the outcome variables, I conducted a stepwise regression analysis. The results of these two analyses are presented in Table 7.11.

According to Table 7.11, we see that all the variables are predictive of the two outcome variables. The two most important variables in predicting service quality were barista friendliness and wait time. The other two variables, although significantly predictive of service quality, do not account for a substantial amount of the variance in service quality. As for product quality, coffee drink flavor and food quality are the best predictors. The

Table 7.11. Stepwide regression analysis of the Wake Up, Inc. satisfaction questionnaire.

	Subscale	ΔR^2	*p*
Overall service quality	Barista friendliness	.4751	.01
	Wait time	.1364	.01
	Food quality	.0446	.01
	Coffee drink flavor	.0042	.01
	Total for four variables in the equation	.6603	.01
Overall product quality	Coffee drink flavor	.6879	.01
	Food quality	.0470	.01
	Barista friendliness	.0169	.01
	Wait time	.0059	.01
	Total for four variables in the equation	.7577	.01

remaining variables do not account for a substantial amount of the variance in product quality after the first two variables have been included in the equation.

With this knowledge, we can now create control charts using the customer satisfaction data to help us monitor our processes. For illustrative purposes, I will use the current data to calculate the control charts. In Figure 7.8–7.11, I have created control charts for the four quality factors in the Wake Up, Inc. customer satisfaction questionnaire using the month as the sample unit. Each figure includes both the $\bar{x}$ chart as well as the s chart. Recall that the $\bar{x}$ chart monitors the mean of the variable while the s chart monitors the standard deviation of the variable. These two types of control charts are typically presented together to allow you to see how the mean varies from sample to sample as well as how the range of data vary from sample to sample.

The upper and lower control limits vary from month to month due to the fluctuating sample size across the various months. Nonetheless, these control charts are interpreted the same way as those presented in Chapter 6.

We see that the respective processes related to wait time, barista friendliness, coffee drink flavor, and food quality are fairly stable across the first three quarters of the given year. For wait time, in the last month reported (September), however, we see that the s chart indicates a process that is out of control. The variability in September is quite small relative to all the other months. This lack of variability might be associated with the

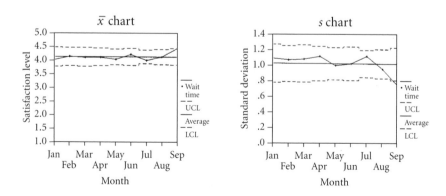

Figure 7.8. Control charts ($\bar{x}$ chart and s chart) for wait time.

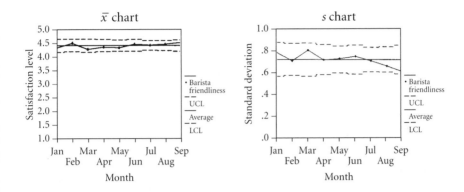

Figure 7.9. Control charts ($\bar{x}$ chart and s chart) for barista friendliness.

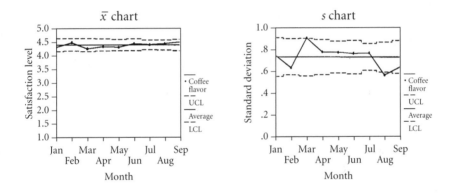

Figure 7.10. Control charts ($\bar{x}$ chart and S chart) for coffee drink flavor.

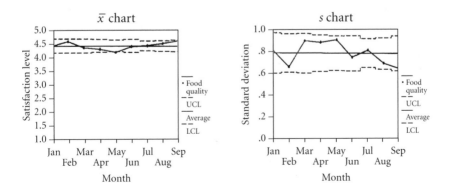

Figure 7.11. Control charts ($\bar{x}$ chart and S chart) for food quality.

high mean in the corresponding month in the $\bar{x}$ chart for wait time (notice that the average score in the corresponding month almost exceeds the UCL). Because possible scores can only be as high as the given scale (five-point scale), a high average score for that particular month indicates that most scores are clustered at the high end of the scale, thus minimizing the variability of possible responses. Subsequent monitoring of these control charts will help us determine if this is a plausible finding.

The monitoring of these variables (such as barista friendliness and food quality) with control charts helps us determine the stability and change of the system that is driving the respective scores. Control charts would help the company determine if changes were due to common causes or special causes. Consequently, the company would know when, and if, changes were needed in the process.

Summary

We have seen that the development of the customer survey helped the survey team identify the important quality characteristics associated with their services and products. The use of a preliminary survey indicated what types of items should be used in the final, shorter version of the customer satisfaction questionnaire. The final six-item customer satisfaction questionnaire is a useful vehicle on which customers can deliver feedback to the company on important quality dimensions. This survey was used for several purposes: (1) Determine current standing on customer satisfaction levels, (2) Identify what factors are most highly associated with overall satisfaction with service and overall satisfaction with the product, and (3) Monitor the work processes that are responsible for the scores through control charting techniques. Through these various uses of survey data, Wake Up, Inc. will ensure that its customers are an integral part of its quality-related measurements. Consequently, these data will allow Wake Up, Inc. to make informed decisions regarding quality improvement strategies in order to increase customer satisfaction.

Conclusions

This book presents practical guidelines to follow when developing customer satisfaction questionnaires. Chapters focused on the steps in the general model of customer satisfaction questionnaire development and use.

Chapter 2 discussed methods of determining customer requirements or quality dimensions. Customers judge services and products according to these dimensions. It is important to identify a comprehensive list of these quality dimensions because they determine the content of the questionnaire. If a customer requirement is not identified in this first step, the questionnaire will be unable to assess an important element.

Developing and evaluating questionnaires presents another important step in understanding customer attitudes. In Chapter 3, measurement issues highlighted the importance of reliability and validity of scales. Reliability is important when determining the amount of error that is associated with our measures. The various methods of estimating the different forms of reliability were presented in this chapter. Validity deals with the meaning of the scores from our questionnaire.

Chapter 4 presented various rating formats used to quantify the quality of the service or product. Depending on the expected use of the data, either a checklist or rating scale may be appropriate. A checklist format is useful for providing attribute data; a rating scale provides variable data. Chapter 4 also included characteristics of good items, as well as information that should be included in the introduction of the questionnaire.

Chapter 5 presented information on sampling. Different methods of sampling were presented as well as two approaches to random selection. The determination of sample size was presented to allow you to see how sample size affects the precision of our findings. Methods to increase response rates for mail surveys was also presented in this chapter.

Customer satisfaction has many applications (Chapter 6). Questionnaires can be used to monitor ongoing business processes, highlight general strengths and weaknesses, evaluate intervention programs, and help determine the most important customer requirements.

Chapter 7 included examples of some companies that have used customer satisfaction questionnaires in various capacities. The examples in this chapter allowed you to see how companies have applied some of the guidelines presented in this book and how the information obtained from the customer surveys was used.

The use of customer satisfaction questionnaires has increased greatly in the past few years. Companies want to distinguish themselves from their competitors in their ability to satisfy customers. The Baldrige Award places a strong emphasis on customer satisfaction. A company's ability to use customer-related information depends on the quality of the measurement system. The measurement system is often represented by customer satisfaction questionnaires designed to assess various dimensions of service or product quality. If information obtained from questionnaires is to be useful, questionnaires should reflect reliable and valid information. I hope this book has provided users of customer satisfaction questionnaires with useful guidance for developing and using these instruments.

Introduction to Appendices

In today's business, there is an increasing use of data in aiding the decision-making process. To understand data and how it can help in decision making, we need to summarize and interpret the data. The appendices provide a basic foundation for the interpretation of data, including specific examples using data resulting from questionnaires and other business processes and general examples.

A basic understanding of statistics is desirable but not necessary to grasp the fundamental principles that will be presented. The appendices are not intended to make the reader proficient in these statistical techniques. Many textbooks cover these topics, and interested readers may consult the bibliography to learn more about these techniques. Although formulae for calculating various statistical indices are presented in this text, these statistical procedures usually require the assistance of a computer and appropriate statistical software because hand calculations are not practical with large data sets. The text presents formulae to allow you to see how these indices are, in fact, calculated. A final note: in some situations, you should consult an expert on these statistical techniques. Expert judgment is often necessary for interpreting statistical results.

The topics of the appendices fall into two major sections. The first (covered in Appendices C through F) deals with descriptive statistics and sampling distributions. Specifically, Appendix C introduces the measurement process and presents four levels of measurement often used in data collection. Appendix D discusses frequency as a way of summarizing data and also covers probability and distributions. Appendix E introduces measures of central tendency and variability as a means of summarizing data. Appendix F introduces one of the most important topics in the use of data in decision making: sampling error. Readers must thoroughly understand this topic to appreciate subsequent appendices.

The second section of topics deals with the use of data in hypothesis testing. Appendix G covers decision making and hypothesis testing. It outlines the elements involved in making a decision and formally presents the concept of hypothesis testing, including the types of errors that may occur in any decision-making situation. Appendix H introduces the *t*-test procedure, which allows us to examine the difference between two groups of numbers. Appendix I presents the analysis of variance (ANOVA) procedure, which helps us examine the difference between two or more groups of numbers. Appendix J introduces the topic of correlational analysis, a procedure for summarizing the linear relationship between two variables. This appendix also includes a discussion on the regression equation for a straight line. Appendix K discusses the use of factor analysis. This appendix provides only a brief introduction to a powerful technique in questionnaire development. Appendix L contains a table of random numbers, which will help you in establishing your random samples.

Critical Incidents Interview Forms

Interview #_____ for critical incidents

Positive examples

1.
2.
3.
4.
5.
6.
7.
8.
9.
10.

Negative examples

1.
2.
3.
4.
5.
6.
7.
8.
9.
10.

Satisfaction Items and Customer Requirement Forms

Satisfaction item 1: _____

Critical incidents:

Satisfaction item 2: _____

Critical incidents:

Satisfaction item 3: _____

Critical incidents:

Customer requirement 1:

Satisfaction items:

1.

2.

3.

4.

5.

6.

7.

8.

Customer requirement 2:

Satisfaction items:

1.

2.

3.

4.

5.

6.

7.

8.

Customer requirement 3:

Satisfaction items:

1.

2.

3.

4.

5.

6.

7.

8.

Measurement Scales

Measurement scales are the means by which we assign a number to an object or entity. The number on the scale represents some characteristics of that object or entity. Stevens (1951) divided measurement scales into four types: nominal, ordinal, interval, and ratio. The degree to which these scales differ is reflected in the degree to which arithmetic operations make sense with the values of the entity represented by the numbers on the scale. The discussion of each scale will clarify this.

Nominal Scale

A nominal scale categorizes objects. These objects are mutually exclusive, and the numbers on the nominal scale reflect only that the objects are different from one another. For example, we might use a nominal scale to categorize customers on the basis of their marital status.

Single people are assigned a 1.
Married people are assigned a 2.
Divorced people are assigned a 3.

We may also use a nominal scale to label a set of stores.

Bob's Barn is assigned a 1.
Tom's Tent is assigned a 2.
Stephen's Store is assigned a 3.
Marissa's Mall is assigned a 4.

Let's look at arithmetic operations using the scale values for customers' marital status. Some operations that would *not* make sense are addition and subtraction. For example, a Stephen's Store (3) minus a Tom's Tent (2) would not equal a Bob's Barn (1). The only arithmetic operations that can be used on a nominal scale are the equality and inequality operations. For example, within our present store categorization system, a Stephen's Store (3) is the same as another Stephen's Store (3). Also $1 \neq 2$ indicates that a Bob's Barn is not the same as a Tom's Tent.

Because the values on the nominal scale represent categories, they can also be identified by different symbols, such as letters of the alphabet. For example, a Bob's Barn might be labeled an "A," a Tom's Tent as "B," a Stephen's Store as "C," and a Marissa's Mall as "D."

Ordinal Scale

An ordinal scale uses numbers to order objects with respect to some characteristic. For example, we can place customers in order according to their satisfaction level. If person A is more satisfied than person B, and person B is more satisfied than person C, then person A is more satisfied than person C. Using an ordinal scale, we may assign a number to each of these people and rank them from least satisfied (person C) to most satisfied (person A). The numbers corresponding to this satisfaction ordinal scale could be

Person C is a 1.
Person B is a 2.
Person A is a 3.

Let's look at some arithmetic operations applied to ordinal scales. Equality/inequality operations can be applied to ordinal scales. For example, in an equality/inequality operation, we can say that person C (1) is not equal to person A (3). We can also use the operations of less than (<) and greater than (>) on ordinal scales. Statements such as $3 > 2$ and $1 < 3$ make sense, indicating that person A is more satisfied than person B and person C is less satisfied than person A, respectively.

Another example of ordinal scales is reflected in the ranking of companies on some variable. For example, in studying a wide variety of companies, a research firm may assess the satisfaction level of its customers. In a final report, the research firm ranks the companies from highest to lowest in terms of its customers' overall satisfaction level. Suppose the study included five companies. The company with the highest average score on the customer satisfaction questionnaire would be ranked 5; the company with the second highest score would be ranked 4; and so forth:

Company A is a 5.
Company B is a 4.
Company C is a 3.
Company D is a 2.
Company E is a 1.

Although ordinal scales allow us to order objects, they do not allow us to determine the distance between the objects with respect to the characteristic being measured. For the example of ranking customers in terms of satisfaction, we know the order of the people but do not know how much more satisfied one person is relative to another. Also, ranking the companies does not tell us how much more satisfied company A's customers are compared to customers of other companies. This inability to determine differences between objects relates to the ordinal scale's lack of a unit of measurement.

Interval Scale

An interval scale orders things so that differences between scale values are equal, because the interval scale has a unit of measurement. One example is the Fahrenheit scale.

We can use more arithmetic operations with interval scale values. In addition to the equality/inequality and ordering operations, we can perform subtraction. For example, the difference between 50°F and 40°F equals the difference between 120°F and 110°F.

Attitude questionnaires are assumed to possess the features of an interval scale. If this assumption is true, we can perform useful arithmetic operations with the data from such questionnaires, which will aid in the interpretation of the data.

Ratio Scale

A ratio scale is similar to the interval scale in that it possesses a unit of measurement. The ratio scale has one additional feature: a meaningful zero point. An example of a ratio scale is the measurement of length. All arithmetic operations are meaningful for the ratio scale. This includes equality/inequality, ordering, subtraction, addition, and division. Table C.1 summarizes the characteristics of measurement scales.

Measurement Scales in Customer Satisfaction

Some of the measurement scales can be used in customer satisfaction questionnaires to categorize customers (nominal scale) and differentiate customers along some continuum (interval scale). Development of questionnaires to assess customers' perceptions and attitudes is based on the notion that the scales possess features found in the interval scale. In addition, we imply the use of a scale when we rank companies on the basis of their quality (ordinal scale). The ranking of companies is best accompanied by evidence that the ranking reflects meaningful, statistically significant differences between companies (see Appendix F).

Example

A hospital wanted to determine the quality of its physicians and front office staff. The survey was to be used to track this information over time and to compare the various office locations across the western region, where the company has its offices. The survey is presented in Figure C.1.

Table C.1. Types of measurement scales and the functional uses of each.

		Functional uses			
		Establish equality/ inequality	Establish rank ordering	Establish equal differences between scale points	Establish zero point
	Nominal	yes	no	no	no
Scale	Ordinal	yes	yes	no	no
types	Interval	yes	yes	yes	no
	Ratio	yes	yes	yes`	yes

The goal at Doc in a Box is to ensure you get the best service possible. Please take the time to answer the following questions. Your opinions are important to us. We will use this information to help us learn how to meet your needs in the best way we possibly can. To mail, please fold at the lines on the back of this sheet and seal with tape and drop in any mailbox. Thank you.

Date of exam: _____ Location of exam: _____

Name of patient: _____

Physician's name: _____

For each of the following questions, please indicate whether the phrase describes your experience at Doc in the Box. Please use the rating scale below. Circle your response for each question.

Y = Yes, describes my experience   N = No, does not describe my experience   ? = Not sure

Physician Quality

	Yes	No	Not Sure
1. Introduced him/herself to me.	Y	N	?
2. Asked me how I was injured/became ill.	Y	N	?
3. Listened to me.	Y	N	?
4. Treated me with respect.	Y	N	?
5. Was professional in doing the examination.	Y	N	?
6. Spent enough time with me (not rushed).	Y	N	?

7. Please rate your overall experience of the exam, using the following scale (circle your response.)

Terrible	Poor	Fair	Good	Excellent
1	2	3	4	5

Office Quality

	Yes	No	Not Sure
1. Appointment was at a convenient time.	Y	N	?
2. Waiting area was clean.	Y	N	?
3. Waiting room was comfortable.	Y	N	?
4. Examination room was clean.	Y	N	?
5. Office staff treated me with respect.	Y	N	?
6. I received a call from Doc in the Box reminding me of my appointment.	Y	N	?
7. Office staff answered my questions.	Y	N	?
8. Office staff was professional.	Y	N	?

9. Time of your appointment _____ A.M. P.M. Time you saw your doctor: _____ A.M. P.M.

Thank you for your time and for completing this survey. Please place in a mailbox. There is room for comments on the reverse side of this form.

Figure C.1. Patient satisfaction questionnaire.

We can divide the various questions into the types of measurement scales. Nominal scales are illustrated by the following questions: location of exam, name of patient, gender of patient, and name of physician. There is some debate as to the classification of rating scales for surveys. While some might classify rating scales as ordinal measures, we make the assumption that rating scales possess features of interval measures. Ratio scales are illustrated by the following questions: time with doctor and wait time (time you saw your doctor minus the time of your appointment).

Frequencies, Percentages, Probabilities, Histograms, and Distributions

Data can be overwhelming. Often we are confronted with large data sets consisting of hundreds of scores. We need a way of summarizing the data to make some sense of it. This appendix will discuss one way of summarizing large data sets with the use of frequencies and histograms .

Frequencies

Table D.1 lists scores from a hypothetical study examining the level of customer satisfaction of a given company. The data set contains 48 scores, each representing one person's average score on the customer satisfaction questionnaire. Upon examination, we see that scores vary somewhat, ranging from a low of 1.4 to a high of 4.6. To gain a better understanding of the data, we need to summarize the scores in a simple format.

One way of summarizing data is to calculate the frequency of occurrence of a specific value, or how often that given value occurs in our data set. To calculate frequencies, we first rank the scores from lowest to highest (see Table D.2). After the ranking, we determine the frequency of occurrence of each value. We see that the value of 1.4 occurred only once. Therefore, 1.4 has a frequency of one. Likewise, the value of 2.5 has a frequency of four.

Although calculating frequencies for each specific value will help summarize the information, the amount of information can still be overwhelming. For example, with characteristics measured in small increments,

Table D.1. Hypothetical data set.

2.3	4.3	3.3	1.5
2.5	2.7	3.4	3.2
4.1	3.8	3.7	2.9
3.0	2.7	2.5	3.4
4.6	2.3	2.1	2.3
3.7	3.6	1.4	3.2
1.5	1.6	1.7	3.6
4.0	4.1	3.4	2.1
3.3	3.1	3.5	4.4
2.5	2.8	3.9	2.0
1.7	2.5	2.9	3.8
4.2	2.1	3.9	2.4

Table D.2. Data from Table D.1 ranked from smallest to largest.

1.4	2.3	3.1	3.7
1.5	2.4	3.2	3.8
1.5	2.5	3.2	3.8
1.6	2.5	3.3	3.9
1.7	2.5	3.3	3.9
1.7	2.5	3.4	4.0
2.0	2.7	3.4	4.1
2.1	2.7	3.4	4.1
2.1	2.8	3.5	4.2
2.1	2.9	3.6	4.3
2.3	2.9	3.6	4.4
2.3	3.0	3.7	4.6

we may obtain a lot of values, each occurring with little frequency. Calculating the frequency of each value might not be enough to simplify the data. Therefore, when calculating frequencies, we usually group values with similar scores into a particular class. Then we calculate frequencies for these class values.

Class Intervals

A class interval represents a range in which a set of values is included. Creating class intervals is a process of dividing the scores into specified equal intervals. Each class interval is defined by a lower bound and an upper bound. The lower bound represents the lowest possible score that can be included in the interval; the upper bound represents the highest possible score. Using the data set in Table D.2, we can create a class interval with the width of 0.4 to represent the scores. Starting with a lower bound of 1.0, the first class interval would include scores ranging from a low of 1.0 to a high of 1.4. The second class interval would include scores ranging from 1.5 to 1.9. The last class interval would include scores ranging from 4.5 to 4.9. Table D.3 presents these class intervals and the frequency of values that occur in the class.

Table D.3. Frequencies for the class variable.

Class interval	Frequency	Percentage
1.0 to 1.4	1	2.1%
1.5 to 1.9	5	10.4%
2.0 to 2.4	8	16.7%
2.5 to 2.9	9	18.8%
3.0 to 3.4	9	18.8%
3.5 to 3.9	9	18.8%
4.0 to 4.4	6	12.5%
4.5 to 4.9	1	2.1%
Total	48	100.0%

We use arbitrary numbers to select class intervals and determine the width of each class interval. It has been shown that, if continuous data are divided into intervals, you lose less information about the data by creating more intervals. A reasonable number of intervals is seven (Shaw, Huffman, and Haviland 1987), although more intervals would result in less information loss.

Percentages

Another way of looking at the frequency of values is through the use of percentages. A percentage reflects the proportion of scores of a particular value. The percentage for a particular value is calculated by dividing the frequency of a given value by the total number of scores in the data set. For our data, we see that the percentage of people with scores of 2.5 to 2.9 is 18.8 percent (9/48), and the percentage of people with scores ranging from 4.0 to 4.9 is 14.6 percent (7/48). The total of the percentages for a given question should be 100 percent (given rounding errors).

The percentage is sometimes preferred to the frequency since it incorporates the total number of scores into its calculation. A frequency of 50 may not tell us all we want to know about the data. A frequency of 50 in one sample of scores may indicate a large percentage (for example, when sample size is 60), while in another sample a frequency of 50 may indicate a minute percentage (for example, when sample size is 1,000,000). Thus, before interpreting the magnitude of the frequency, we should be aware of the total sample size.

Constructing Frequency Distributions of the Intervals

We can graphically represent the frequencies of the class intervals. The graph is formally called a *histogram*. The histogram aids in summarizing the data beyond the lone use of frequencies since it captures many pieces of information in a single picture. The histogram not only indicates the frequency of each value, but also roughly indicates the range of the data (lowest to highest value) and the shape of the distribution.

The histogram has two axes. The horizontal axis (sometimes referred to as the *X axis* or *abscissa*) represents the variable or class interval. The vertical axis (sometimes referred to as the *Y axis* or *ordinate*) represents the frequency for a variable or class interval.

The horizontal axis is scaled by the midpoint of each class interval. Therefore, for the data in Table D.3, the horizontal axis would be scaled by eight values, each value representing the midpoint of each class interval. The midpoints are 1.2, 1.7, 2.2, 2.7, 3.2, 3.7, 4.2, and 4.7. The histogram appears in Figure D.1.

Frequency tables and the histograms are both useful tools for summarizing data. The frequency table reflects the frequency of occurrence of specific values or the frequency of values for a specific class interval. The histogram is a graphic illustration of the frequency table.

We can calculate frequencies for variables that are on any scale of measurement (nominal, ordinal, interval, and ratio). For example, a questionnaire could include various questions pertaining to satisfaction

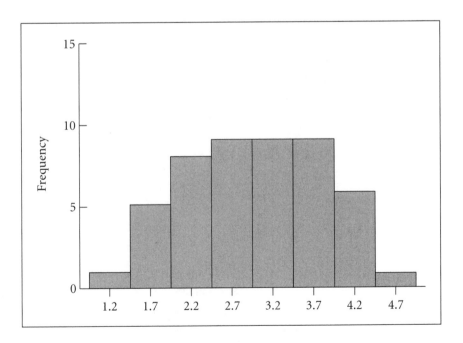

Figure D.1. Histogram of the class intervals in Table D.3.

levels as well as questions asking for demographic information. The demographic portion could include questions pertaining to sex and age.

If the questionnaire was distributed to 150 people, we could subsequently calculate the frequency or proportion of males versus females and also determine the frequency or proportion of a given. age group.

The frequencies for the sex variable (nominal) and age variables (ratio) are listed in Table D.4. The frequencies indicate that the sample consists of more males than females. In terms of percentages, we see that males represent 58 percent (87/150) of respondents and females represent 42 percent of respondents. Also, this sample consists of a large group of people aged 36 to 45 years.

Distributions

The histogram in Figure D.1 can also be called a *distribution of scores*. Although there are many forms of distributions, such as a bimodal (two-humped) distribution and a unimodal (one-humped) distribution, I will present a special type called a *normal distribution*. The normal distribution is a symmetric, bell-shaped distribution. Many of the things we measure in our environment can be described by a symmetric, bell-shaped distribution. For example, if the heights of many people were plotted, the shape of the histogram would form a normal distribution.

Table D.4. Frequencies and percentages for the variables of sex and age.

Sex	Frequency	%		Age	Frequency	%
M	87	58.0		0–15	0	0.0
F	63	42.0		16–25	3	2.0
				26–35	44	29.3
				36–45	64	42.7
				46–55	25	16.7
				56–older	44	9.3
Total	150	100.0%		Total	150	100.0%

Determining Probabilities from Distributions

Given a distribution, we can calculate probabilities of various events. For example, we may have measured the height of 1000 people. The data of height forms a normal distribution described by some mean and variance (see distribution of $n = 1$ in Figure F.1). Now let's say we were to select one person at random from this sample. What is the probability that the height of that person is greater than 65″?

We determine the probability by dividing the number of people who are taller than 65″ by the total number of people in the sample. We can also determine the probability by calculating the area under the curve to the right of 65″. We can describe this area as a percentage of people who are taller than 65″. We can then transform this percentage into a probability by dividing the value by 100.

As we increase the height of our criterion to 70″, we see that the probability of selecting a person greater than that criterion decreases, since the area under the curve to the right of the criterion decreases.

Example

The percentage of respondents for each of the questions is presented in Table D.5.

As we can see in Table D.5, the distribution of scores is fairly evenly spread across the three quarters of the year. Additionally, the surveys are composed of surveys from all of the offices in the western region. Most of the surveys represent our San Jose, Yakima, Tacoma, and Spokane offices. San Diego and Sonoma have the least amount of surveys in our sample. Furthermore, a little over half of the sample of surveys (53.4 percent) is from offices located in the state of Washington. Looking at the percentage of responses for our survey questions, many of the customers indicate a "Yes" to the questions. The percent of "Yes" responses range from a low of 53.4 percent to a high of 99.1 percent.

Figure D.2 shows a histogram of the responses for the overall rating. As is indicated, most of the respondents indicate a "Good" or "Excellent" response.

Table D.5. Frequencies and percentages for the patient satisfaction questionnaire.

Quarter of survey	Frequency	Percentage
1st quarter	462	34.4
2nd quarter	466	34.7
3rd quarter	414	30.8

Month of survey	Frequency	Percentage
January	153	11.4
February	149	11.1
March	160	11.9
April	155	11.5
May	169	12.6
June	142	10.6
July	133	9.9
August	138	10.3
September	143	10.7

Office location	Frequency	Percentage
Yakima	180	13.4
Seattle	176	13.1
San Francisco	150	11.2
Tacoma	180	13.4
San Jose	181	13.5
Sacramento	155	11.5
Spokane	180	13.4
San Diego	58	4.3
Sonoma	82	6.1

Office location	Frequency	Percentage
Washington	716	53.4
California	626	46.6

Physician Quality

	Yes	No	Not Sure
1. Introduced him/herself to me.	1297 (97.4%)	23 (1.7%)	12 (0.9%)
2. Asked me how I was injured/became ill.	1268 (95.3%)	52 (3.9%)	11 (0.8%)
3. Listened to me.	1186 (90.5%)	60 (4.6%)	64 (4.9%)
4. Treated me with respect.	1256 (94.5%)	33 (2.5%)	40 (3.0%)
5. Was professional in doing the examination.	1261 (95.2%)	33 (2.5%)	31 (2.3%)
6. Spent enough time with me (not rushed).	1078 (83.2%)	118 (9.1%)	100 (7.7%)

7. Please rate your overall experience of the exam, using the following scale (circle your response.)

Terrible	Poor	Fair	Good	Excellent
21 (1.6%)	41 (3.2%)	178 (13.9%)	608 (47.4%)	435 (33.9)

Table D.5. *Continued.*

Office Quality	Yes	No	Not Sure
1. Appointment was at a convenient time.	1156 (87.9%)	143 (10.9%)	16 (1.2%)
2. Waiting area was clean.	1319 (99.1%)	10 (0.8%)	2 (0.1%)
3. Waiting room was comfortable.	1288 (96.9%)	27 (2.0%)	14 (1.1%)
4. Examination room was clean.	1312 (98.7%)	10 (0.8%)	7 (0.8%)
5. Office staff treated me with respect.	1302 (98.1%)	18 (1.4%)	7 (0.5%)
6. I received a call from Doc in the Box reminding me of my appointment.	703 (53.4%)	554 (42.1%)	60 (4.6%)
7. Office staff answered my questions.	1205 (94.8%)	33 (2.6%)	33 (2.6%)
8. Office staff was professional.	1291 (97.9%)	16 (1.2%)	12 (0.9%)

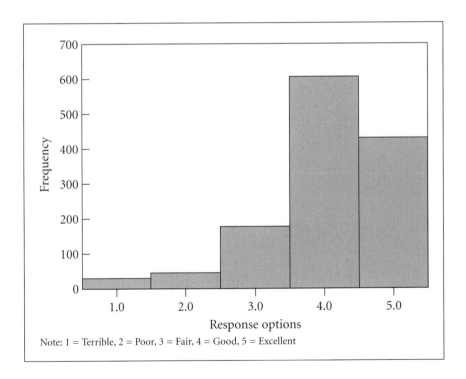

Note: 1 = Terrible, 2 = Poor, 3 = Fair, 4 = Good, 5 = Excellent

Figure D.2. Histogram of the overall rating of the exam.

Summary

This appendix introduced various ways of describing and presenting data. Frequencies and percentages convey the occurrence of values in the data set. Histograms are a useful way of presenting data. They convey the frequency of values as well as the range of the data set. Histograms can also be thought of as distributions. The probability of a given event occurring can also be determined using the distribution.

Descriptive Statistics

The use of frequencies and histograms is one way of summarizing data (see Appendix D). Another way to summarize large data sets is with the use of summary indices, which describe the shape of the histogram. Two types of summary indices help us understand the data: central tendency and variability.

Central Tendency

One way of summarizing data is to determine the center or middle point of scores. Measures of central tendency allow us to determine roughly the center of the scores in the data set. For example, we may measure the satisfaction level of 10 customers. The data are presented in Table E.1. The scores vary considerably. We can capture a lot of information about these scores by determining the middle point. By doing so, we get an estimate of where the scores fall. Three statistics that describe the central tendency are the mean, median, and mode.

Table E.1. Hypothetical data set.

Customer	X
1	4
2	1
3	3
4	2
5	4
6	1
7	5
8	4
9	3
10	2

Mean

The mean is the arithmetic average of all scores in the data set. It is calculated by adding all the scores in the data set and dividing by the total number of observations in the data set. The formula is

$$\bar{x} = \frac{\Sigma x_i}{n}$$

where n = the number of observations in the data set and Σx_i is the sum of all scores in the data set.

Using the formula, we can calculate the mean of the data in Table E.1.

$$\bar{x} = \frac{4 + 1 + 3 + 2 + 4 + 1 + 5 + 4 + 3 + 2}{10} = 2.9$$

Median

Another measure of central tendency is the median. The median is the middlemost score after the data have been rank ordered from either highest to lowest or lowest to highest. In other words, half of the scores have values larger than the median and half have values smaller than the median.

If the data set has an odd number of scores, the median is the $(n + 1/2)$th largest score in the data set. If the data set has an even number of scores, the median is the average of two numbers, the $(n/2)$th largest score and the $(n/2 + 1)$th largest score. Table E.2 provides the rank order of data from Table E.1. Since the number of scores in the data set is even, the median is calculated as the average of the two middlemost scores. The median value in the data set is 3.

Mode

The third measure of central tendency is the mode. The mode is the score that occurs most often in the data set. In Table E.2, there are two 1s, two 2s, two 3s, three 4s, and one 5. Therefore, the mode of this data set is 4, since it is the most frequently occurring score. It is possible that a data set could have more than one mode. This occurs when two or more values in the data set have the highest frequency and the same frequency.

Variability

While measures of central tendency indicate the middle of the distribution, we also would like to know about the spread of data. The spread of

Table E.2. Rank order of data from Table E.1.

Score	Customer	X	
1	7	5	
2	1	4	
3	5	4	
4	8	4	
5	3	3	← $(n/2)$th score
6	9	3	← $(n/2 + 1)$th score
7	4	2	
8	10	2	The median is $(3 + 3)/2 = 3$
9	2	1	
10	6	1	

data is indexed by measures of variability. Measures of variability indicate the extent to which scores are tightly packed together versus spread out. The measures of variability presented here are the variance and the standard deviation. Both measures indicate the spread of data around the mean.

Variance

Table E.3 contains four columns of numbers. The first column is x, the score; the second column contains a deviation score from the mean $(x - \bar{x})$; the third column contains the squared deviation score; and the last column is the squared value of each score.

One measure of variability is the variance. Variance, s^2, is the sum of the squared deviations about the mean (SS) divided by the number of scores in the data set less one. The formula for the variance is

$$s^2 = \frac{\Sigma(x_i - \bar{x})^2}{n - 1} = \frac{SS}{n - 1}$$

The numerator is the sum of the squared deviations about the mean (SS) and the denominator is called the *degrees of freedom*. In general, the degrees of freedom for a particular statistic is the number of observations in the data set minus the number of estimated parameters used in the equation. The total number of observations used in the calculation is the sample size (n), and the number of estimated parameters used in the

Table E.3. Deviation scores and squared deviation scores for hypothetical data.

	x	$x - \bar{x}$	$(x - \bar{x})^2$	x^2
	1	−2	4	1
	2	−1	1	4
	3	0	0	9
	4	1	1	16
	5	2	4	25
Totals	15	0	10	55

equation is one (the sample mean). It should be noted that some people, in calculating the variance, divide the *SS* by *n* instead of *n* – 1. Usually, *n* is used when the variance is used to describe the present data set, while *n* – 1 is used to make inferences about the population variance from which the sample is drawn. A more complete discussion between the difference is available in various introductory statistics books. Using the previous equation, the variance of the data is calculated.

$$s^2 = \frac{4 + 1 + 0 + 1 + 4}{10} = 2.5$$

The formula for the sum of squared deviations (*SS*) can be simplified to facilitate hand computation of the variance. The formula for the sum of squares is

$$SS = \Sigma x_i^2 - \frac{(\Sigma x_i)^2}{n}$$

Using the data, the *SS* is calculated to be

$$SS = 55 - \frac{225}{5} = 10$$

The numerator for the formula of the variance is the squared deviation of each score from the mean. As the scores are widely spread out from the mean, the numerator increases. Therefore a large variance indicates that the scores are widely spread out, and a small variance indicates that the scores are tightly packed around the mean.

Standard Deviation

Another measure of variability is the standard deviation. The standard deviation is simply the square root of the variance and is denoted by *s*. The standard deviation for the data in Table E.3 is calculated to be *s* = 1.58. The larger the standard deviation, the larger the spread in the data.

If the data are normally distributed, the standard deviation can be used to estimate the percentage of scores that fall within a specified range. By definition, 68 percent of the scores fall within a range whose limits are (mean – 1*s*) and (mean + 1*s*), and 95 percent of the scores fall within a range whose limits are (mean − 2*s*) and (mean + 2*s*). If the standard deviation is small, a high percentage of the data falls closely around the mean. For our data, approximately 68 percent of the data falls within a range from 1.4 to 4.4.

Example

Before descriptive statistics were calculated, summary scores for physician quality and office quality were calculated by averaging the items within the respective scales. The descriptive statistics for the patient satisfaction questionnaire are presented in Table E.4.

As we can see from Table E.4, the descriptive statistics indicate that customers seem to be satisfied with the overall experience of the exam. Additionally, they seem to indicate that they are satisfied with the physician quality and overall quality of the exam. This information is not surprising to us given the information regarding the frequency of responses. Although this method of presenting the data (mean, median, and mode), compared to frequencies and percentages, summarizes the data even more, we conclude the same thing. This method of reporting the descriptive statistics is easier compared to reporting the frequencies if we just want to get a general idea of what the satisfaction data tell us. The wait time indicates that the patients typically had to wait about 15 minutes before seeing the physician. Once in to see the physician, the typical patient spent about 44 minutes with the physician.

Table E.4. Descriptive statistics of items in the patient satisfaction questionnaire.

Variable	Mean	Median	Mode	SD
Physician quality	2.81	3.00	3.00	.44
Overall experience of exam	4.09	4.00	4.00	.86
Office quality	2.74	2.75	3.00	.32
Time spent with physician (minutes)	43.53	40.00	30.00	28.93
Wait time (minutes)	16.24	15.00	0.00	23.90

Summary

This section included measures of central tendency and measures of variability. Both types of measures summarize information contained in a sample of scores. The central tendency measures determine the score in the data set around which all other scores cluster. Measures of variability determine the extent of spread of the data.

Statistics, Parameters, and Sampling Distributions

A subset of observations can be randomly selected from a larger set of observations. The larger set of observations is called the *population;* the smaller set is called the *sample*. We are usually concerned with making conclusions about the population. Since the population can be extremely large, we often examine a sample to make conclusions about the larger population. For example, we may want to know the level of satisfaction of all our customers. Due to limited resources, we may only be able to measure the satisfaction level of a small set of customers. The population consists of all the customers; the sample consists of the small set of customers we measure.

We may examine the mean and the variance of a sample to make inferences about the mean and variance of the population. Numbers calculated from a sample of data are referred to as *statistics*. Therefore, the mean, variance, and standard deviation of the sample are statistics. Numbers calculated using the entire population are called *parameters*. Statistics are denoted with the following symbols: the mean is $\bar{x}$, the variance is s^2, and the standard deviation is s. Parameters are usually denoted with Greek symbols. The population mean is μ, the variance is σ^2, and the standard deviation is σ. Because the population parameters may not be easily obtained (due to limited resources), we have to estimate the parameters. We use the statistics as estimators of the parameters.

Sampling Error

Suppose we have a population of 1000 people and want to make conclusions about their mean height. We may have only the resources to measure 50 of these people. We use the mean from the sample to estimate the mean of the population.

For the sake of argument, suppose we knew the mean height of the population to be $\mu = 60''$ with a $\sigma^2 = 50''$. Based on our sample of 50 randomly selected people, we calculate the mean of their height. Suppose we found the mean height of the sample to be $\bar{x}_1 = 62''$. Now, let's place this sample back into the population of 1000 people and take another sample of 50 randomly selected people. Suppose we found the mean of this sample to equal $\bar{x}_2 = 55''$. We notice that there is some difference between the means of the first and second sample of people, both differing from the true population mean.

The difference of the sample means from population mean is referred to as *sampling error*. This error is expected to occur and is considered to be random. For the first sample, we happen to select, by chance, people who are slightly taller than the population mean. In the second sample, we selected, again by chance, people who are slightly shorter than the population mean.

Standard Error of the Mean

In the preceding example, we witnessed the effect of sampling error; in one sample the mean $(\bar{x}_1) = 62''$ and in the second sample the mean $(\bar{x}_2) = 55''$. If we did not know the population mean (which is usually the situation), we could not determine the exact amount of error associated with any one given sample. We can, however, determine the degree of error we might expect using a given sample size. We could do so by repeatedly taking a sample of 50 randomly selected people from the population, with replacement, and calculating the mean for each sample. Each mean would be an estimate of the population mean.

If we collected 100 means, we could then plot them to form a histogram or distribution. This distribution is described by a mean and a standard deviation. This distribution of sample means is called a *sampling distribution.* The mean of this sampling distribution would be our best estimate of the population mean. The standard deviation of the sampling distribution is called the *standard error of the mean* (sem). The sem describes the degree of error we would expect in our sample mean. If the population standard deviation is known, we can calculate the sem. The standard error of the mean can be calculated easily using the following formula.

$$\text{Standard error of the mean } = \frac{\sigma}{\sqrt{n}}$$

where n is sample size and σ is the population standard deviation. If we do not know the population standard deviation, we can calculate the sem using the sample standard deviation as an estimate of the population standard deviation.

The sampling distributions for two different sample sizes are presented in Figure F.1. The population mean (μ) is 60″ and the population variance (σ^2) is 50″. The size of sample 1 is 10 and the size of sample 2 is 100. Using the equation above, the standard error of the mean is 2.24″ for sample 1 and .71″ for sample 2. As seen in Figure F.1, the degree of sampling error is small when the sample size is large. This figure illustrates the effect of sample size on our confidence in the sample estimate.

When the sample size is 100, we see that any one of our sample means will likely fall close to the population mean (95 percent of the sample means will fall within the range of 58.58″ to 61.42″). When the sample size is 10, our sample means will deviate more from the population mean than do our sample means when using a sample size of 100 (95 percent of the sample means will fall within the range of 53.68″ to 66.32″). In fact, when the sample size equals the population size, the standard error of the mean is 0. That is, when sample size equals population size, the sample mean will always equal the population mean.

Figure F.2 illustrates the relationship between sampling error and sample size. As sample size increases, sampling error decreases. When sample size equals one, the standard error of the mean is, by definition, the standard deviation of the observation. When sample size equals the size of the population, there is no error in the estimate of the population

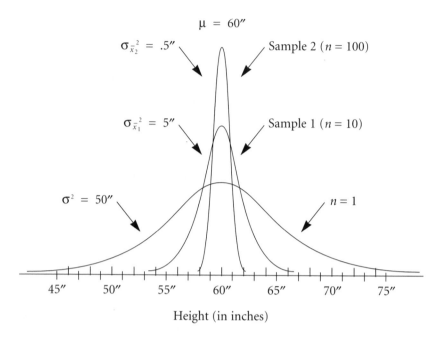

Figure F.1. Sampling distributions for sample sizes of $n = 100$ and $n = 10$ with a population mean of 60 and population variance of 50.

mean. Thus, the standard error of the mean is 0 when sample size equals the size of the population.

Example

The sampling error for some of the variables in the Patient Satisfaction Questionnaire are presented in Table F.1.

As we can see from the table, the sampling error is quite small, suggesting that there is not much error associated with our estimates of the population parameters. Given that we have a fairly large sample size, we can be fairly confident that our results will not vary if we were to conduct the same study using another sample of the same size. That is, if we were to take another 1500 or so surveys from our population of customers, our results would be very similar to the results we have here. For example, we would expect our mean for the physician quality score to vary only .01 (on the scale we are using) from sample to sample.

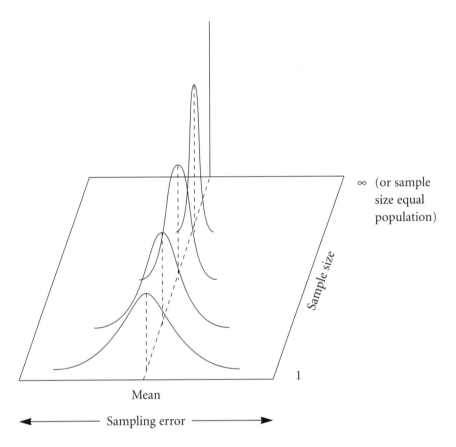

Figure F.2. The relationship between sample size and sampling error: as sample size increases, sampling error decreases.

Table F.1. Sampling error of the variables in the patient satisfaction survey.

Variable	Mean	SD	*n* (sample size)	Sampling error
Physician quality	2.81	.44	1335	.01
Overall experience of exam	4.09	.86	1283	.02
Office quality	2.74	.32	1337	.01
Time spent with physician (minutes)	43.53	28.93	1093	.88
Wait time (minutes)	16.24	23.90	827	.83

Summary

Statistics are numbers derived from a sample of numbers. Parameters are numbers derived from a population. A sampling distribution is a distribution of a given statistic. Sampling error describes the degree of error associated with a given statistic for a specified sample size. As sample size increases, sampling error decreases. The concept of sampling error can be applied to many statistics (mean, t-value), and the concept of sampling error will be applied throughout the remaining appendices.

Decision Making and Hypothesis Testing

Decisions are made every day in the business world. On a small scale, we decide whether or not to leave early for a meeting being held on the other side of town. On a larger scale, companies select one supplier instead of another. We implicitly make decisions about some aspect of the world. In the former scenario, we might decide to leave early if the roads are icy and we need extra time to get to the meeting. In the second scenario, a company might select one supplier instead of another because one supplier makes parts of higher quality.

When we make decisions, we hope they are correct. A decision is correct if it is congruent with the state of the world. For example, a decision to leave early for the meeting is correct if the roads are icy and incorrect if the roads are not icy. In addition, a decision not to leave early for the meeting is correct if the roads are not icy and incorrect if the roads are icy.

Reality and Decisions

One morning, you are deciding whether or not to take your umbrella to work. To help you make this decision, you rely on some evidence (data). This evidence consists of several weather forecasts from various sources, each providing you with some data on the weather for the day. You must decide, based on this data, whether or not to take your umbrella with you.

You can make one of two choices based on your evaluation of the data. If you decide the data indicate it will rain today, you will take your umbrella. If you decide the data indicate it will not rain today, you will leave your umbrella at home.

There are four possible outcomes for this scenario. We can diagram these, crossing the two states of the world with the two possible decisions. The two states of the world constitute reality—the way the world truly is. The two decisions are based on the evaluation of the evidence (data), leading us to decide whether or not an umbrella is warranted. The diagram depicting the four possible outcomes is presented in Figure G.1 and illustrates the two correct decisions and the two types of errors. For the sake of discussion, the errors are labeled as *Type I* and *Type II*.

The Process of Decision Making

We can look at decision making as a process consisting of two important elements: the evidence and the criterion. The evidence is the data we evaluate in making our decision. In our previous umbrella-toting example, we may have gathered data from many local weather reports, the *Farmer's Almanac,* and other sources. The criterion reflects the amount of evidence or data we need to decide whether to carry an umbrella. Therefore, differences in our criterion will influence the likelihood of making a Type I versus a Type II error. We could have a stringent criterion, which means we need a lot of evidence to convince ourselves to carry an umbrella (for example, we will carry an umbrella only when all of the forecasts predict

		State of the world	
		No rain	Rain
	Carry umbrella	Error (Type I)	Correct decision
Your decision			
	Do not carry umbrella	Correct decision	Error (Type II)

Figure G.1. Four possible outcomes, crossing the two states of the world with the two decisions.

rain). With this stringent criterion, we will rarely end up carrying an umbrella on a day without rain (not likely to make a Type I error), but will likely end up not carrying an umbrella on a rainy day (likely to make a Type II error). On the other hand, we could have a lenient criterion, which means we need little evidence to convince us to carry an umbrella (for example, we will carry an umbrella if at least one forecast predicts rain). With this criterion, we would likely carry an umbrella on a day with no rain (likely to make a Type I error), but we will rarely end up without an umbrella on a rainy day (not likely to make a Type II error).

Decision Making in Hypothesis Testing

In business, we would like to know the real state of the world. To understand the true state of the world, we collect data. The data constitute the evidence we need to make conclusions about the world. Based on this evidence, we decide which state of the world is true.

Let's look at an example to illustrate the role of decision making in hypothesis testing. We may own two stores and have limited financial resources. We would like to give resources to the store that needs the most help (has the lowest level of customer satisfaction). We develop a customer satisfaction questionnaire and administer it to the stores' customers. Questionnaire scores constitute the data we need to make conclusions about the state of the world.

We can formally state our question: Do the two groups of customers have different levels of satisfaction? In hypothesis testing, we set up the world as consisting of two mutually exclusive hypotheses: the null hypothesis and the alternative hypothesis. The null hypothesis (HO) states

> *There is no difference in satisfaction levels between the customers of the two stores.*

The alternative hypothesis (HA) states

> *There is a difference in the satisfaction levels between the customers of the two stores.*

In the world, only one of these hypotheses is true. In our study, we will collect evidence to help us decide which is correct. In our hypothesis

testing situation, we have a possibility of four outcomes. We have two possible states of the world crossed with two possible decisions. Each state of
the world is represented by one of our hypotheses (there is no difference
versus there is a difference). We also have two decisions we can make
(deciding there is a difference between the two stores or that there is not a
difference between the two stores). These decisions are unique to hypothesis testing. Formally, we state our decisions as either rejecting the null
hypothesis (or accepting the alternative hypothesis that there is a difference between the two stores) or not rejecting the null hypothesis (not
accepting the alternative).

We can construct a decision outcome matrix for this situation. This is
presented in Figure G.2. The four cells, similar to the four cells in our
umbrella-toting situation, can be characterized by probabilities, or likeli-
hoods of occurrence. The probability of rejecting the null when the null is,
in fact, true (upper left corner) is labeled as α. The probability of not
rejecting the null when the null is true is $1-\alpha$. In addition, the probability
of failing to reject the null when the alternative is true is labeled as β. The
probability of rejecting the null when the alternative is true is $1-\beta$.

		State of the world	
		Null hypothesis true	Alternative hypothesis true
Your decision	**Reject null hypothesis**	Type I error (α)	Correct decision ($1-\beta$)
	Do not reject null hypothesis	Correct decision ($1-\alpha$)	Error (Type II) (β)

Figure G.2. The four possible outcomes in a hypothesis testing situation, crossing
the two states of the world with the two decisions.

Some Evidence

We need to collect data to provide us with evidence of the true state of the world. Let's use our example concerning the level of satisfaction of customers from our two stores. We collect data from two samples, each representing one store. Higher scores on the questionnaire reflect higher levels of satisfaction. The data are presented in Table G.1.

Before examining the data, let's discuss the kind of evidence that would indicate whether or not we should reject the null. If the null is correct, then the two groups of scores should be roughly the same. If the alternative is true, then the two groups of scores should be different; one set should contain higher scores than the other.

We need a way of summarizing the data to allow us to decide which hypothesis is true. In this situation, we could look at the overall average of each group. The average score for Store 1 is $\bar{x}_1 = 3.5$, and the average for Store 2 is $\bar{x}_2 = 3.1$. The difference between these two scores is 0.4. We could use this difference score as the summary score. This summary score reflects the degree of difference between the two groups and is, essentially, the evidence.

Table G.1. Hypothetical data of satisfaction scores for two stores.

Store 1	Store 2
4	3
5	4
2	3
4	4
5	2
4	2
3	3
4	5
2	2
2	3

Determination of the Criterion

Summary scores are used to represent the state of the world, supporting either the null hypothesis or the alternative hypothesis. We need a criterion to judge whether the summary score reflects that the null hypothesis is true or that the alternative hypothesis is true. In hypothesis testing, we usually set the criterion to reflect that the alpha level (probability of rejecting the null when it is true) equal .05. That is, given that the null is true, we want to set a criterion with which we will incorrectly reject the null hypothesis, at the most, five times out of 100.

For our study, we found that the summary score (the difference between the two groups), is 0.4. Recall that, in Appendix F, the effect of sampling error would result in differences between two samples of scores even if the samples were selected from the same underlying population. Therefore, the difference of 0.4 revealed in our study might not indicate any real difference at all. The difference between the two samples could be due to sampling error.

For our example, the criterion we choose should reflect a difference between two samples that would occur by chance only five times out of 100 if the null were true. This criterion is established through formal methods discussed in the next three appendices.

Example

We could state some hypotheses for our study using our patient satisfaction data. Some explicit hypotheses are presented in Figure G.3.

There are many more hypotheses that can be generated using our current patient satisfaction questionnaire. We could examine the difference across the various offices using the other variables in the survey such as the office quality score, wait time, and time spent with the physician. Additionally, we could generate hypotheses examining the difference across the different months or quarters using these same variables.

Summary

Hypothesis testing involves determining the extent to which the differences between our samples is not likely due to sampling error. When the

Null hypothesis (H_{01}): There is no difference in patient satisfaction levels for physician quality among the different offices.

Alternative hypothesis (H_{A1}): There is a difference in the patient satisfaction levels for physician quality among the different offices.

Null hypothesis (H_{02}): There is no difference in the patient satisfaction levels for physician quality among the difference months.

Alternative hypothesis (H_{A2}): There is a difference in the patient satisfaction levels for physician quality among the different months.

Null hypothesis (H_{03}): There is no difference in the patient satisfaction levels for overall rating of the exam among the difference offices.

Alternative Hypothesis (H_{A3}): There is a difference in the patient satisfaction levels for overall rating of the exam among the different offices.

Null hypothesis (H_{04}): There is no difference in the patient satisfaction levels for overall rating of the exam among the difference months.

Alternative hypothesis (H_{A4}): There is a difference in the patient satisfaction levels for overall rating of the exam among the different months.

Null hypothesis (H_{05}): There is no difference in the patient satisfaction levels for overall rating of the exam between the two states.

Alternative hypothesis (H_{A5}): There is a difference in the patient satisfaction levels for overall rating of the exam between the two states.

Figure G.3. Hypotheses for the patient satisfaction questionnaire.

difference is likely due to sampling error, we do not reject the null hypothesis; the two samples are likely from the same population. When the difference is not likely due to sampling error (difference is large), then we reject the null hypothesis in favor of the alternative hypothesis.

The steps to hypothesis testing are presented in Figure G.4. The first step is to generate a null and an alternative hypothesis. The second step is to collect data to provide evidence of the state of the world (supporting the null or alternative hypothesis). The third step is determining a summary

1. Generate null and alternative hypothesis.
   - Null is: there is no difference
   - Alternative is: there is a difference
2. Collect data to provide evidence of the state of the world.
3. Using the data, determine the summary score which summarizes the difference between the groups.
4. Determine criterion to which to compare your summary score.
5. Decide to reject the null or not reject the null.

Figure G.4. Steps in hypothesis testing.

score using data that reflect the difference between the groups. The fourth step is determining the criterion, reflecting the point at which the summary score is likely to occur five times out of 100 if the null hypothesis is true. Fifth, if the summary score exceeds the criterion, we reject the null hypothesis and accept the alternate hypothesis.

T-Tests

We may want to compare two groups of people on some variable. Two companies in the retail business have a friendly competition with each other. In fact, Bob of Bob's Barn claims that his customers are highly satisfied, while Tom, owner of Tom's Tent, claims he has more satisfied customers. Both owners would like to obtain empirical information to determine which company has the highest level of customer satisfaction.

An independent research firm was contacted to see if it could settle the score. The research firm developed a customer satisfaction questionnaire to assess overall customer satisfaction. Higher scores on the questionnaire reflect higher satisfaction. This questionnaire was administered to two sets of customers. One set had received service from Bob's Barn and the other had received service from Tom's Tent. The research firm obtained 20 customers from each company to complete the questionnaire. The data appear in Table H.1.

The mean for the group from Bob's Barn is 2.85, and the mean for the group from Tom's Tent is 3.45. If we inspect only these mean values, we might conclude that customers from Tom's Tent are more satisfied with service than customers from Bob's Barn.

Recall that, when two small sets of data are compared, their means will almost always be different from each other, even if the two data sets come from the same population. This difference is due to sampling error (see Appendix F). This error arises because the observed mean is only an

Table H.1. Hypothetical data for two companies.

	Bob's Barn		Tom's Tent	
	1	3	2	3
	2	4	4	3
	3	3	5	4
	2	2	3	5
	4	1	3	3
	3	3	4	2
	3	4	2	1
	3	2	5	3
	4	4	4	4
	4	2	5	4
Total =		57.00		69.00
n =		20		20
$\bar{x}$ =		2.85		3.45
SS =		18.55		24.95

estimate of the population mean, which has inherent error because it is based on only a sample of data. Therefore, merely seeing if there is a difference between the two groups is not enough to say that the two data sets arise from two different populations.

The *t*-test provides a method by which we can more rigorously compare two data sets. Conducting a *t*-test informs us whether the degree of difference between the two data sets could be due to factors other than sampling error. If the results indicate that the difference between the groups is not likely due to sampling error, we believe that the two data sets probably do not come from the same population.

Calculation
The formulae for the calculation of the *t*-test vary, depending on whether the sample sizes for each group are equal. The following general equation

can be applied to situations in which the sample sizes are either equal or not equal. The calculation of the *t*-test is

$$t(N - 2) = \frac{\bar{x}_1 - \bar{x}_2}{\sqrt{\left(\dfrac{SS_1 + SS_2}{n_1 + n_2 - 2}\right)\left(\dfrac{1}{n_1} + \dfrac{1}{n_2}\right)}}$$

where $\bar{x}_1$ and $\bar{x}_2$ are the means for each group, SS_1 and SS_2 are the sum of squares for each group, n_1 and n_2 are the sample sizes for each group, and N is the sum of n_1 and n_2.

Also, $(N - 2)$, associated with the t statistic, is the degrees of freedom. Recall that the degrees of freedom is the total number of observations (N) minus the number of estimated parameters. Using the data in Table H.1, the observed t value is calculated to be

$$t(38) = \frac{3.45 - 2.85}{.338} = 1.77$$

If we assume that the null hypothesis is true (there is no difference between the two groups), we would expect the t statistic to equal 0.0 (since $\bar{x}_1 - \bar{x}_2 = 0$). The t statistic, like the sample mean, can also be described by a sampling distribution with associated sampling error. That is, even though the null might be true, we would not expect to obtain a t statistic of zero every time we randomly sample two samples from the same population. Given that the null hypothesis is true, the mean of the t distribution is symmetric around zero. If we were to randomly sample t values from this distribution, we would likely see a majority of t values clustering around 0. We would not likely see extreme t values. Recall that 95 percent of the data falls within two standard deviations above or below zero. If the t value we obtain from our study is more than $2s$ away from the mean, we know this finding is highly unlikely; therefore, we think the two sample means do not come from the same population.

When the t values are extreme, we think the two samples come from different populations (reject the null hypothesis and accept the alternative hypothesis). We say the two sample means are *statistically significantly* different from each other. In significance testing, we set a critical value which our observed t value should exceed if we are to say the means are significantly different from each other. This critical *t* value is determined to be the *t* value above which the probability of obtaining a *t* value, by chance, is .05.

The spread of the *t* distribution is determined by the sample size used in the calculation of the *t* statistic. The spread of the *t* distribution is wider when sample size is small and becomes narrower as the sample size increases. A given *t* distribution (with associated degrees of freedom) describes the frequency with which we would see varying *t* values if we repeatedly performed independent *t*-tests with a given sample of subjects (20 in each group). For our example we would be interested in the probability of obtaining *t* values using a *t* distribution with 38 degrees of freedom.

The observed *t* value we obtain in our study is 1.77. We compare this *t* value to a critical *t* value. A *t* table containing critical t values is located in Appendix H. We select our critical *t* value to be 2.04 (.05 level with 30 degrees of freedom and a two-tailed test). Although our actual degrees of freedom is 38, we select 30 to provide a conservative test of significance. This critical *t* value represents the point above which our chance of obtaining an obtained *t* value is less than 5 percent if the null hypothesis were true. Our observed *t* value is below this critical *t* value. Thus, we conclude that the difference between our observed means (2.85 and 3.45) is likely due to sampling error, or that both sets of customers come from one underlying population; the customers from Bob's Barn and Tom's Tent are equally satisfied.

Factors Affecting Significance Testing

Power is the probability of finding a significant difference with our samples when there truly is a difference between the two populations. We always strive to have a high degree of power when we conduct significance testing. One way of increasing power is by increasing the sample size on which the *t*-test is conducted. Another is to use scales with high reliability. In our example, perhaps customers from Tom's Tent were more satisfied but our test lacked sufficient power to detect this difference.

Example

A *t*-test can be conducted to test hypothesis 5 (see Appendix G). Specifically this hypothesis tests to see if there is a difference between the two states (Washington and California) in the customers' overall rating of the exam. The summary information for this *t*-test is presented in Table H.2.

From the *t*-test, we compare the obtained *t* value with our critical value. Because we did not have a directional hypothesis, we will compare this obtained *t* value with the critical value for a two-tailed test. To be conservative, we use a critical *t* value associated with a smaller degree of freedom. The critical value for *t* given 180 degrees of freedom is 1.96. We see that the absolute value of the obtained *t* statistic does not exceed the critical value. Therefore, we conclude that there was no statistically significant difference between the two states with respect to the overall rating of the exam. That is, the observed differences we see between the states is just due to chance factors (sampling error).

Table H.3 contains the critical values for the *t* statistic. The table is used to compare the absolute value of the obtained *t* statistic (from the study) with the critical value of the *t* statistics for a given critical value. If the absolute value of the observed *t* statistic exceeds the critical value, we reject the null (there are no differences between the groups) and conclude that the difference between the two groups is probably not due to chance.

Table H.2. Summary information for the *t*-test examining state differences for overall ratings of the exam.

	Washington	California
Mean	4.07	4.11
SD	.89	.84
SE of the mean	.03	.03
n	678	605

$$t(1281) = -.72, p > .05$$

Note: SD = standard deviation; SE = standard error; *n* = sample size.

Table H.3. Critical values of the *t* statistics (generated by a program written by the author).

Degrees of freedom	One-tailed significance level *p*		Two-tailed significance level *p*	
	.05	.01	.05	.01
3	2.35	4.54	3.18	5.84
4	2.13	3.75	2.78	4.60
5	2.02	3.36	2.57	4.03
6	1.94	3.14	2.45	3.71
7	1.89	3.00	2.36	3.50
8	1.86	2.90	2.31	3.36
9	1.83	2.82	2.26	3.25
10	1.81	2.76	2.23	3.17
11	1.80	2.72	2.20	3.11
12	1.78	2.68	2.18	3.05
13	1.77	2.65	2.16	3.01
14	1.76	2.62	2.14	2.98
15	1.75	2.60	2.13	2.95
16	1.75	2.58	2.12	2.92
17	1.74	2.57	2.11	2.90
18	1.73	2.55	2.10	2.88
19	1.73	2.54	2.09	2.86
20	1.72	2.53	2.09	2.85
21	1.72	2.52	2.08	2.83
22	1.72	2.51	2.07	2.82
23	1.71	2.50	2.07	2.81
24	1.71	2.49	2.06	2.80
25	1.71	2.49	2.06	2.79
26	1.71	2.48	2.06	2.78
27	1.70	2.47	2.05	2.77
28	1.70	2.47	2.05	2.76
29	1.70	2.46	2.05	2.76
30	1.70	2.46	2.04	2.75
40	1.68	2.42	2.02	2.70
50	1.68	2.40	2.01	2.68
60	1.67	2.39	2.00	2.66
70	1.67	2.38	1.99	2.65
80	1.66	2.37	1.99	2.64
90	1.66	2.37	1.99	2.63
100	1.66	2.36	1.98	2.63
120	1.66	2.36	1.98	2.62
140	1.66	2.35	1.98	2.61
160	1.65	2.35	1.97	2.61
180	1.65	2.35	1.97	2.60
>10000	1.65	2.33	1.96	2.58

Summary

The *t*-test can determine if the difference between two samples is meaningful. We calculate the observed *t* value using our data and compare it to a critical *t* value. This critical *t* value is the cutoff point above which the probability of obtaining a *t* value is .05. If our observed *t* is greater than this critical *t* value, then we say the difference between the two means is not likely due to sampling error. That is, the data likely come from two different populations. On the other hand, if the observed *t* value falls below the critical *t* value, we say the observed difference between the two means is likely due to sampling error. That is, the data from the two groups likely come from the same population and the observed difference is the result of chance. The power of detecting true differences can be increased by increasing the sample size on which the *t*-test is conducted and also by using measures with high reliability.

APPENDIX I

Analysis of Variance

Analysis of variance (ANOVA) is used to compare groups. When conducting an ANOVA, we can compare more than two groups simultaneously. As the name of the analysis implies, ANOVA is a method of analyzing components of variance.

Let's look at an example. Suppose we have four independent sets of data. The data are presented in Table I.1. We will calculate the variance of the observations with two methods. The first method is to calculate the variability within each group. Four separate variances, one for each group, can be calculated. These four separate variances are each an estimate of the same variance. Therefore, we can get an overall variance measure by averaging these four variances. This average variance is the pooled variance estimate (s_p^2). This approach results in a variance estimate of .625.

The second method is to calculate the variance of the means ($s_{\bar{x}}^2$). The variance of the means, however, is dependent on the sample size (see Appendix F). As sample size increases, the variance of the means decreases. Thus, to correct for sample size, we multiply the variance of the means by the sample size for each group ($n = 10$). This estimate now reflects the variability of the group means corrected for sample size ($ns_{\bar{x}}^2$). This approach results in a variance estimate of 7.49.

If there is no true difference between the group means, then the two variance measures should be roughly the same. We see, however, that the variability using the group means approach is 7.49, and the variance using the within-group approach is .625. The magnitude of the former variance

Table I.1. Hypothetical data of four groups.

	Set 1	Set 2	Set 3	Set 4
	2	4	2	3
	1	5	3	2
	2	5	1	3
	1	4	4	2
	2	4	3	4
	2	4	3	3
	2	5	4	4
	3	3	3	2
	3	4	3	3
	2	3	2	4
Mean =	2.0	4.1	2.8	3.0
$n =$	10	10	10	10

$SS_1 = 3.996 \qquad SS_2 = 4.896 \qquad SS_3 = 7.S96 \qquad SS_4 = 6.003$

$s_1^2 = .444 \qquad s_2^2 = .544 \qquad s_3^2 = .844 \qquad s_4^2 = .667$

$s_p^2 = (s_1^2 + s_2^2 + s_3^2 + s_4^2)/4 = .625$

$SS_B = 20.03 + 41.02 + 28.02 + 30.02 - (20 + 41 + 28 + 30)2/4 = 6.741$

$s_{\bar{x}}^2 = SS_B/3 = .749$

indicates that there is considerable variability between groups, more so than variability within groups. In ANOVA, we are comparing these variance components. If the variance calculated using the means is larger than the variance calculated using individual scores within groups, this might indicate that there is a significant difference between the groups.

Calculations

The standard method for presenting the results of the ANOVA is the tabular format. The ANOVA table appears in Table I.2. The first row of the ANOVA table contains information about the variance of the groups. The second row contains information concerning the variance of the subjects

Table I.2. Analysis of variance (ANOVA) table.

Source	Sum of squares	Degrees of freedom (df)	Mean square	$F(df_B, df_W)$
Between	SS_B	$k - 1$	$SS_B/(k - 1)$	MSB
Within	SS_W	$N - K$	$SS_W/(N - k)$	MSW
Total	SS_{TOT}	$N - 1$		

Note: N = total sample size, k = number of groups, df = degrees of freedom.

within each group. The third row of the table represents total variance. Each of the rows contains specific information about the variability of its respective components.

The first column identifies the sources of variation. The differences between groups is denoted by Between (B). The variation due to subjects within each group is denoted by Within (W). The total variation is denoted by Total. The second column in the ANOVA table represents the sum of squared deviations (SS). The SS_B and the SS_W should sum to SS_{TOT}. The third column represents the degrees of freedom for each SS. The degrees of freedom (df) for SS_B are the number of groups minus one. The df for SS_W are the total sample size minus the number of groups. The df for SS_{TOT} are the total sample size minus one. The df_B and the df_W should sum to df_{TOT}. The fourth column, mean square, represents the measure of variation of a particular source. The mean squares are calculated by dividing the sum of squares by the df. The last column represents the ratio of the MS_B to the MS_W and is referred to as the F *ratio.*

Testing

The F value is a ratio of the variance of the means corrected for by sample size to variance within the groups. A large F value indicates that the between-group variance is larger than the within-group variance. Like the t statistic, the F value can also be described by a distribution, the F distribution. The F distribution has two different degrees of freedom, one associated with the estimate of the variance of the means ($k - 1$) and the other associated with the variance within groups $(N - k)$. The exact shape of the distribution is determined by the df_B and df_W.

The concept of testing in ANOVA is the same as the testing using the *t*-test. We compare the observed *F* value from our study to a critical *F* value. This critical *F* value is a cutoff point, above which the probability of obtaining an *F* value is only .05 if the null hypothesis is true. Therefore, an observed *F* value above the critical value, because it is such an unlikely event, would lead us to believe that the different groups in our study do not come from the same population.

The ANOVA table for the data in Table I.1 is presented in Table I.3. We see that the resulting *F* value is large. The critical *F* value with 3 and 36 degrees of freedom is approximately equal to 2.9. Our observed *F* value equals 11.99, which is larger than the critical *F*. Thus, we conclude that all four groups do not come from the same underlying population; at least one group comes from a different population from the rest.

Post-Hoc Comparisons

When we compare three or more groups and find a significant effect using the ANOVA method, we can conclude only that the group means are significantly different from each other. Unlike the *t*-test, in which only two groups are compared, the ANOVA method can be inconclusive. For example, if we find the *t*-test to be statistically significant, we examine the means of the two groups to see which group is higher. In the ANOVA with three or more groups, a significant *F*-test tells us only that the groups do not come from the same population. In other words, significant effect indicates that there is at least one statistically significant difference between two of the groups in our study. Some of the groups may not be significantly different from each other, while others might be significantly different.

To determine where the underlying differences lie, we must do further testing, referred to as *post-hoc testing*. There are various methods of post-hoc testing. All are somewhat related to the *t*-test method in which individual groups are compared to determine if they are significantly different from each other. Readers are referred to the bibliography to learn more about these techniques.

Table I.3. ANOVA table for the data in Table I.1.

Source	Sum of squares	Degrees of freedom	Mean square	$F(3, 36)$
Group	22.475	3	7.492	11.987
Within	22.5	36	.625	$p = .0001$
Total	44.975	39		

Note: p = the probability of our observed F value occurring by chance.

Example

An ANOVA can be conducted to test the other hypotheses stated in Appendix G. The ANOVA table is presented in Table I.4. In the table, the summary F-test is presented. If the result is significant, more information regarding analysis is presented. Specifically, the descriptive statistics of the customer satisfaction measure are presented for each level of the independent variable, including the mean, standard deviation, standard error of the mean, and the 95 percent confidence interval. Additionally, the result of the post-hoc comparisons (Tukey-HSD test) is presented to show you where the differences are located.

As can be seen in Table I.4., there are significant differences seen across the different offices on the measure of physician quality and overall rating of the exam. Patients in the Sonoma office rated their physician lower compared to all other offices (except Seattle patients). Additionally, Sonoma and Seattle patients tended to be less satisfied with the overall exam compared to the rest of the patients from the other offices. There was a significant difference across the months with respect to the overall rating of the exam. The months of June and September had significantly lower scores compared to the month of January of that same year, suggesting a downward trend.

Table I.4. ANOVA table for the hypotheses in Appendix G.

Null Hypothesis 1: No difference in physician quality across offices

Source	df	Sum of squares	Mean squares	*F* ratio	*F* prob.
Between groups	8	6.1902	.7738	4.1106	.0001
Within groups	1326	249.6067	.1882		
Total	1334	255.7969			

Group	Count	Mean	Standard deviation	Standard error	95% confidence interval for mean
Yakima	178	2.8577	.3060	.0229	2.8124 to 2.9029
Seattle	173	2.7371	.5685	.0432	2.6518 to 2.8224
San Francisco	150	2.8224	.5023	.0410	2.7414 to 2.9035
Tacoma	179	2.8467	.3420	.0256	2.7963 to 2.8972
San Jose	181	2.8726	.3172	.0236	2.8260 to 2.9191
Sacramento	155	2.7989	.4004	.0322	2.7354 to 2.8625
Spokane	180	2.7988	.4421	.0330	2.7338 to 2.8638
San Diego	58	2.9233	.2619	.0344	2.8544 to 2.9922
Sonoma	81	2.6140	.6830	.0759	2.4630 to 2.7650
Total	1335	2.8119	.4379	.0120	2.7884 to 2.8355

(*) Indicates significant differences, which are shown in the lower triangle

```
                          S
                          a
                          n
                      S
                      a   F           S
                      c   r       S   a
                  S   S   r   a       a   n
              S   e   p   a   n   T   Y   n
              o   a   o   m   c   a   a       D
              n   t   k   e   i   c   k   J   i
              o   t   a   n   s   o   i   o   e
              m   l   n   t   c   m   m   s   g
              a   e   e   o   o   a   a   e   o
```

Mean	Office	
2.6140	Sonoma	
2.7371	Seattle	
2.7988	Spokane	*

Table I.4. *Continued.*

2.7989	Sacramento	*
2.8224	San Francisco	*
2.8467	Tacoma	*
2.8577	Yakima	*
2.8726	San Jose	*
2.9233	San Diego	*

Null Hypothesis 2: No difference in physician quality across months

Source	df	Sum of squares	Mean squares	F ratio	F prob.
Between groups	8	2.8366	.3546	1.8586	.0627
Within groups	1326	252.9604	.1908		
Total	1334	255.7969			

No significant differences

Null Hypothesis 3: No difference in overall rating of exam scores across offices

Source	df	Sum of squares	Mean squares	F ratio	F prob.
Between groups	8	27.7563	3.4695	4.7607	.0000
Within groups	1274	928.4666	.7288		
Total	1282	956.2229			

Group	Count	Mean	Standard deviation	Standard error	95% confidence interval for mean	
Yakima	170	4.0824	.8244	.0632	3.9575 to 4.2072	
Seattle	166	3.8976	1.0481	.0813	3.7370 to 4.0582	
San Fran	147	4.2041	.8019	.0661	4.0734 to 4.3348	
Tacoma	168	4.0893	.7802	.0602	3.9704 to 4.2081	
San Jose	172	4.2035	.7409	.0565	4.0920 to 4.3150	
Sacramento	150	4.0400	.7408	.0605	3.9205 to 4.1595	
Spokane	174	4.2069	.8553	.0648	4.0789 to 4.3349	
San Diego	58	4.2931	.6756	.0887	4.1155 to 4.4707	
Sonoma	78	3.6923	1.1877	.1345	3.4245 to 3.9601	
Total	1283	4.0873	.8636	.0241	4.0400 to 4.1346	

(*) Indicates significant differences, which are shown in the lower triangle

Table I.4. *Continued.*

```
                            S
                            a
                            n
                  S
                  a  F        S
                  c  r     S  a
            S  S  r  a     a  n
      S  e  p  a  n  T  Y  n
      o  a  o  m  c  a  a     D
      n  t  k  e  i  c  k  J  i
      o  t  a  n  s  o  i  o  e
      m  l  n  t  c  m  m  s  g
      a  e  e  o  o  a  a  e  o
```

Mean	Office		
3.6923	Sonoma		
3.8976	Seattle		
4.0400	Sacramento		
4.0824	Yakima	*	
4.0893	Tacoma	*	
4.2035	San Jose	*	*
4.2041	San Fran	*	*
4.2069	Spokane	*	*
4.2931	San Diego	*	

Null Hypothesis 4: No difference in overall rating of exam scores across months

Source	df	Sum of squares	Mean squares	*F* ratio	*F* prob.
Between groups	8	16.9757	2.1220	2.8782	.0035
Within groups	1274	939.2472	.7372		
Total	1282	956.2229			

Table I.4. *Continued.*

Group	Count	Mean	Standard deviation	Standard error	95% confidence interval for mean
January	144	4.2708	.7684	.0640	4.1443 to 4.3974
February	144	4.1736	.8050	.0671	4.0410 to 4.3062
March	157	4.1783	.7638	.0610	4.0579 to 4.2988
April	149	4.0940	.8648	.0708	3.9540 to 4.2340
May	158	4.0506	.9155	.0728	3.9068 to 4.1945
June	135	3.9407	.9601	.0826	3.7773 to 4.1042
July	128	4.0781	.8749	.0773	3.9251 to 4.2312
August	134	4.1045	.8341	.0721	3.9620 to 4.2470
September	134	3.8657	.9322	.0805	3.7064 to 4.0250
Total	1283	4.0873	.8636	.0241	4.0400 to 4.1346

(*) Indicates significant differences, which are shown in the lower triangle

```
              S
              e                F
              p              e   J
              t          A   b   a
              e        A u r M   n
              m J    J p g u a   u
              b u M u r u a r    a
              e n a l i s r c    r
              r e y y l t y h    y
```

Mean	Month
3.8657	September
3.9407	June
4.0506	May
4.0781	July
4.0940	April
4.1045	August
4.1736	February
4.1783	March
4.2708	January * *

Regression Analysis

To understand the application of regression analysis, let's first look at an example of the relationship between two variables: (1) A person's level of satisfaction with perceived quality of service received from a company in terms of availability; and (2) The person's level of overall satisfaction with service. Perceived quality of availability is defined as the extent to which the customer perceives the company as being available to provide service whenever he or she needs it. Overall satisfaction with the service is defined as the extent to which the customer is generally satisfied with the way he or she was treated by the company. Measures were developed to assess both variables on a five-point scale. A higher number on either scale represents better service.

We use these measures on a sample of 10 people and subsequently obtain two scores: X_i, which represents perceived quality of availability, and Y_i, which represents overall satisfaction. The data are presented in Table J.1. The first column in the table provides the names of 10 people who were given the questionnaire. The second and third columns present the scores on perceived availability and overall satisfaction, respectively, for each of the 10 people.

A graphic representation called a *scatterplot* indicates the relationship between these two variables. This is seen in Figure J.1. As one would expect, there is a positive relationship between these two variables. That is, customers who perceive the company as more available to provide services when needed have higher levels of satisfaction. The relationship can be

Table J.1. Hypothetical data for variables X and Y.

Customer	Xi	Yi	$(Xi)^2$	$(Yi)^2$	$XiYi$
Lance A.	3	5	9	25	15
Jackson B.	1	2	1	4	2
Brian F.	3	3	9	9	9
Joe F.	5	4	25	16	20
Kim P.	2	2	4	1	2
Lamona F.	2	2	4	4	4
Bob H.	4	4	16	16	16
Tom H.	3	4	9	16	12
Jenifer K.	1	1	1	1	1
Wade G.	4	3	16	9	12

$$\Sigma Xi = 28 \quad \Sigma Yi = 29 \quad \Sigma Xi^2 = 94 \quad \Sigma Yi^2 = 101 \quad \Sigma XiYi = 93$$

$$r = \frac{10(93) - (28 \times 29)}{\sqrt{([10(94) - (28)^2][10(101) - (29)^2])}} = .726$$

summarized by a line, a regression line, which indicates the degree of relationship between X and Y. This relationship can also be described by an equation

$$Y = a + bX + e$$

where b and a are constants representing the slope and intercept of the regression line, respectively. The error associated with the prediction is labeled as e.

The intercept is the predicted score for Y when X is equal to zero, the point at which the line intersects the Y axis. The slope represents the change in Y given a unit change in X. The values of a and b describe the regression line. Different values of each will necessarily lead to different regression lines. For a given relationship between two variables, there is a regression line that best fits the scatterplot. The parameters, a and b, for the best fitting regression line are calculated by the following equations.

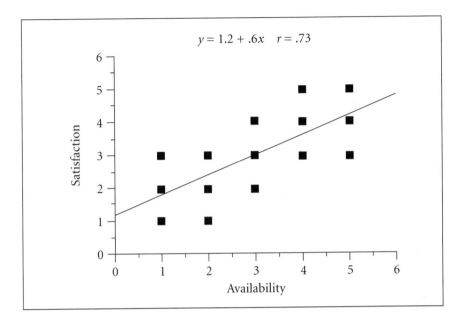

Figure J.1. A scatterplot representing the relationship between perceived avail-ability and overall satisfaction with service.

The formula for b is

$$b = \frac{n\Sigma X_i Y_i - (\Sigma X_i)(\Sigma Y_i)}{n\Sigma X_i^2 - (\Sigma X_i)^2}$$

We use b to calculate a.

$$a = \frac{\Sigma Y_i - b\Sigma X_i}{n}$$

These two equations are used to calculate the best fitting regression line. For the data in Table J.1, the regression slope is calculated to be

$$b = .756$$

and the intercept is calculated to be

$$a = .782$$

Therefore, the regression equation for predicting Y (overall satisfaction) from X (perceived availability) is

$$Y = .782 + .76X$$

This equation can be used to make predictions of Y for any given level of X. If a person had an X score of 4.5, their predicted score for Y would be 4.2. If a person had an X score of 1.25, their predicted score for Y would be 1.73.

Determining the Degree of Fit

An important step in regression analysis is to determine how well the regression line represents the data or how well the regression line fit the data. We determine this fit with an index called *Pearson r^2*. This index varies from 0 to 1.0. This index approaches 1.0 as the data lie closely near the regression line. The index approaches 0 as the data are widely dispersed around the regression line. The formula for the Pearson r^2 is

$$r^2 = \frac{[n\Sigma X_i Y_i - \Sigma X_i \Sigma Y_i)]^2}{[n\Sigma X_i^2 - (\Sigma X_i)^2][n\Sigma Y_i^2 - (\Sigma Y_i)^2]}$$

This index can be interpreted as the percentage of variance in Y (the criterion) that is accounted for by X (the predictor). So, if r^2 is equal to .70, we say that 70 percent of the variance in Y is accounted for by differences in X. Conversely, we could also say that 30 percent of the variance in Y is not accounted for by differences in X (this is essentially the variance that is unexplained by the X variable). The r^2 for data presented in Table J.1 is calculated to be

$$r^2 = \frac{[10(93) - (28)(29)]^2}{[10(94) - (28)^2][10(101) - (29)^2]} = .528$$

The r^2 indicates that about 53 percent of the variance in Y is accounted for by differences in X.

Pearson *r*

The r^2 is an index that describes how well the data fit a straight line. However, the r^2 does not tell us the direction of the relationship between the two variables. The linear relationship between two variables can be indexed by a single number, the Pearson correlation coefficient, denoted by the letter *r*. The Pearson *r* indicates the strength and direction of relationship between two variables. It can vary from −1 (a perfectly negative relationship between two variables) to 1 (a perfectly positive relationship between two variables). A negative relationship indicates that, as one variable increases, the other variable decreases. A positive relationship indicates that, as one variable increases, the other variable also increases.

The equation for the Pearson *r* is

$$r = \frac{n\Sigma X_i Y_i - \Sigma X_i \Sigma Y_i}{\sqrt{[n\Sigma X_i^2 - (\Sigma X_i)^2][n\Sigma Y_i^2 - (\Sigma Y_i)^2]}}$$

Table J.1 includes data on two variables, *X* and *Y*. Using the previous equation, we determine the extent to which variables *X* and *Y* are related to each other. The direction of their relationship is positive, and the strength of their relationship is *r* = .73. The amount of variance in *Y* accounted for by *X* (r^2) is calculated by squaring the correlation coefficient ($r^2 = .73^2 = .53$).

Figure J.2 illustrates various strengths and directions of relationships. A high correlation (either positive—Figure J.2(a)—or negative—Figure J.2(b)) indicates that there is a substantial relationship between the two variables. Figures J.2(c) and (d) indicate that there is a moderate relationship between the two variables. In fact, we know, by the size of the correlation coefficient, that the relationship between *X* and *Y* is stronger in the two former figures. For example, the two variables in Figure J.2(a) have a positive correlation of .84, while the two variables in Figure J.2(c) have a moderate positive correlation of .45.

Testing Significance of Fit

We test the significance of the *r* by first transforming the *r* statistic to a *t* statistic. The formula for the transformation is

$$t(n - 2) = \frac{r\sqrt{n - 2}}{r\sqrt{1 - r^2}}$$

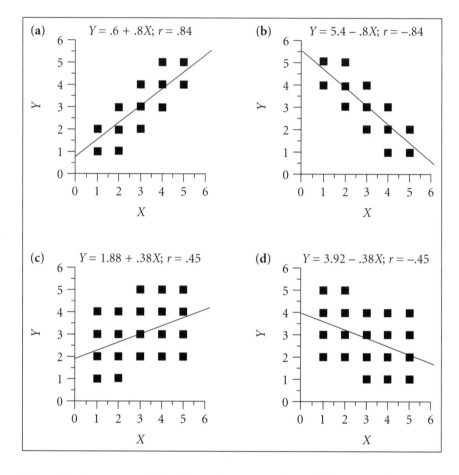

Figure J.2. Scatterplots indicating various strengths and directions of relationships between two variables.

We can calculate the *t* from the *r* in our present example. In our example *n* = 10 and

$$t(8) = \frac{.73\sqrt{8}}{\sqrt{1 - .53}} = 3.01$$

We can determine if the *t* represents a significant effect (see Appendix H).

Summary

The relationship between two variables can be described by a straight line, a regression line. The regression line allows us to predict values of *Y* (with a degree of error) from given values of *X*. The degree of fit of data around the regression line is indexed by the correlation coefficient, denoted by *r*. It is an index of the linear association between the two variables. The correlation coefficient can range from –1 (perfect negative relationship) to 1 (perfect positive relationship). A correlation of zero indicates no linear relationship between two variables.

Multiple Regression

In simple linear regression, we examine the relationship between two variables. We might want to examine the relationship of overall satisfaction with many other factors within the customer survey, such as reliability, availability, and professionalism. Instead of examining each factor separately (for example, calculating simple correlation coefficients), another approach would be to examine all factors simultaneously in their prediction of overall customer satisfaction. This method is referred to as *multiple regression analysis*. Multiple regression analysis allows us to determine which variable or variables best predicts overall customer satisfaction. For example, it might be conceivable to think of overall satisfaction as a result of several factors, some factors more important than others. Although all the variables may be significantly correlated with overall customer satisfaction, multiple regression analysis determines which factors are *the best* predictors of overall customer satisfaction. *Best* is defined as factors that uniquely predict customer satisfaction.

Essentially, multiple regression analysis examines all the factors and selects the factors that account for most of the variance in customer satisfaction with the criterion that the factors account for a unique and significant amount of the variance in customer satisfaction. So, it is possible that, although five factors may be significantly correlated with overall customer satisfaction, a multiple regression analysis could result in a finding that only one factor accounts for a unique portion of the variance in customer satisfaction. The other factors, due to overlap with the first factor, may not add any explanation to the prediction of customer satisfaction. Graphically, we could look at this in a Venn diagram (see Figure J.3).

In this diagram, the circles represent the variance in each of the variables. The overlapping portions of the circles represent shared variance among the variables. We see that the factor, availability, explains most of the variance in customer satisfaction (larger overlap) compared to professionalism. Additionally, we see that professionalism does share a large amount of variance with customer satisfaction. However, we see that the unique variance professionalism shares with customer satisfaction is almost cut in half after we take into account the variance professionalism and availability both share with customer satisfaction. Multiple regression could be used to see if the unique variance of professionalism significantly predicts customer satisfaction.

There are various methods of multiple regression analysis. The different multiple methods vary with respect to how the factors are included (or retained) in the final regression equation. These methods are forward selection, backward elimination, and stepwise selection. Using the forward selection method, the variable that has the highest correlation with customer satisfaction is entered into the equation first. Next, the factor that explains the greatest and unique amount of variance (after the first

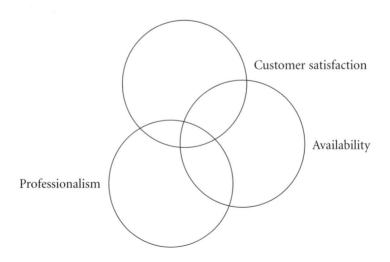

Figure J.3. A Venn diagram.

factor has been entered) is entered into the equation and tested for its significance. If the factor is significant, it remains in the equation and the next factor that explains the greatest and unique amount of variance (after the first two factors have been entered) is entered in the equation and tested for significance. This process is conducted until the remaining factors do not contribute any significant variance to the prediction of customer satisfaction.

Using backward elimination, all factors are included into the equation from the start. Each factor's unique contribution to the explanation of customer satisfaction (after controlling for the other factors) is tested. The factor whose unique variance does not account for a significant amount of variance and explains the least amount of variance in customer satisfaction is dropped from the equation. Each factor is again tested to see if its unique variance accounts for a significant amount of variance. The process of elimination is iterated until all factors in the equation account for a significant amount of variance in customer satisfaction.

In stepwise selection, both forward selection and backward elimination procedures are used. In the first step, the variable that has the highest correlation with customer satisfaction is entered into the equation. Next, the factor that explains the greatest and unique amount of variance (after the first factor has been entered) is entered into the equation and tested for its significance. In the next step, however, the first variable that was entered into the equation is tested to see if it explains a unique amount of variance in customer satisfaction after the second variable has been added to the equation. If the first variable does add unique explanation to customer satisfaction, it remains in the equation. If it does not, it is dropped. This process is conducted with the remaining variables. With this method, it is possible to determine which factors were initially good at predicting customer satisfaction at the early stages of the analysis but may have lost their usefulness at later stages after more variables have entered the equation.

These methods of multiple regression are presented here to show you the various methods you can use to determine the factors that best predict overall customer satisfaction. Readers are referred to the bibliography to learn more about multiple regression analysis.

Example

Using the patient satisfaction questionnaire, we are able to use simple linear regression to determine the relationship of office quality and physician quality. Specifically, we will use regress office quality (Y) on physician quality (X). First, the relationship between these two variables is plotted to give us a general idea of the relationship between the two variables. This scatterplot is presented in Figure J.4. As can be seen in this figure, the relationship between the two variables is positive.

In the next step, we conduct a simple regression analysis. The results of this regression analysis are presented in Table J.2. As we can see, the relationship between physician quality and office quality is slightly positive ($r = .27$). Also, the percent of variance of physician quality that is accounted for by office quality is only 7 percent. Table J.2 also includes the final regression equation for the prediction of physician quality (Y) from office quality (X).

Next, we could determine which variables are related to the overall rating of the exam. First, let's examine the simple correlations among the variables. These are located in Table J.3. As we can see from the correlation matrix, overall rating of the exam is positively correlated with physician

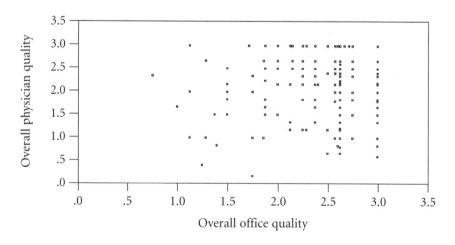

Figure J.4. Scatterplot of the relationship between physician quality and office quality.

Table J.2. Regression analysis predicting physician quality from office quality.

r	.27
r^2	.07
Regression equation:	$Y = a + bX$; $Y = 1.78 + .376X$
Significance test:	$t(1329) = 10.21$; $p < .0001$

Table J.3. Correlations among the patient satisfaction variables.

	Physician	**Office**	**Wait time**
Physician quality	—		
Office quality	.34	—	
Wait time (minutes)	−.07	−.14	—
Overall rating of the exam	.60	.30	−.11

Note: N for correlations ranges from 797 to 1336. All correlations significant at the .05 level.

quality and office quality. Overall rating of the exam is negatively correlated with wait time; patients who spend more time waiting for the doctor also report lower levels of satisfaction with the exam compared to patients who spend less time waiting for their doctor.

Next, we conduct a multiple regression analysis (using a stepwise approach) using physician quality, office quality, and wait time as the predictor variables and overall rating of the exam as the outcome variable. The results of the analyses are presented in Table J.4. As we can see from the multiple regression approach, the best predictor of the overall rating of the exam is physician quality, followed by office quality, and wait time. The effects of the latter two variables are significant but not that substantial. Thus most of the variance in overall rating of the exam can be explained by the satisfaction level with the physician.

Table J.4. Stepwise regression analysis of the patient satisfaction questionnaire.

	Scale	ΔR^2	p
Overall rating of the exam	Physician quality	.3554	.01
	Office quality	.0189	.01
	Insurance quality	.0031	.05
	Total for four variables in the equation	.3774	.01

The next appendix covers another procedure that extends the concept of correlational analysis. This procedure, factor analysis, determines the relationship between observed variables and hypothetical variables.

Factor Analysis

Factor analysis is a general term used to refer to a number of statistical techniques that can be used in questionnaire development. There are several types of factor analysis methods, each with its own particular method for generating results. Even though each of these methods is different, they often result in the same conclusions regarding interpretation of the data. Therefore, the present discussion will be very general and will not focus on one particular method of factor analysis but will instead describe the general factor analytic technique.

Generally, factor analysis is used when you have a large number of variables in your data set and would like to reduce the number of variables to a manageable size. For example, the 12 items presented in Figure K.1 might be used to assess service quality of a particular organization. You might think that they represent 12 dimensions of customers' attitudes, but upon inspection, we see that they might not really represent 12 different dimensions.

For example, items 1, 2, and 3 are similar to each other and might be represented by a broader dimension called *availability of the provider*. In addition, items 4, 5, and 6 might represent *responsiveness of the provider*, and items 7, 8, and 9 represent *professionalism*. Items 10, 11, and 12 represent *overall satisfaction with the service*.

Let's say that we had a large number of people complete the questionnaire. A factor analysis of the resulting data would tell us whether there is a smaller set of more general dimensions (like availability and responsiveness).

1. I could get an appointment with the merchant at a time I desired.
2. The merchant was available to schedule me at a good time.
3. My appointment was at a convenient time for me.
4. The merchant was quick to respond when I arrived for my appointment.
5. The merchant immediately helped me when I entered the premises.
6. My appointment started promptly at the scheduled time.
7. The merchant listened to my opinion about what I wanted.
8. The merchant conducted herself/himself in a professional manner.
9. The merchant was courteous.
10. The quality of the way the merchant treated me was high.
11. The way the merchant treated me met my expectations.
12. I am satisfied with the way the merchant treated me.

Figure K.1. Customer opinion statements concerning service quality and overall satisfaction.

We reduce the original number of variables to a smaller number of dimensions so we can more easily interpret the information contained in the data. If we want to see the interrelationship (correlation coefficients) between these 12 variables, we would have to calculate and interpret 60 correlations. This may be difficult, since we are not able to understand what all of the interrelationships would indicate. By reducing the number of dimensions—say, reducing the 12 variables to the four dimensions suggested earlier—we now only have to calculate and interpret six relationships.

In general, factor analysis examines the relationships between a large set of variables and tries to explain these correlations using a smaller number of variables. Initially, factor analysis uses the overall correlation matrix of the variables and determines which items share an underlying dimension. Factor analysis mathematically identifies the number of factors or underlying dimensions that best represents the observed correlations between the initial set of items. Generally, in the set of existing items, those that are highly correlated with each other will be represented by a single factor or dimension.

After the number of factors or dimensions has been identified, the next step in factor analysis is to determine which items fall within their respective dimensions. This is done by a mathematical procedure called *rotation*. This rotation will clarify the dimensions' relationships with the items. As with the general method of factor analysis, various methods of rotation exist. Generally, these different rotation methods result in the same conclusions regarding which dimensions represent a given set of items.

Exploratory and Confirmatory Uses of Factor Analysis

Factor analysis explores the possibility that our variables can be reduced to a smaller, undetermined number of factors. That is, we do not know the number of factors that represents our variables nor which variables load on which factors. Factor analysis, in this situation, will identify which variables load on their respective factors. Factor analysis can also be used in a confirmatory manner in which we go into the analysis with some guess as to the outcome of the factor analysis. In other words, we think we know the number of factors and which variables load on which factors. (The term *confirmatory factor analysis* is used here to illustrate how factor analysis can be used and is different from the more sophisticated approach of confirmatory factor analysis using significance testing.) This use of factor analysis is guided more by hypothesis testing. We expect the results from the factor analysis to confirm our hypothesis of the variables in our data set. For example, if we develop a questionnaire designed to assess certain dimensions of service quality, we expect that the items on our scale represent their respective factor or dimension.

Hypothetical Factor Analysis

The results of the factor analysis (the number of factors and factor rotation) are presented in a tabular format called a *factor pattern matrix*. The elements in the factor pattern matrix represent the regression coefficient (like a correlation coefficient) between each of the items and the factors. These elements indicate the degree of relationship between the variables and the factors.

Table K.1 presents a hypothetical factor pattern matrix representing the results of a factor analysis that identified the existence of three factors that represented nine items. Items 1 through 3 have a high loading on factor I and small loadings on the other factors. Items 4 through 6 load highly on factor 11, and items 7 through 9 load highly on factor 111. A factor's definition is determined by the content of the items which load on it.

This hypothetical factor analysis indicates it would be reasonable to think of the data set as containing three variables rather than nine. Therefore, instead of looking at each variable as its own separate dimension, we would believe that there are three dimensions, each composed of three items. To obtain a score for each of the dimensions, we might combine the variables associated with a given factor to represent that dimension. That is, we would combine all the items that loaded highly on factor I to get a measure of that dimension. We would do the same for the items associated with factor II and factor III.

Now we would have three dimensions with which to work. These dimensions are useful summary variables for drawing conclusions about the data. Furthermore, we could now more easily interpret the interrelations (correlation coefficients) among these dimensions.

Table K.1. A factor pattern matrix with the factor loadings from the results of a hypothetical factor analysis of the responses to nine items.

| | Factor | | |
Items	I	II	III
1.	.80	.05	.07
2.	.77	.04	.21
3.	.45	.11	.13
4.	.02	.55	.04
5.	.10	.77	.21
6.	.11	.88	.16
7.	.09	.08	.72
8.	.30	.21	.77
9.	.21	.22	.67

Actual Factor Analysis

This next example is taken from actual data obtained from a beauty salon using a customer satisfaction questionnaire. Although the questionnaire contained the items listed in Figure K.1, only items 1 through 6 are included in this example. The first three items were written to reflect an availability dimension, while the last three items were written to reflect a responsiveness dimension. A method of factor analysis, called *principle factor analysis,* was performed. This initial factor analysis resulted in the factor pattern matrix presented in Table K.2.

As this factor pattern indicates, the factor analysis identified the existence of two factors or dimensions representing these six items. We expected this. However, it might be unclear as to which items represent factor 1 and which represent factor 2. All of the six items seem to load fairly high on factor 1. Factor 2 seems to reflect a bipolar scale; some items load positively on the factor, while others load negatively on the factor. The interpretation of the factor pattern matrix becomes even more difficult as the number of items and factors increases. To make the results of the factor analysis more meaningful, we use rotation.

On the initial factor pattern matrix, a method of rotation, called *varimax rotation,* was conducted. Other methods of rotation were used

Table K.2. The factor pattern matrix resulting from the factor analysis of six items designed to measure perceived availability and perceived responsiveness.

Unrotated factor matrix

	Factor 1	Factor 2
Item 1	.727	.683
Item 2	.842	.425
Item 3	.321	.861
Item 4	.807	−.537
Item 5	.604	−.652
Item 6	.84	−.361

and, as expected, resulted in the same pattern of results as varimax rotation. Therefore, this presentation will only include the results of varimax rotation. The rotated factor pattern matrix appears in Table K.3. In this factor pattern matrix, the interpretation of the factors is more clear. Factor 1 is clearly represented by the last three items, while factor 2 is clearly represented by the first three items.

As expected, we found the existence of two factors that underlie these six items. In a sense, we used factor analysis to confirm our expectations. By design, the first three items reflected an availability dimension of service while the last three items reflected a responsiveness dimension. The factor analysis confirmed our hypothesis as to the number of factors that these six items represent, thus making us more confident that the items measure what they were designed to measure.

Example

From the patient satisfaction questionnaire, we derived an overall measure of physician quality by averaging the responses to the six questions related to physician quality. We can use factor analysis to determine if this method of averaging the items is reasonable. The factor analysis would tell us the number of underlying factors that describe the correlations among the six items of physician quality. The six items measuring physician quality are presented in Figure K.2.

Table K.3. The result of the factor analysis after rotating the factors.

Orthogonal transformation solution—varimax

	Factor 1	Factor 2
Item 1	.14	.987
Item 2	.391	.858
Item 3	−.288	.873
Item 4	.966	.086
Item 5	.879	−.131
Item 6	.881	.244

Physician quality			
	Yes	No	Not sure
1. Introduced him/herself to me.	Y	N	?
2. Asked me how I was injured/became ill.	Y	N	?
3. Listened to me.	Y	N	?
4. Treated me with respect.	Y	N	?
5. Was professional in doing the examination.	Y	N	?
6. Spent enough time with me (not rushed).	Y	N	?

Figure K.2. Physician quality items.

The next step would be to determine the correlations among these six items. The correlation matrix for the six physician quality items is presented in Table K.4.

As we can see from the correlation matrix, all items are positively correlated with each other. The pattern of correlations, however, is not clear. Some items show high correlations with other items ($r = .58$) while other items show low correlations with other items (.14). A factor analysis examines the entire correlation matrix and helps us make sense of these

Table K.4. Correlation matrix for the six physician quality items.

	1	2	3	4	5	6
Question 1	1.00					
Question 2	.22	1.00				
Question 3	.15	.22	1.00			
Question 4	.31	.20	.56	1.00		
Question 5	.26	.14	.48	.58	1.00	
Question 6	.17	.22	.47	.42	.41	1.00

correlations. Perhaps one underlying factor can explain the pattern of correlations we see in Table K.4.

The results of the factor analysis (factor pattern matrix) is presented in Table K.5.

The results of the factor analysis suggest that the six items could be described by one underlying factor. As is indicated in the factor pattern matrix, one factor can explain the correlations among the variables, suggesting that all six items are measuring one underlying factor that is responsible for the variance in the items. Therefore, the creation of a new variable called *overall physician quality* by averaging the six items does make sense, both logically and statistically.

Table K.5. Factor pattern matrix for the six physician quality items.

	Factor 1
Question 1	.35531
Question 2	.26187
Question 3	.69985
Question 4	.78311
Question 5	.69716
Question 6	.59329

Summary

Factor analysis identifies the number of underlying dimensions that account for the relationship between many items. Since factor analysis allows you to determine which items measure similar things, it is often used as a means of data reduction.

Table of Random Numbers

These random numbers were generated with a computer program and range from 1 to 99,999. Each number had an equal chance of being generated.

92513	21156	20618	78167	87337	80703	00468	84107	58120	15456
17743	07198	90623	93143	58624	99172	90774	32892	43015	03868
64861	63732	82018	99240	11925	87715	08917	64625	51627	20766
79728	09753	43999	23550	20290	45512	06476	50545	49641	68162
20515	97350	04927	87226	11553	40866	70782	20944	65761	08406
55469	10628	09666	09906	94742	11203	99330	38092	26386	38890
95834	67434	10367	25356	03517	11773	12159	61605	79374	73538
38344	94791	86959	90375	39792	31626	16217	75227	59118	48758
58805	62440	80292	69705	80900	53725	19260	63853	52996	41111
13310	73409	14683	72271	83141	31214	06020	36270	89706	59971
63713	76433	82594	13916	49596	51822	19609	27454	85470	89592
74104	73061	81653	70740	30044	11351	97125	92733	73051	84786
78861	42464	71587	29797	69687	98987	73885	91051	56021	55387
36915	77574	29370	77071	38475	39808	26999	61025	74503	48624
04771	12920	35438	84635	57077	71178	05781	95589	19444	50655
38792	98613	08548	65459	46643	31589	26608	93722	71904	98448
22358	87444	47701	58366	28319	66264	90515	16041	62258	35767
85925	79736	54218	88132	33224	19743	29210	26962	79052	44391
52972	54548	85857	60644	12414	63024	30719	47093	57483	98950
01504	34410	87397	45152	13270	70784	40097	74700	36362	27201
47310	81172	43366	95102	12440	66368	71484	84735	78198	65864
52773	71303	43874	52350	50081	87145	08226	45971	87660	77714
10822	41517	94528	27204	34618	21898	92037	77282	00834	91593
45122	47428	78536	16203	47494	40969	75182	44961	04057	75998
57860	98766	70665	22204	50186	92901	43092	01484	94901	38907
97394	86975	63503	83789	66147	18745	98056	56883	09887	68377
04824	69980	08281	08365	81162	14938	15126	14297	97930	87086
72933	93269	88155	37800	46676	45646	93489	83874	82111	62150
16305	67104	66060	28206	53165	79230	01372	53440	27867	09628
02674	21739	07376	51503	39818	77886	66043	53012	66435	65773
72311	39822	42810	19800	96401	27412	36409	69962	93899	11187
20706	35672	86437	61921	65572	92677	95636	57183	58219	63017
42718	18888	63674	90418	40960	08617	24701	31349	72595	34379
24010	42118	44494	68694	33997	26586	86540	52297	74910	56444
32067	87027	19144	18467	40376	35642	05817	27684	19042	03323
44569	68369	59771	39055	17045	64723	65400	66571	75542	65935
08487	63190	89557	44757	52447	62902	87699	50010	63877	96156
85834	44712	33304	54909	75046	49907	64365	42403	61689	72287
05150	00751	15552	87821	72474	73283	88592	61628	12753	78396
17670	88611	90535	04493	23554	07028	19741	00796	12694	65857
05221	65192	51547	52682	81566	94180	78802	47901	76064	54259
20977	74751	03998	78282	64292	48037	09946	02345	61880	45268
57906	12627	93767	06761	55512	53175	26354	73948	55615	53165
28352	33164	93269	93833	58574	62083	13382	00109	46278	49877
94165	27864	64602	68693	53619	64668	07040	33622	33066	40964
56693	42385	00601	65723	54104	63014	05768	07673	88769	42281
09131	74506	63078	30882	59738	70331	63669	16305	60160	72148
17652	95540	87088	89126	16730	79871	48653	37999	25753	89591
63576	61256	93052	49509	39740	39844	73818	30614	29605	62099
40912	46784	97819	67113	23390	79137	50734	33970	71863	79725

Bibliography

American Educational Research Association, American Psychological Association, and National Council on Measurement in Education. 1985. *Standards for Educational and Psychological Testing*. Washington, DC: American Psychological Association.

Anastasi, A. 1988. *Psychological Testing*. New York: Macmillan.

Balakrishnan, P. V.; Chawla, S. K.; Smith, M. F.; and Michalski, B. P. 1992. Mail survey response rates using a lottery prize giveaway incentive. *Journal of Direct Marketing* 6(3): 54–59.

Brennan, M. 1992. The effect of a monetary incentive on mail survey response rates: New data. *Journal of the Market Research Society* 34(2): 173–177.

Brennan, M.; Hoek, J.; and Astridge, C. 1991. The effects of monetary incentives on the response rate and cost-effectiveness of a mail survey. *Journal of Market Research Society* 33(3): 229–241.

Brown, F. G. *1983. Principles of Educational and Psychological Testing*. New York: Holt, Rinehart and Winston.

Camp, R. C. *1989. Benchmarking: The Search for Industry Best Practices That Lead to Superior Performance*. Milwaukee, Wis.: ASQC Quality Press.

Campbell, D. T., and Fiske, D. W. 1959. Convergent and discriminant validation by the multitrait-multimethod matrix. *Psychological Bulletin* 56: 81–105.

Campbell, D. T., and Stanley, J. C. 1966. *Experimental and Quasi-Experimental Designs for Research.* Boston: Houghton Mifflin Co.

Chandler, C. H. 1989. Beyond customer satisfaction. *Quality Progress* 22(2): 30–32.

Chapko, M. K.; Bergner, M.; Green, K.; Beach, B.; Milgrom, P.; and Skalabrin, N. 1985. Development and validation of a measure of dental patient satisfaction. *Medical Care* 23(1): 39–49.

Chawla, S. K.; Balakrishnan, P. V.; and Smith, M. F. 1992. Mail response rates from distributors. *Industrial Marketing Management* 21(4): 307–310.

Corah, N. L.; O'Shea, R. M.; Bissell, G. D.; Thines, T. J.; and Mendola, P. 1988. The dentist-patient relationship: Perceived dentist behaviors that reduce patient anxiety and increase satisfaction. *Journal of the American Dental Association* 116: 73–76.

Corah, N. L.; O'Shea, R. M.; Pace, L. F.; and Seyrek, S. K. 1984. Development of a patient measure of satisfaction with the dentist: The Dental Visit Satisfaction Scale. *Journal of Behavioral Medicine* 7(3): 367–373.

Cottle, D. W. 1990. *Client-Centered Service: How to Keep Them Coming Back for More.* New York: John Wiley and Sons.

Cronbach, L. J. 1951. Coefficient alpha and the internal structure of tests. *Psychometrika* 16: 297–334.

Cronbach, L. J. 1984. *Essentials of Psychological Testing.* 4th ed. New York: Harper & Row.

Cronbach, L. J., and Meehl, P. E. *1955.* Construct validity in psychological tests. *Psychological Bulletin* 52: 281–302.

Davies, A. R., and Ware, J. E. Jr. 1981. Measuring patient satisfaction with dental care. *Social Science and Medicine* 15(A): 751–760.

Dawes, R. M. 1972. *Fundamentals of Attitude Measurement.* New York: John Wiley and Sons.

Edwards, A. L., and Kenney, K. C. 1946. A comparison of the Thurstone and Likert techniques of attitude scale construction. *Journal of Applied Psychology* 30: 72–83.

Flanagan, J. C. 1954. The critical incident technique. *Psychological Bulletin* 51: 327–358.

Fishbein, M. 1967. *Readings in Attitude Theory and Measurement.* New York: John Wiley and Sons.

Fox, R. J.; Crask, M. R.; and Kim, J. 1989. Mail survey response rate: A meta-analysis of selected techniques for inducing response. *Public Opinion Quarterly* 52(4): 467–491.

Gale, E. N.; Carlsson, S. G.; Eriksson, A.; and Jontell M. 1984. Effects of dentists' behavior on patients attitudes. *Journal of the American Dental Association* 109: 444–446.

Goodman, J. 1989. The nature of customer satisfaction. *Quality Progress* 22(2): 37–40.

Guion, R. M. 1965. *Personnel Testing.* New York: McGraw-Hill.

Gulliksen, H. 1987. *Theory of Mental Tests.* Hillsdale, New Jersey: Lawrence Erlbaum Associates, Publishers.

Guttman, L. L. 1950. The basis for scalogram analysis. Vol. 4 of Stouffer, S. A.; Guttman, L.; Shuchman, E. A.; Lazarfeld, P. W.; Star, S. A.; and Clausen, J. A. (eds.) *Studies in Social Psychology—World War II.* Princeton, N.J.: Princeton University Press.

Handleman, S. L.; Fan-Hsu, J.; and Proskin, H. M. 1990. Patient satisfaction in four types of dental practices. *Journal of the American Dental Association* 121: 624–630.

Hannan, M., and Karp, P. 1989. *Customer Satisfaction: How to Maximize, Measure, and Market Your Company's "Ultimate Product."* New York: American Management Association.

Hawkins, D. I.; Coney, K. A.; and Jackson, D. W. Jr. 1988. The impact of monetary inducement on uninformed response error. *Journal of the Academy of Marketing Science* 16(2): 30–35.

James, J. M., and Bolstein, R. 1990. The effect of monetary incentives and follow-up mailings on the response rate and response quality in mail surveys. *Public Opinion Quarterly* 54(3): 346–361.

Johnson, J. D.; Scheetz, J. P.; Shugars, D. A.; Damiano, P. C.; and Schweitzer, S. O. 1990. Development and validation of a consumer quality assessment instrument for dentistry. *Journal of Dental Education* 54(1): 644–652.

Kennedy, D. A., and Young, B. J. 1989. Managing quality in staff areas. *Quality Progress* 22(10): 87–91.

Kenny, D. A. 1987. *Statistics for the Social and Behavioral Sciences.* 2d ed. Boston: Little, Brown and Co.

Kepes, S. Y., and True, J. E. 1967. Anonymity and attitudes toward work. *Psychological Reports* 21(2): 353–356.

Koslowsky, M.; Bailit, H.; and Vallugo, P. 1974. Satisfaction of the patient and the provider; Evaluation by questionnaire. *Journal of Public Health Dentistry* 34: 188–194.

Latham, G. P., Fay, C.; and Saari, L. 1979. The development of behavioral observation scales for appraising the performance of foremen. *Personnel Psychology* 32: 299–311.

Latham, G. P.; Saari, L.; and Fay, C. 1980. BOS, BES, and baloney: Raising Kane with Bernardin. *Personnel Psychology* 33: 815–821.

Latham, G. P., and Wexley, K. N. 1977. Behavioral observation scales for performance appraisal purposes. *Personnel Psychology* 30: 255–268.

Likert, R. A. 1932. Technique for the measurement of attitudes. *Archives of Psychology.* No. 140.

Lissitz, R. W., and Green, S. B. 1975. Effect of the number of scale points on reliability: A Monte Carlo approach. *Journal of Applied Psychology* 60: 10–13.

Locke, E. A.; Shaw, K. N.; Saari, L. M.; and Latham, G. P. 1981. Goal setting and task performance: 1969–1980. *Psychological Bulletin* 90: 125–152.

Loftus, G. R., and Loftus, E. F. 1988. *The Essence of Statistics.* 2d ed. New York: Alfred A. Knopf.

Lorenzi, P.; Friedmann, R.; and Paolillo, J. 1988. Consumer mail survey responses: More (unbiased) bang for the buck. *Journal of Consumer Marketing* 5(4): 31–40.

Montgomery, D. C. 1996. *Introduction to Statistical Quality Control,* 3d ed. John Wiley & Sons.

Morrison, D. F. 1976. *Multivariate Statistical Methods.* 2d ed. New York: McGraw-Hill.

Morrison, D. F. 1983. *Applied Linear Statistical Methods.* Englewood, N.J.: Prentice Hall.

Murine, G. E. 1988. Integrating software quality metrics with software QA. *Quality Progress* 21(11): 38–43.

Neter, J.; Wasserman, W.; and Kutner, M. H. 1985. *Applied Linear Statistical Models.* 2d ed. Homewood, Ill.: Richard D. Irwin, Inc.

Nunnally, J. M. 1978. *Psychometric Theory.* 2d ed. New York: McGraw-Hill.

Parasurman, A.; Zeithaml, V. A.; and Berry, L. L. 1985. A conceptual model of service quality and its implications for future research. *Journal of Marketing* (fall): 41–50.

Parasuraman, A.; Zeithaml, V. A.; and Berry, L. L. 1988. SERVQUAL: A multiple-item scale for measuring consumer perceptions of service quality. *Journal of Retailing* 64: 12–40.

Pedhazur, E. J. 1982. *Multiple Regression in Behavioral Research: Explanation and Prediction.* 2d ed. New York: Holt Rinehart Winston.

Pritchard, R. D.; Jones, S. D.; Roth, P. L.; Stuebing, K. K.; and Ekeberg, S. E. 1988. Effects of group feedback, goal setting, and incentives on organizational productivity. *Journal of Applied Psychology* 73: 337–358.

Reckase, M. D. 1990. Scaling techniques. In Goldstein, G. and Herson, M. (eds.) *Handbook of Psychological Assessment.* New York: Pergamon Press.

Rouse, R. A., and Hamilton, M. A. 1990. Dentists' technical competence, communication, and personality as predictors of dental patient anxiety. *Journal of Behavioral Medicine* 13(3): 307–319.

Shank, M. D.; Darr, B. D.; and Werner, T. C. 1990. Increasing mail survey response rates: Investigating the perceived value of cash versus non-cash incentives. *Applied Marketing Research* 30(3): 28–32.

Shaw, D. G.; Huffman, M. D.; and Haviland, M. G. 1987. Grouping continuous data in discrete intervals: information loss and recovery. *Journal of Educational Measurement* 24(2): 167–173.

Society for Industrial and Organizational Psychology, Inc. 1987. *Principles for the Validation and Use of Personnel Selection Procedures.* 3d ed. College Park, Md.: SIOP.

Soelling, M. E., and Newell, T. G. 1983. Effects of anonymity and experimenter demand on client satisfaction with mental health services. *Evaluation and Program Planning* 6(3–4): 329–333.

Stevens, S. S. 1951. *Handbook of Experimental Psychology.* New York: John Wiley and Sons.

Thurstone, L. L. 1929. Theory of attitude measurement. *Psychological Bulletin* 36: 224–241.

Watkins, D. 1978. Relationship between desire for anonymity and responses to a questionnaire on satisfaction with university. *Psychological Reports,* 42(1): 259–261.

Yammarino, F. J.; Skinner, S. J.; and Childers, T. L. 1991. Understanding mail survey response behaviors: A meta-analysis. *Public Opinion Quarterly* 55(4): 613–639.

Zeithaml, V. A.; Parasuraman, A.; and Berry, L. L. 1990. *Delivering Quality Service: Balancing Customer Perceptions and Expectations.* New York: The Free Press.

Index

A

Abscissa, 193

Adjectives, for critical incidents, 17–18

Administration, of questionnaires, 45, 100–5, 150, 159, 169. *See also* Response rates; Sampling

Allocation process, in critical incident technique, 22–23

Alpha level, in hypothesis testing, 216, 218

Alternative hypothesis, 215–20

Ambiguity, of questionnaire items, 62–63, 65–66

Analysis of variance (ANOVA), 163–64, 229–37

Arithmetic average. *See* Mean

Arithmetic operations, and measurement scales, 183–86

Assignable causes, and variability, 126, 129

Attribute data, 126, 127–34

Automobile industry
critical incident technique in, 26–28
example questionnaire for, 114–16

Average, arithmetic. *See* Mean

B

Baldrige Award. *See* Malcolm Baldrige National Quality Award

Banking industry
control charts for, 127–29, 130–33, 136–39
critical incident technique for, 24–26
example questionnaire for, 112–14
satisfaction items for, 25, 63, 64

Behavioral terminology, for critical incidents, 17–18

Benchmarking, 140–41

Best practices, 140–41

READER FEEDBACK

Fax to ASQ Quality Press Acquisitions: 414-272-1734

Comments and Areas for Improvement:
Measuring Customer Satisfaction

Please give us your comments, feedback, and suggestions for making this book more useful. We believe in the importance of continuous improvement and in meeting your needs. Your comments will help determine what improvements can be made in all ASQ Quality Press books.

Please share your opinion by circling the number below:

Ratings of the book	Needs Work		Satisfactory		Excellent	Comments
Structure, flow, and logic	1	2	3	4	5	
Content, ideas, and information	1	2	3	4	5	
Style, clarity, ease of reading	1	2	3	4	5	
Held my interest	1	2	3	4	5	
Met my overall expectations	1	2	3	4	5	

I read the book because:

The best part of the book was:

The least satisfactory part of the book was:

Other suggestions for improvement:

General comments:

Thank you for your feedback. If you do not have access to a fax machine, please mail this form to:
ASQ Quality Press, 611 East Wisconsin Avenue, P.O. Box 3005, Milwaukee, WI 53201-3005   Phone: 414-272-8575